AN OUTLINE
OF THE BOOK OF
LEVITICUS

AN OUTLINE
OF THE BOOK OF
LEVITICUS

C. A. COATES

STOW HILL BIBLE AND TRACT DEPOT
2 UPPER TEDDINGTON ROAD HAMPTON WICK
KINGSTON-ON-THAMES

Printed in Great Britain
at the Villafield Press Bishopbriggs, Glasgow

PREFATORY NOTE

IT was the writer's privilege to be present at a series of readings on the Book of Leviticus during the years 1921–22. The substance of what came out in those readings—after free revision in view of publication—is contained in this " Outline."

Quotations from Scripture are generally, throughout this book, from the New Translation by J. N. Darby.

C. A. COATES

AN OUTLINE OF
THE BOOK OF LEVITICUS

CHAPTER 1

THE Book of Leviticus has in view a people in
covenant relations with God, in whose midst God
dwells, and who have movements of heart Godward.
God had said to Moses, " When thou hast brought
forth the people out of Egypt, ye shall serve God
upon this mountain," Exod. 3 : 12. He had said
to Pharaoh, " Let my son go, that he may serve
me," Exod. 4 : 23. Here we see the manner and
order of that service—the service of a free and willing
people ; and we learn that every outgoing of heart in
the service of God is concerning Christ. Blessed
service ! Blessed those whose privilege it is to take
it up !

What we get here about the offerings has its place
in the forty-nine days during which the cloud rested
on the tabernacle (see Num. 10 : 11) ; a time typical
of the complete period of tabernacle service in the
wilderness.

The instruction in Leviticus is for us ; it is doubtful
if the children of Israel ever carried it out. In a
coming day when Israel's heart turns to the Lord they
will enter into the meaning of these types. The veil
will then be taken away from their heart, and they
will read Moses, seeing the Lord as the end of the old

covenant, and the Spirit of all the Old Testament
Scriptures. In the meantime saints of the assembly,
being in the good of the ministry of the Spirit and of
righteousness, are able to read the old covenant
without a veil, and find their affections quickened in
the apprehension of the Lord as the Spirit of it all.
Nor do I doubt that the church's apprehension of these
types has a fulness and expansion which goes beyond
what Israel will apprehend in the coming day.

God speaks from the " tent of meeting " ; the
appointed centre to which His people gathered, where
He met them, and where they came into contact
with one another in relation to His things. The
communication of His mind was found there.

" The assembling of ourselves together " (Heb. 10 :
25) answers, I think, to the " tent of meeting." We
also get many references to saints coming together in
1 Cor. 11 ; 14. Saints are taught of God to love one
another, and if this divine teaching were not neutral-
ized by human influences it would bring all Christians
together in every city, town, or village where they
are found. The " tent of meeting " would thus have
its antitype in every local assembly. Things are very
broken to-day, but it is still possible, through infinite
mercy, for saints to come together as loving one
another in relation to God, and as they do so they get
instruction and enlargement in the knowledge of God.
He has great pleasure in seeing His saints together in
love ; it sets Him free to communicate His mind to
them.

If we think of our own times it is as saints have come
together in love to one another as being of God's
assembly that there have been communications of
God's mind ; great light has been given in regard to

Christ and the assembly. We ought to recognise that the privilege of the " tent of meeting " has been restored in these last days. Saints can come together as saints, and in the truth of their relations with God and with one another, and this in the wilderness. If believers disregard the " tent of meeting " they will not get much increase of divine light, and what they possess of Christ will not be available for the common good, or for God's praise in the assembly of His saints.

The " tent of meeting " suggests the coming together of saints according to divine order, not human arrangement or organisation. The word translated " meeting " means what is set or appointed ; it is used of the feasts of Jehovah (Lev. 23) and other divinely-appointed occasions. To have the good of the tent of meeting it is not enough that saints should be together in one room. They must be together in accord with divine principles, and the truth of God's assembly. Every principle connected with divine order in the assembly is really essential to the safeguarding and development of spiritual affections. There must be holy conditions if God is to meet His people. If saints are at variance with one another they must settle their differences before they can really " come together." We cannot offer at the altar if we remember that our brother has aught against us. We could not be there in the undistracted appreciation of Christ. If we speak of being gathered together to the Name of our Lord Jesus Christ it necessitates that ourselves and our associations must be suitable to that Name.

These early chapters of Leviticus have to do with movements of heart towards God on the part of His people. They suppose that Christ has been received, for if one is not in possession of Christ he has nothing to bring. The morning and evening lamb of the continual burnt-offering (Exod. 29 : 38–46) give us rather the divine side—the burnt-offering in its abiding and unchanging perfection as the ground on which God meets His people, and speaks to them, and dwells with them. " A continual burnt-offering throughout your generations." It is necessary to be established in the grace of that before we contemplate what is before us in these chapters.

But on our side we have been the subjects of divine working, and the result of this is that certain exercises have been produced in our souls to which Christ is the answer. One exercise is as to acceptance, and Christ as the burnt-offering is the answer to that. Another is with regard to perfection in an object for the heart, and the meat-offering is Christ as the answer to that exercise. A third is with reference to fellowship, and the peace-offering is Christ in relation to that. And, lastly, there are exercises arising from the humbling discovery of what is in ourselves, and the consciousness of our own failure, to which the answer is Christ as the sin-offering. All God's called ones have these exercises ; I believe the germ of them is inherent in that divine teaching which *all* His people have ; though there may be with many saints a lack of spiritual diligence to follow them up, and to gain Christ as the answer to them. Our acquisition of divine wealth depends on the diligence with which we pursue the exercises which God gives us. In proportion as they are followed up, and Christ apprehended in relation to them, we have material for offerings, and are able to take part in the service of God according to His pleasure.

The consideration of this will make it apparent that

every acceptable offering has cost the offerer something. David said, " I will not take that which is
thine for Jehovah, to offer up a burnt-offering without
cost," 1 Chron. 21 : 24. It is true that, in a very
blessed sense, the gospel furnishes us with everything.
It brings Christ to us in all His fulness and perfection,
and by the hearing of faith we receive the Spirit.
But there is a history of exercise behind every true
acquisition of Christ, so that the soul has a real sense
of the value of what it has gained. See Proverbs
23 : 23 ; Revelation 3 : 18. As to what grace has made
available for us, there is no difference and no limitation ;
it is the infinite fulness and blessedness of Christ. But
as to the actual wealth of souls in the knowledge of
Christ many of us are far short of the full measure of
grace. Many of God's people have not had " the fulness
of the blessing of Christ " (Rom. 15 : 29) presented to
them, and many others who have been more favoured
in this respect have only received in their souls a
small part of what has been set before them. Hence
there are different measures of apprehension of Christ,
and no one can bring more than he has got. The
consideration of this is very exercising, for it raises
the question as to how much I can bring to the " tent
of meeting " as an offerer ? If my offering is small,
is it that my heart has not been prepared for the cost
at which a larger one might have been acquired ?

I have often thought of the people we read of in the
Gospels who came on the scene with appreciation of
Christ. What a volume of spiritual history lies
behind the record of each incident ! Would you not
like, for instance, to get alongside the woman of
Luke 7—we shall in courts above—and ask her how
she was led to such a blessed appreciation of Christ ?

And there was a corresponding history in the case of each man and woman who came to light as having an appreciation of Him. A similar history of divine instruction and spiritual acquisition lies behind each offering that we bring to the tent of meeting. Of course it is ever true, as David said, " All is of thee, and of that which is from thy hand have we given thee." It was God's, and through grace it has become ours, and now we bring it back to God for His pleasure and service.

There is a beautiful word in Jer. 30 : 21, 22. " Who is this that engageth his heart to approach unto me ? saith the Lord. And ye shall be my people, and I will be your God." As the blessedness of the covenant is known we shall surely engage our hearts to approach God. It is delightful to God to see His people, moved by His known grace and love, thus engaging their hearts. God has engaged Himself to us in the most blessed way, and the effect of our knowing it is that we engage our hearts to approach Him both as offerers and priests. May it be ever more so with us, to His glory and praise !

The burnt-offering comes first, the offering for acceptance. The sin-offering comes last ; it is only as we know Christ as set forth in the previous offerings that we can rightly estimate sin. It is in the light of the obedient and perfect One that we can alone truly learn the character of the lawless one. In the light of One wholly devoted to God in obedience and love we discern how hateful lawlessness is, and how intense, searching and all-consuming is the judgment which has come upon sinful flesh.

The *offerer* in this chapter has the consciousness that he approaches God in divine favour. In the *priest* we

see typically a further thought, for he had been washed,
clothed in holy garments, anointed and consecrated.
All this suggests moral suitability to God ; a state in
which God can be complacent. Such can minister in
holy things for God's pleasure. And then in Aaron's
"*sons*" there may be a hint that it is our privilege
to be with God in the relationship of sons for the
satisfaction of His love. Saints are entitled to be
offerers, priests, and sons ; they are three different
thoughts. But the ground on which we can approach
with acceptance as *offerers*, or serve acceptably as
priests, or taste the blessedness of acceptance in the
Beloved as *sons*, is the perfection of Christ and the
infinite value of His death.

"He shall present it a male without blemish : at
the entrance of the tent of meeting shall he present it,
for his acceptance before Jehovah," Lev. 1 : 3. The
offerer is possessed of *perfection*, and brings it to God
with holy delight ; all his thoughts of acceptance
centre in Another in whom is found unblemished
personal excellence. He is entirely on the ground of
Christ ; he "leans with his hand" on the bullock.
What could be more blessed than to come near to
God with one's hand upon Christ ? To be consciously identified with Him, the heart having possessed
itself of Him, and having no thought of any other ?
Unblemished perfection is there, God's full delight in
Man, and this brought into the world in that holy and
glorious Person to furnish through His death acceptance of a most blessed nature for men. So that, as
to acceptance, we have but One to consider, and the
heart engages itself with Him, and with Him only, in
its movements Godward.

And, blessed be God, it is possible for us to do so in

the deepest spiritual reality. We do not need to hide
from ourselves the truth as to what we are according
to the flesh. " It shall be accepted for him to make
atonement for him." The word " to make atonement
for him " suggests that there is that in the man himself
which is unsuited to be brought near to God. All
that we were as in the flesh was unfit for His eye to
rest upon, but the only way in which we consider it,
when serving God, is as having been covered—nay,
more than covered, absolutely removed—in the death
of Christ to His glory. No self-deception darkens the
heart as we draw near, for we realise that holy love
has taken its own way to judge and remove all that
we were. We fully own what existed on our part,
but the great and blessed fact that we engage our
hearts with is that even that has brought to view in
a glorious way the perfections and love of the Son of
God. He has given Himself for us, and our hearts
are entitled to dwell on this, and they delight to
dwell on it, in the presence of God. And if I know
Christ for my own acceptance I view all my brethren
in the same light, and this gives them a wonderful
place in my heart. Indeed, the way we regard our
brethren reveals where we are in our own souls.

The offerer kills the bullock, and flays it, and cuts
it up into pieces (verses 5, 6). What holy and spiritual
exercises are here suggested ! Saints drawing near to
God with true and Spirit-given thoughts of the death
of Christ ; with intelligent and adoring hearts that
realise something of its blessed character and meaning
as manifesting the obedience, devotedness, love and
glory of that One Man who has lain in death for the
glory of God, and to accomplish His will ! How that
death has revealed the perfection of all the inward

and hidden parts of Christ ! Every detail of thought
and feeling and purpose and judgment perfect ! All can
be uncovered without any discovery of imperfection,
even when tested by the absolute purity of God's
testimonies—washed in water. Every divine testimony
as to what is suitable to God in the state of man
inwardly found its full answer in the hidden parts
of that blessed One. How delightful it is to God to
be served by those who come to Him with the appreciation of all this in their hearts ! And what deep
consciousness of acceptance fills the hearts of those
who approach, identified in thoughts and affection with
the preciousness of Christ ! Many can look back to a
moment when they touch this joy, but it is not
maintained with them because they have not culti-
vated those movements of heart Godward in which
the consciousness of acceptance is renewed and
deepened.

But if we approach God with the appreciation of
Christ in our hearts it involves the displacement of
self. We must be prepared to be tested by Christ.
Are *we* prepared to have all laid bare ? To have
thoughts and motives as well as words and acts all
judged in the light of what He was ? He could say,
" I seek not mine own glory." It was at all points
a giving up of Himself for the glory of God. As we
enter into that it must affect us morally.

But saints are privileged to be *priests* as well as
offerers. These types run one into another ; the man
in conscious acceptance becomes a priest, for he only
has it in nearness to God, and one who is there is a
priest. God's original thought was not a separate
priestly family, but that all Israel should be " a kingdom of priests," Exod. 19 : 6. And it is remarkable

that we find priests in Israel before the calling and
consecration of Aaron and his sons. See Exod. 19 : 22.
" And the priests also, *who come near to Jehovah*,
shall hallow themselves." There was no official order
of priesthood as yet, but there were those who came
near to Jehovah, and all such were priests morally.
Moses was really a greater priest than Aaron, for he
enjoyed personally greater nearness to God. Hence
it is written, " Moses and Aaron among his priests,"
Psa. 99 : 6. It is most blessed that God should have
brought us to Himself, not merely for our deliverance
and happiness, but that we might minister to Him as
priests for His pleasure. And every movement of
heart that minister to God's pleasure must be concerned with CHRIST.

The priest in the early chapters of Leviticus is not
Aaron, but one of his sons, so that he is not typical of
Christ but of spiritual persons who can take up things
with spiritual intelligence for God's pleasure. It is
the privilege of all saints to be priests, but even if all
are not in priestly state the gain of the tent of meeting
is that *all*, in a way, get the benefit of the priestly
element. It would hardly be the tent of meeting if
there were no priestly element there, and if there, it
is there for the good of all, as well as for the pleasure
of God. It has been said that the most spiritual
person in a meeting—whether brother or sister—gives
character to the meeting. Every spiritual person
contributes that which tends to make others
spiritual.

Each individual brings his offering—his apprehension
and appreciation of Christ—but the fact that all
bring their offerings to a common·meeting-place would
indicate that the bearing of it is collective. Whatever

individual exercises we may have, they are all intended
to be contributory to what is collective.

I suppose we all look to get some good out of our
personal exercises and discipline, but it is well to have
before us that *the saints* are to benefit by the fruit of
those exercises. The assembly is the centre to which
all the varied lines of private exercise converge. We
may see this even as to the sin-offering exercise which
is brought before us in Psalm 51. It leads to what is
collective—the good of Zion, and the building of
the walls of Jerusalem. And it indicates, too, that
if one goes through a sin-offering exercise with God
it ends with a burnt-offering. " Then shalt thou
have sacrifices of righteousness, burnt-offering, and
whole burnt-offering ; then shall they offer up bullocks
upon thine altar."

There is priestly ability in spiritual persons to take
up every apprehension of Christ and present it to God
in praise so that it is fragrant before Him, and at the
same time is helped and enlarged in the souls of the
saints. Thus the service ministers to God's pleasure,
and at the same time edifies the saints. The assembly
is the place to increase spiritual wealth, for the apprehension of Christ which each has brought there becomes
available for all. So that each time we come together
we should become richer in the knowledge of Christ,
and thus able to bring larger offerings. One delights
to think of the assembly as a spiritual commonwealth.
The wealth of the assembly is the aggregate of what
is known of Christ in every heart. Spiritual men can
bring there a large appreciation of Christ, but as it
finds expression it becomes available for the enrichment of all, as well as for the service and pleasure
of God.

The priest is one with spiritual intelligence, and apprehension of what is *for God*. He has spiritual affections and capability, and knows how to handle what is pleasurable to God. He presents the blood—the witness of death ; he has the sense that Christ has been in death entirely for the will and pleasure of God. " I come to do thy will, O God." This does not weaken the sense of acceptance ; it intensifies it by connecting it with God's pleasure and glory, and this is a great enlargement. With what unbounded liberty and delight can we approach God when we realise that our acceptance is according to His pleasure in Christ !

In Exodus, as we have observed, the altar is the place where continual sweet odour affords the basis on which God ever meets His people, and speaks in grace to them. See Exodus 29 : 42, 43. But in Leviticus it is the place of offering on our side. It is Christ viewed as the One by whom every spiritual sacrifice is offered to God. See Heb. 13 : 15 and 1 Peter 2 : 5. Not only is Christ the Substance of every offering, but He is also the Altar. This secures divine holiness, for the altar is " holiness of holinesses ; whatever toucheth the altar shall be holy," Exod. 29 : 37. All must be brought to the test, and to the blessedness, of God's Anointed Man. Nor would a true heart wish it to be otherwise.

Every spiritual apprehension of Christ can be brought to the Altar, for it is holy, but nothing can be placed on the Altar that does not accord with it. The best sentiment of the natural mind, even in regard to Christ, could not be placed there for a moment. Nothing really has any place in the service of God, or in the assembly of God, that is not in keeping with Christ as the Altar. The altar being " at the entrance of the tent of meeting " intimates that we come there with a profound sense of the holiness of God, and that it is essential that every movement should be in accord with Christ, and with His cross and death. Nothing that is spiritually unreal can be placed on the Altar. It is possible to use expressions which are not the genuine language of the heart at the moment. The outward service may go beyond the measure of faith and spiritual power. But this will not do for the Altar of God ; it cannot be offered " by Jesus Christ." It is better that the words used should be consciously inadequate to express the heart's apprehension of Christ than that they should be high-sounding but unreal. The Altar tests everything, and cannot be touched by what is unholy and unsuitable to God ; but it also sanctifies every true gift that is placed upon it. The smallest and feeblest true apprehension of Christ can be offered " by Jesus Christ " ; it will bear the holy test of that Person, and of His death, and its sweet odour comes before God as sustained in the power and worth of that Blessed One. The Altar involves the absolute withering and refusal of all that is of the mind and sentiment of the natural or carnal man, but it sustains in sanctification and acceptability every apprehension of Christ that is real and Spirit-given.

Then the fire and the burning on the altar suggest priestly understanding of the intensity of the test which was applied to Christ. He was in the place of sin and death, and all that God is as " a consuming fire " was there. But there was more there than sin and its judgment. We see this in the sin-offering burned without the camp. But in the burnt-offering we see that infinite perfection was there, and that the

fire brought out the sweet odour of it. Everything in
Him was found, even in that place of supreme testing,
perfectly responsive to God in obedience, devotedness,
and love, and though all was offered *to God* it was *for
us*. How wondrous the privilege to bring the memorial
of it to God for His delight, and for our conscious
acceptance !

The bullock is what we might call the normal
offering, but, alas ! how few are possessed of such a
large appreciation of Christ as the bullock would set
forth. The sheep is a smaller measure of apprehension.
There is no leaning upon the victim. The sense of
Christ's death and of His perfection is there, but not
the sense of personal identification. There is a pious
appreciation of the perfections of Christ, but not the
happy consciousness of being altogether on the ground
of what He is. Still the offerer of the sheep has a
certain power of discrimination, and a recognition of
perfection in each feature of Christ that his soul takes
knowledge of, but he is altogether smaller in his
apprehension of Christ.

Then when we come to the fowls it is feebler
still. The priest has to do almost everything in this
case. In the offerer there is the sense that any sweet
savour for God must be from Christ, but there is not
much apprehension of Him. There is lack of ability
to uncover the inward parts of Christ, and to appreciate His inward perfections. In the Psalms personal
to Christ there is a wonderful uncovering of His
inward perfections. To seek them out with intelligent
and affectionate appreciation is a profound study for
the spiritual mind. Believers in general are too
indefinite ; they have a sense of the perfection of
Christ, but do not devote themselves to the un-

covering and searching out of it in detail. It demands spiritual maturity to take account of what was inward in that blessed One—His affections, His sensibilities, His thoughts and feelings. The offerer of the fowls is not equal to this ; the victim is not even divided asunder. And not only is his measure small ; but there would appear to be that which is natural mixed with his apprehension of Christ—that which cannot be offered as sweet savour, and which the priest has to cast aside.

What we see in this type is that a priest knows how to make the best of the offering of a poor person ! If you come to the tent of meeting with a small thought of Christ—and *every* saint comes with *some* thought of Christ—you will find a priest there who can help you because he apprehends according to God what is perhaps feeble and vague in *your* soul. You will find that somebody will take part in a way that brings before God the very thought that was in your mind ; but, if he is in true priestly competency, he brings it out according to God, and free from the natural element which was perhaps along with it in your mind. It thus gets enlargement in your soul, and if rightly exercised you get such increase that next time you can bring a sheep ! It was never God's thought that any of us should remain poor in the spiritual Israel.

But, while increase should be desired and looked for, it is very blessed to see that the turtle-dove or the young pigeon is spoke of in precisely the same terms as the sheep or even the bullock. It is called " a burnt-offering, an offering by fire to Jehovah of a sweet odour." This is most encouraging, for it shows that the smallest appreciation of Christ is acceptable to God, and that His grace estimates the offering according to the means of the offerer. He does not expect that in a " babe " which He would look for in a ". father." The thought of His gracious considera- tion is " good to the feeblest heart," and it encourages all to approach in liberty.

Chapter 2

This chapter brings before us the saints' apprehension of Christ in His personal perfection. It is not a question of atonement or acceptance, but the heart delighting in a perfect Object, and engaging itself with that Object in its movements Godward. Presenting an " oblation " or " gift " supposes that one is con- sciously in the acceptance of the burnt-offering as seen in chapter 1. There is entire freedom from every question that might arise as to one's own acceptance. We are not now thinking of sin, nor of how it has been dealt with, nor even of the way in which God has been glorified as to it. We are occupied with what is perfect under the eye of God, and under our eye, in a Man here on earth.

We may notice as to the " oblation " that it suggests preparation at home. It was *there* the Israelite had his flour and oil and frankincense ; it was there the cakes were baked ; all was prepared before it was brought to the tent of meeting. If we are not engaging ourselves with Christ at home, or in private, there will be no gift to bring to the tent of meeting, and no sweet odour for God. How blessed to be engaged with Christ in secret !

" Fine flour " is the basis of the oblation in each case, save that of the first-fruits, which stands by itself. Then what marks the oblation generally is that, while there was a memorial burned as sweet savour to Jehovah, it was given as food to the priests. It speaks of Christ in an aspect in which He can be the food of saints, and particularly of saints viewed as spiritual persons in charge of the testimony and service of God.

There is a difference between Christ viewed as the " manna " and Christ as typified in the " oblation." The manna was given from heaven to sustain men in wilderness conditions. But in the oblation we see rather what there was in Man viewed as " the fruit of the earth "—this expression is applied to Christ in Isaiah 4 : 2—for the delight of God, and to engage the affections of all who are divinely taught to appreciate it. It is what can be offered as a sweet odour for the pleasure of God, and what becomes, as such, the food of the holy priesthood.

When at the baptism of Jesus the voice came out of heaven, " Thou art my beloved Son, in thee I have found my delight," the fine flour of the oblation was there with the oil poured on it, and the frankincense was there also, for He was praying (Luke 3 : 22). But when, tempted of the devil, He answered, " It is written, Man shall not live by bread alone, but by every word of God;" we see Him true to the wilderness place into which He had come, and sustained there " by every word of God." Probably each saint has known what it is to be sustained by some word of God, but with Him it was " every word." He lived by it ; every minute detail in His life was formed by the word of God. If He had not a word from God He did nothing. " Every word of God " found its perfect answer in Him, and came into expression in

His life. That is the "fine" grain of the manna. (Compare Deut. 8 : 3.) It suggests perfection in minute detail " on the face of the wilderness." In the pathway of Jesus we see a life sustained from above, and which was in every way the perfect expression of that which sustained it. Now He is in heaven to minister from thence to His saints here so that they may live in the wilderness in the strength of that grace which was so perfectly expressed in Him.

But the " fine flour " of the oblation speaks of what has sprung up here and come to maturity, in the Person of Jesus, for the delight of God. It is viewed in this type as apprehended in the minute detail of its perfection and evenness. This is the fruit of a precious occupation of heart and spiritual intelligence. What a study of the perfections of Jesus does it necessitate! What more delightful engagement of affectionate meditation could there be ?

We may trace it in numberless features in the Gospels ; the law of Moses, the prophets, and the Psalms are full of presentations in detail of that which is for God's delight in man ; and every exhortation which the Epistles contain as to the spirit and walk which are comely in saints is an unfolding of the perfections of Jesus. I am not speaking, for the moment, of His official dignity or royal glory, but of His moral perfection. Everything which Scripture presents from Genesis to Revelation as being morally excellent in man, and for God's pleasure, had its place in that unique Manhood of which the " fine flour " is typical. It can only be brought as an offering by the saint who has apprehended it, and in the measure of his apprehension. But this should surely be, with each one of us, continually increasing.

We lose a great deal by not paying more attention to the perfection of Christ in detail. We should make it the study of our hearts. For example, take the First Book of the Psalms (Ps. 1–41) and ponder every separate quality of Christ that you find. There will expand in your soul the apprehension of a Blessed Man who always lived in relation to God—a Man marked by separation, meditation, obedience, dependence, delighting in good, and ever finding His place with those who feared and loved God. The following scriptures in that book may be considered amongst others : Psalms 1 : 1–3 ; 3 : 4–6 ; 4 : 3, 7, 8 ; 5 : 1–3, 7, 8, 11 ; 6 : 8, 9 ; 7 : 1, 4, 8 ; 9 : 1, 2, 13, 18 ; 11 : 1, 2 ; 13 : 5 ; 16 : 1–11 ; 17 : 3–6, 8, 15 ; 18 : 1–6, 18–24, 30–36 ; 19 : 7–11, 14 ; 20 : 1–6 ; 21 : 1–7 ; 23 : 1–6 ; 25 : 1–5, 9, 10, 12, 14, 16, 17 ; 26 : 1–8, 11, 12 ; 27 : 1–8 ; 28 : 6–8 ; 31 : 1, 5–7 ; 34 : 1–3 ; 38 : 13–15 ; 40 : 4, 9, 10 ; 41 : 12.

As born into this world He was " the holy thing " (Luke 1 : 35), and could truly be presented as holy to Jehovah (Luke 2 : 22, 23). Excellence was found here as " the fruit of the earth " in Him. Even as a child He was filled with wisdom, and God's grace was upon Him (Luke 2 : 40). At the age of twelve we find Him occupied in His Father's business, sitting in the temple in the midst of the teachers, hearing them and asking them questions, and astonishing all who heard Him by His understanding and answers. Yet would He keep the place suited to One of such an age : " He went down with them and came to Nazareth, and he was in subjection to them," Luke 2 : 51.

Then, at the age of thirty, we see Him going along with those in whom grace had wrought repentance, and being baptised. Not, surely, that He had personally anything to repent of, but the movement in *their* souls was of God ; it was for *them* the path of righteousness, and He would walk with them in it. Not patronising them, as some great one of the earth might condescend to consort for a season with those far beneath him, but going along with them because they were to Him the saints on the earth, the excellent and all His delight was in them (Ps. 16 : 3).

Then it was characteristic of Him that He should be seen as praying at the time of His baptism. It was no new attitude of spirit for Him, for His language, as given prophetically, was, " Thou didst make me trust, upon my mother's breasts. I was cast upon thee from the womb ; thou art my God from my mother's belly," Ps. 22 : 9, 10. From His mother's breasts to the last cry upon the cross, " Father, into thy hands I commit my spirit," He was never for one moment removed from the spirit of dependence. There was not only perfection in every detail of the life of the Holy Child and Youth and Man, but it was perfection that had all its spring and strength in God. God was a necessity to Him at every moment ; His object, His delight, the One whose will was His only guide and rule, His resource for all things and at all times.

How fragrant to God was this entire dependence of One who took up every detail of His path and every exercise in the affections proper to a Son ! I think the apprehension of this is typified by the frankincense put upon the fine flour, all of which was burnt as sweet odour on the altar. There was not a movement of the spirit of Christ inwardly or outwardly— whether the thoughts of His heart or their expression in word or deed—that did not first breathe itself out to God in prayer, and find its strength in so doing.

So that every movement of His heart and spirit was
not only perfect in itself, but perfect in its reference
to God, and in the dependent affections which characterised it. We may see this in the frequent mention
of His praying in Luke's gospel, and we see it brought
out with peculiar fragrance in John 11 : 41, 42, and
12 : 27, 28.

" And he shall pour oil on it." God would have us
to recognise the perfect suitability of that blessed
Man to be anointed by the Holy Spirit. The Holy
Spirit could come into contact with every grain of
that " fine flour " ; all was suitable. There was no
necessity in His case for " the Holy Spirit *and fire* " to
set aside in consuming power through self-judgment a
mass of unsuitability such as we find in ourselves.
" The Holy Spirit descended in a bodily form as a
dove upon him " (Luke 3 : 22) ; He could come into
sympathetic contact with every exercise in the heart
of that blessed One. Love made Him a mourner in
a world of woe, and the Holy Spirit descended upon
Him in a form sympathetic with His sorrow, but as
power that God might be made known in a world of
human woe in the way of gentleness and grace and
healing and deliverance. In the Person of Jesus the
Holy Spirit came upon a Man who felt according to
God everything that was in a world of sin. A Man
in perfect sympathy with God as to everything here,
was the suited Vessel in whom all the grace of heaven
could come near to men in dove-like gentleness.

The offerer pouring oil on the fine flour is typical of
the saint coming, as divinely taught, into the apprehension and appreciation of Christ as the blessed Man
marked by perfection in every minute detail, and
thus suitable to be anointed by the Holy Spirit. A

Man who is the contrast in every way to the man after the flesh. It is the work and delight of God to bring us to appreciate Him—to bring us, in measure, to His own appreciation of Him—so that He may become the Substance of affectionate movements on our part Godward. Then, in . result, all this becomes " most holy " food for the priesthood. The heart that assimilates it, and is nourished by it, acquires capability for sanctuary service. It is strengthened to understand spiritually God's pleasure in Christ, and to serve Him in a priestly way with reference to it. Probably the lack of vigour for priestly service amongst Christians generally is largely due to the absence or feebleness of those apprehensions and appreciations of Christ which would manifest themselves in movements answering to the offering of an oblation.

Then is verses 4–10 we get a further aspect of the oblation as baken or prepared in different ways under the action of fire " in the oven," " on the pan," or " in the cauldron." This would seem to indicate the desire of God that His saints should apprehend the perfection of Christ as it came out under different kinds and degrees of testing. " Unleavened cakes " set forth the entire absence of any element of inflation or corruption. But " mingled with oil " suggests the positive energy of the Spirit as giving character to His Manhood. " Mingled " is more than " anointed." It is the same word in Psalm 92 : 10, where it suggests that the " whole system is invigorated and strengthened by it : it formed his strength." See note to Lev. 2 : 4, in the New Translation. That which was begotten in the virgin was of the Holy Spirit (Matt. 1 : 20). The angel Gabriel said to her, " The Holy Spirit shall come upon thee, and power of the Highest over-

shadow thee, wherefore the holy thing also which shall be born shall be called Son of God," Luke 1 : 35. The true and holy humanity of the Lord Jesus is to be cherished and sacredly guarded by the faithful affections of His saints in face of the infidelity which abounds. It is as essential to Christianity as His deity. Both, alas ! are called in question in religious high places. But it is in the spiritual apprehension of a Manhood that derived its character and energy from the Holy Spirit that we can understand the delight of God in Him, and bring our oblation as " a sweet odour."

One would suggest that the most complete apprehension of Christ in oblation character is set forth in that which is " baken in the oven." This would be according to the analogy of the other offerings, where in each case the greatest apprehension is the one first presented. There is also a definiteness of form in " cakes " and " wafers " which is lacking in the succeeding offerings. The offerer has typically a very definite apprehension of Christ as imbued with the Holy Spirit or as anointed, and subjected to the most intense testing. The " oven " being an enclosed chamber would suggest what was hidden from public view—the secret testings through which He passed, which were the most intense of His personal sufferings, with the exception of His atoning sufferings, which are not presented in this type. Those secret testings require the deepest spirituality for their apprehension and for the discernment of how the Lord's perfection came to light in them. His feelings and sensibilities were as perfect as His works and words. What must it have been to God to have One here in Manhood who felt about everything just as it ought to be felt about.

B

The feeding on Christ as thus known would give us
priestly sensibilities. Natural feelings, with reference
to what is trying, lead to impatience and irritability.
They lack reference to God, and the sobriety which His
presence gives. But the offerer who brings " an oblation baken in the oven " has apprehended spiritually
emotions and feelings brought out in Christ under
testing which were in perfect contrast to all that is
natural in man, and which were wholly delightful to
God. And the priest who burns the memorial of it
has presented it to God with holy and reverent
appreciation, and is to feed on it for his own inward
nourishment and formation. But spirituality in both
offerer and priest is needed for this, for it is " most
holy of Jehovah's offerings."

For example, to enter into how He " suffered, being
tempted " (Heb. 2 : 18) requires great spirituality.
The positive *suffering* that it was to Him to be tempted
could only be understood by one who was, at least in
measure, a partaker of God's holiness. Then how He
felt the rejection of Israel, not merely because they
rejected Him—though surely He felt this deeply—
but because His heart entered into all that His
rejection means *for them*. Then the unbelief and lack
of understanding in His own, so often manifested ; the
inability of those He loved to watch with Him one
hour ; the treachery of Judas. Then the bearing in
His own spirit the weight of every infirmity and
disease which He removed by His power—that found
expression in His groan over the deaf man (Mark
7 : 34), and His groan over the unbelief of that generation (Mark 8 : 12), and His being " deeply moved in
spirit " in presence of the desolation and power of
death (John 11 : 33, 38). All these things show how

deeply He was tried in His own spirit by that which
He passed through, but they are to be apprehended as
bringing out nothing but unalloyed perfection for the
delight of God in that blessed One. A deeper testing
still remained for Gethsemane, where all the terrible-
ness of death, and of what was involved in drinking
the cup, was known by Him in anticipation with
unutterable agony. But what did the testing bring
out ? " Not my will, but thine be done."

These things would all belong, as it seems to me, to
the " oven " character of the oblation. The thinness
of the " cakes " and " wafers " would perhaps suggest
how completely every part of the humanity of our
blessed Lord was brought under the action of intense
trial.

Then the " oblation on the pan " would have reference to such testings as were more public, requiring
less spirituality for their apprehension. Such would
be the daily contact with the contradiction of sinners,
the varied forms of open or concealed enmity by
which He was confronted, His being reviled, etc., the
demands of many kinds from many quarters. Each
separate part is seen in this type as distinguished,
and as apprehended to be in the power of the holy
anointing.

And, finally, the offering prepared " in the cauldron "
lacks the definiteness and discrimination of the two
previous forms of the oblation. It corresponds thus
with the burnt-offering of fowls as compared with the
sheep or bullock of chapter 1. It suggests an apprehension of Christ as characterised by the Spirit which
is true as far as it goes, and therefore acceptable, but
which lacks maturity in development, and in power
of spiritual discrimination. Nevertheless it is the

perfection of *Christ* that is apprehended, and the Holy
Spirit in relation to Him, however feebly estimated
by the offerer, and this constitutes it an offering " of
a sweet odour." How precious the grace that gives
to one a more mature appreciation of Christ ! And
how precious, too, the grace that accepts the feebler
apprehension of another because it is the perfection
of Christ that is apprehended and not that of self.
Every apprehension of Christ that is brought to the
tent of meeting contributes " sweet odour " to God,
and food for the priesthood. But we must not forget
that an apprehension of Christ, which might be delightful and acceptable in a newly converted soul, might be
the sad evidence in an older saint of spiritual indolence
and of the allowance of things that have hindered
divine growth.

Then no oblation was to be made with leaven ;
" for no leaven and no honey shall ye burn in any
fire-offering to Jehovah " (verses 11, 12). " Leaven "
is the corrupting and inflating principle of self-importance which is never absent from man in the flesh. It
could not possibly have place in a " most holy "
offering. It was entirely absent from Christ, and it
must be entirely absent from those movements of
heart Godward which have Christ only as their Theme
and Substance. I think leaven might come into our
oblation if we say more than is really true. There
might be an attempt to make our apprehension of
Christ appear to be greater than it really is. This
would be a puffing up of the flesh in a very sorrowful
way. It is possible to say wonderful things of Christ
which we have heard other persons say, or which we
have read in books, but if they are beyond our own
apprehension they are not a true " gift." There

would be danger of it becoming like Psalm 78 : 36.
" But they flattered (the word means " make pre-
tence," elsewhere " entice," " deceive ") him with
their mouth, and lied unto him with their tongue ;
for their heart was not firm toward him, neither were
they stedfast in his covenant." How blessed that we
can read on, " But he was merciful ; he forgave the
iniquity and destroyed them not " ! " Honey " represents the sweetness of nature as found in amiability
and natural affections. It may be agreeable, and even
refreshing, in its own sphere, and given of God in
mercy ; but it enters not into the oblation. When
it is a question of what God delights in, the line is
sharply drawn between the natural and the spiritual,
and the former is excluded. " Honey " would be the
intrusion of natural sentiment, which I am afraid
often comes into hymns and prayers. It may be
sweet, but it is the sweetness of nature. When Peter
said, " God be favourable to thee, Lord ; this shall
in no wise be unto thee " (Matt. 16 : 22), it was a
sweet sentiment, but it was nature. There was no
savour of the salt of the covenant about it, and it was
an offence to the Lord.

" The offering of the first-fruits " refers to the two
wave-loaves of Pentecost (Lev. 23 : 15–17) which
were baken with leaven. That was " a new oblation
to Jehovah," representing the assembly as composed
of those in whom leaven had once been active, though
now rendered inactive by self-judgment in the power of
the Spirit. But leaven being recognised they cannot
be " offered upon the altar for a sweet savour," though
presented to Jehovah as first-fruits. The Spirit of
God would thus lead us to distinguish between Christ
Himself, who can alone be " offered upon the altar for

a sweet savour," and the assembly which is of Him, and in which He is reproduced as " a new oblation," but which cannot be a " fire-offering."

" And every offering of thine oblation shalt thou season with salt ; neither shalt thou suffer the salt of the covenant of thy God to be lacking from thine oblation ; with all thine offerings thou shalt offer salt." " The salt of the covenant of thy God " is an expression which arrests attention. It suggests that an offering can only be acceptable as being offered in true faithfulness of heart to the covenant relations in which divine grace has set us, and to which we have committed ourselves. I think " salt " is the preservative power of fidelity and purpose of heart to be true to the covenant. It includes self-judgment, but it involves also a faithful purpose to accept and adopt in our own hearts and lives that which is in accord with what we offer. It is that principle of faithfulness which shuts out the activities of the flesh, and brings in Christ in a practical way. For example, if I offer to God in praise an apprehension and appreciation of Christ as the One who was ever about His Father's business, the " salt " that must be with it to make it acceptable is the faithful purpose to be on the same line—to maintain dedication to the interest and pleasure of God. If my oblation is to praise God for the meekness and gentleness of Christ the " salt " would be that I am fully set to cultivate and exhibit a like spirit. This is the test of the reality of the offering, and it indicates whether one is faithfully committed to the covenant. In a word, it tests whether we really appreciate the Christ that we offer, and whether we prefer Him to ourselves. In many things we may come infinitely short of what we appreciate in Christ,

but the " salt " is that we are set in purpose of heart
to pursue moral conformity to Him.

The " oblation of thy first-fruits " seems to come
in as a kind of appendix, and I think it presents Christ
as apprehended by Israel as *their* First-fruits. God
had looked for His pleasure in a peculiar way in
Israel ; as regards the earth Israel was to be, and will
yet be, " the first-fruits of his increase," Jer. 2 : 3.
But Israel will become this as they learn, under divine
teaching, to regard Christ as their First-fruits. What
a day it will be for them when they see that all in
which they have so miserably failed to answer to God's
pleasure has been secured for Him in Christ ! All
that should mark the " Israel of God " has appeared
in this world in the Christ of God. No trace of it
could be seen in Israel after the flesh. But Israel
viewed as " the children of the promise " are entitled
to regard Christ as *their* First-fruits, and in a coming
day they will do so. As they learn to give Christ this
place, they will, through Him, become fruitful for God.
The after-fruits will follow, and take character from the
First-fruits.

The " green ears of corn " would suggest the freshness and vigour of life in which everything wherein
Israel had failed to answer to the pleasure of God
was found here in Christ. But " roasted in fire "
would indicate how the nation after the flesh had
treated Him. Instead of the First-fruits being appreciated, and ripening amidst a responsible people into
the fruition of the kingdom, they were " roasted in
fire." I take it that this corresponds with the action
of fire as seen in the oven, the pan, and the cauldron,
only now it is in an intensified degree ; it is subjected
to the direct action of fire.

We may repeat, What a day it will be for Israel
when they see that the very intensity of their hatred
and rejection has brought out the holy perfection of
Him whom they will then gladly recognise as their
First-fruits ! " Corn beaten out of full ears " speaks
of the maturity and fulness in which God's delight
was found in Him. Israel will learn, too, to give the
oil and the frankincense their place in relation to Him.
There will be affectionate movements of approach to
God in reference to all this when Israel presents the
oblation of his first-fruits. But before that day it is
the privilege of saints of the assembly to present an
oblation, and as priests to bring it to the altar and
offer it as " a sweet odour," and to make it their
" most holy " food. May we have grace to take up
this hallowed service !

CHAPTER 3

THE offerer of a peace-offering desired to be in communion with the altar. " See Israel according to
flesh : are not they who eat the sacrifices in communion with the altar ? " 1 Cor. 10 : 18. Offering
precedes eating. Indeed, we do not get the eating in
this chapter ; it is " the altar " here ; the eating or
communion is in chapter 7. The one gives character
to the other. Though it may be noted that " all that
are clean may eat the flesh," chap. 7 : 19. That is, the
communion is not limited to the offerer or the priests,
but it is available for " all that are clean." No doubt
there is instruction in this.

To be an offerer supposes some degree of spiritual
wealth in the apprehension of Christ, and an energy

in the affections Godward that brings one near the altar to present to God that which has been found in Christ through death for Him. In approaching us God had nothing to say to us about anyone but Christ, and if we approach God what we say to Him in adoration and praise is the echo of what He has first said to us in grace and love. Christ came to us from the heart of God in the unspeakableness of divine giving, and we bring Him back to God in grateful affection and praise. But what we thus bring to God forms a divine bond of communion between saints. We cannot spiritually take up with one another what has not first been taken up with God. He must have the first and best portion. But Christ being brought in, the communion which can be enjoyed together is extended to " all that are clean." Even those who were poor in Israel could partake, if clean, of that which another had brought, and enjoy the privilege of communion with the altar. What a character of grace this gives to the communion of saints ! The prosperity in Christ of one becomes the joy and gain of all ! But that which is enjoyed has no divine value unless its immediate relation to God as offered on His " most holy " altar is maintained in the consciousness of those who partake of it. And to bring what is unclean into connection with it is to be " cut off from his peoples."

The offerer in this case commits himself to communion with the altar of God. It is emphasised that " his own hands " were to bring Jehovah's offerings (Lev. 7 : 30). There is a definite personal committal first of all at the altar ; that is, *with God*. Then in the eating we commit ourselves *with our brethren* to communion with the altar. If we are committed with

God and with our brethren to such a holy communion it determines the character of our associations. Hence Paul says, "Ye cannot drink the Lord's cup and the cup of demons : ye cannot partake of the Lord's table and of the table of demons." And he adds to this a very solemn enquiry, "Do we provoke the Lord to jealousy ? are we stronger than he ? " 1 Cor. 10 : 21, 22.

All who have broken bread have committed themselves to this, that they have done with the world as a source of happiness. "The bread which we break, is it not the communion of the body of the Christ ? " The One on whom we feed as the Source of our enjoyment, and who is the Substance of our communion with God and with one another, has died out of this world and has no part in it whatever. We have a happiness which is of the deepest character, for it is a divine happiness known in nearness to God and shared with our fellow-saints, but it is a happiness completely outside the world. "The cup of blessing which we bless, is it not the communion of the blood of the Christ ? " He went into death according to God's will that He might open up to us an entirely new character of joy—joy in God as revealed in infinite love.

If we consider the intense holiness of the altar, how absolutely exclusive it is of all that is not in accord with it, we must understand that there can be no playing fast and loose as to communion with it. At the altar it is Christ and His death bringing in blessing according to the holiness of God. Every element in this world is idolatrous and unclean. How can the two be linked together ? How could a soul pass from the one to the other, and have its portion in each? It is morally impossible.

The burnt-offering for acceptance, whether of the herd or of the flock, must be " a male without blemish." For conscious acceptance there must be the apprehension of Christ in the energetic activity in which He was found here to do the will of God. But the fact that the peace-offering might be either " male or female " would suggest that the offerer in this case might have Christ before him either from the side of what was taken up for God in " male " energy, or from the side of what was necessitated by the state of fallen humanity. The known reference of the female in types to *state* would lead one to conclude that the " female " as an offering might intimate what was connected with the latter side. The " female " offering for the sin of " any one of the people of the land " (Lev. 4 : 28, 32 ; chap. 5 : 6), and the " red heifer " of Numbers 19 would perhaps confirm this.

The spiritual action typified in this chapter is of great importance, for it is the basis of fellowship in the souls of saints. It is only hearts that have Christ before them that can know what fellowship is in any true or divine sense. I take it that this is the import of the offerer's hand being laid on the head of his offering. He is fully committed to Christ, not only for acceptance, but as his present portion and joy with God, and as the substance of his communion with fellow-saints. We identify ourselves with Christ ; we commit ourselves to Him in relation to the question of communion or fellowship.

A faithful God has called us into the " fellowship of his Son Jesus Christ our Lord," 1 Cor. 1 : 9. That shows the greatness and dignity of the fellowship into which we are called. But in 1 Cor. 10 : 16 *we* bless the cup, and *we* break the bread. It is what *we* do. Each

one who drinks of the cup and eats the bread puts
his own hand to it, and commits himself definitely to
Christ, and to all that is the fruit of His death. And
that constitutes the essence of our fellowship with
one another. The exercise as to fellowship is often
later in the soul's history than that as to acceptance,
and as to perfection in an Object for the heart. But
there is an intuitive desire in saints for enjoyment in
common of that which is our portion with God, and
that which binds us together in separation from all
that is of the world. If one had no desire to share
spiritually with others it would indicate that he had
not as yet much personal enjoyment of Christ. Even
in the world it is recognised that company is
essential to enjoyment. Man is so constituted that
he derives the greatest part of his pleasure from
sharing it. One may safely say that an isolated
man has very little true enjoyment. One might
have a crowd of people round one and yet be
completely isolated because none of them shared
one's thoughts and feelings. " In the day of your
gladness " (Num. 10 : 10), and " Thou shalt sacrifice
peace-offerings, and shalt eat there, and rejoice before
Jehovah thy God " (Deut. 27 : 7), and other passages
show how peace-offerings were connected with the
happiness of the people. The formal organisations
of the religious world deprive those who are in them
of a great deal of spiritual happiness because they
furnish so little opportunity for Christian fellowship.

If Christ has become our consciously enjoyed portion
with God it kindles desire for the fellowship of saints—
for participation in a holy partnership here in which
we can feed on Christ together. Christian fellowship
is in reference to Christ ; the apostles' doctrine forms

the fellowship. It is not so many persons agreeing to walk and act on certain principles together ; still less is it agreeing to differ : but it is that *Christ* has got a place with each one. It is all hearts appreciating One Person, and preferring what is of that Person to what is of the natural thoughts and tastes of men. Not all having the same measure, but all having the same Person in view, and declining to give place to any other.

The offerer's purpose in offering is that he and others may eat together in communion with the altar. He desires a fellowship that is uncontaminated by the selfish and idolatrous associations of the world. He has found that which he can hold and enjoy *with God*.

> " In Thy grace Thou now hast called us
>   Sharers of Thy joy to be ;
> And to know the blessed secret
>   Of His preciousness to Thee."

Christian fellowship is the fellowship of the death of Christ ; it is the fellowship of His body and of His blood. This is indicated by the offerer killing the animal which he offers. He discerns, in type, the Lord's body given in death. How completely this removes the fellowship from all that is natural and material ! The offerer recognises that he could have no peace or prosperity, no festivity or communion of divine character, apart from the death of Christ. Indeed if we could conceive of Christ as excluding all thought of His death He would be of no value to men. In order to accomplish the will of God and our blessing He has died here. Are we in communion with that ? Not simply owning that it is the ground of our blessing, but in communion with it ? It puts one in spirit outside all that is of the world.

Then the priests " sprinkle the blood on the altar round about." This implies spiritual intelligence as to the import of the act, for " the priests' lips should keep knowledge," Mal. 2 : 7. In 1 Cor. 10 : 15, 16, we read, " I speak as to intelligent persons : do ye judge what I say. The cup of blessing which we bless, is it not the communion of the blood of the Christ ? " The blood of the Christ has borne witness to all the wealth of new covenant blessing in the heart of God and has shown that God would bless men infinitely through death. Now there is priestly ability to spread abroad, as it were, the witness of what is in His heart.

The blood presented on man's side Godward is for atonement ; it is wholly *for God*. Hence " no blood shall ye eat." So long as man is on the earth he must own the rights of God over life. The blood is for atonement, and therefore reserved for God. But in the New Testament we learn that the blood which has made atonement is also the witness of the love of God. This is what the blood is on God's part towards us— the new covenant in the blood of Christ. This can be drunk ; indeed, a man has no life if he does not drink it ; it is open to us to appropriate it freely and fully. The cup of the new covenant in the blood of Christ is a cup of blessing, and we bless—eulogise—it. It speaks of all that is in the heart of the blessed God for men, now expressed in the blood of the Christ. This is the basis of our fellowship. It speaks of blessing outside the sphere of sin and death—blessing of a spiritual order which we can enjoy together—what God is as revealed in grace and love. The hearts of the saints break forth to speak well of all that the cup expresses ; we bless the cup, and rejoice in the infinite thoughts of love which have come to light through the death of Christ.

Those who have to do with God in relation to Christ in peace-offering character can bring near to Him their apprehension of how the death and blood of Christ have made possible for men a new and divine joy in the blessing of God. The blood round the altar in this type intimates that it is God known in blessing that we approach, but that it is blessing that cannot be intermingled with the festivities of an idolatrous world. His blessing coming through death is spiritual ; it lies outside the region of sight and sense ; it is of a nature that death cannot touch. All this is realised by the one who draws near with his peace-offering, for the altar is that most holy spot where things are known *with God* in their true value and blessedness. We must know first what is true of us at the altar— that is, in nearness to God—before we can be marked in this world as those who have their associations in communion with the altar.

Then there is the presentation and burning of the fat of the peace-offering. It is that which the blessed God feeds upon, and in which none other can partici- pate. Our communion together would lose its true and holy character if we did not think first of God's portion ; and if we did not recognise that it is due to Him that the richest and most excellent portion in Christ should be His. There is a peculiar joy in the recognition of this—that there is that in Christ which is reserved for God's delight. If we think of WHO He was it must be so. Because all that He was in His Person gave character to what He became, and who but God could appreciate and appropriate all that ? I say " appropriate " because it is twice in this chapter called the " food " or " bread " of the offering.

Think of the Person who said, " Lo, *I* come to do, O God, thy will " : His was a perfect and holy will, but it was surrendered in devoted obedience, at all possible cost to Himself. We see something of the cost in Gethsemane. In the world where man had been saying for four thousand years, " *My* will be done "—and that the will of a fallen and corrupt being—we see a Divine Person come in flesh, with a perfect and holy will, subordinating that will entirely, and saying in the supreme moment when all the cost of doing God's will was present to His spirit, " Not my will but thine be done ! " Do we not realise that there was something in that which it is beyond the creature to appropriate ? We cannot measure what was given up for God's glory, and therefore we cannot estimate what its giving up in sufferings and death was to God. But we can delight to offer it, and to know that the very mention of it is unspeakable delight to God. It is a very blessed feature of our fellowship.

There is infinitely much that we can enjoy together, and that we can appropriate as the food of our souls, in that holy Person who offered Himself, but our enjoyment of it is enhanced by the thought that there is that in His offering which only God can estimate at its full worth, and which is God's peculiar portion and delight. We have communion with God, for we feed on the same blessed Person, but we love to own adoringly that there is that in Him, and in His offering, which is beyond us, and which is wholly for God. We cannot appropriate it, but we can offer it. Wondrous privilege ! that we should be priests to offer that which only God can feed upon ! " All the fat shall be Jehovah's " (verse 16).

" And Aaron's sons shall burn it on the altar upon the burnt-offering which lieth on the wood that is upon the fire." What we have apprehended of Christ in burnt-offering and meat-offering character, as seen in chapters 1 and 2, is carried on in our souls, and underlies the peace-offering. What a wondrous basis the three offerings constitute for the communion of saints —the sweet odour of Christ on the altar ! We shall find much instruction as to communion with the altar when we come to the seventh chapter.

CHAPTER 4

THIS chapter sets forth exercises which we all have to take up personally, for James tells us that " we all often offend." Wilful sins are not referred to here, for God would not contemplate His people sinning wilfully or presumptuously. Wilful sin in Scripture is really apostasy. I believe the working of the will is typified in leprosy (Lev. 13 and 14), and when leprosy breaks out we do not know what the issue may be. Healing can only be brought about by God's sovereign mercy and power. In such a case man is powerless. Here it is, " If a soul shall sin *through inadvertence* against any of the commandments of Jehovah in things that ought not to be done, and do any of them." It refers to sins which are committed through unwatchfulness, through lack of proper exercise in the fear of God. The loins have been ungirded, and what is of nature has been allowed, leading to something being done that ought not to be done. The most serious

aspects of such a case are presented first—the sin of
the priest that is anointed, of the whole assembly, and
of a prince. There are degrees of exercise according
to the greater or less responsibility of the position
held by the one who sins.

" The priest that is anointed " is the first case
considered. It is very sad when such a one sins
" according to the trespass of the people." For a
saint who has known what it is to be anointed—to
have the Spirit, and to be in priestly relations with God
as one possessed of holy knowledge—to forget, as it
were, the anointing, and act wrongly like a common
person, is very serious.

Do we always remember the peculiar and blessed
place that we have as being anointed ? I like to
remind myself sometimes as I go along that I belong
to the Man at God's right hand ! I am of that Man,
and I have His Spirit ! Paul, referring to the saints,
says, " So also is the Christ " (1 Cor. 12 : 12) ; the
saints are the anointed company down here. " Praying in the Holy Spirit " (Jude 20) implies that we have
a priestly place with God, and that our desires do not
move outside the region of the Spirit. There is no
sinning there. Jude contemplates the possibility of
God's called ones, preserved in Jesus Christ, being
kept without stumbling. The second epistle to the
Corinthians speaks of the saints as anointed by God,
and the anointing confers priestly capability. For
such to sin is a very grave defection. It is—for the
moment, at any rate—a bringing into evidence of the
fallen man, not the Man at the right hand of God. It
is not merely that I have done wrong and I am sorry
for it—a man of the world would go as far as that—
but my deep concern is that I have allowed something

of the man who is under judgment with God. And the sin of a priest has an additionally grave character, inasmuch as it directly affects the service of God, and the whole assembly suffers in relation to that service. So that, in its issues, it is much more than a personal fault.

It is noticeable that in connection with the priest it does not speak—as in the case of the assembly, the prince or one of the people—of his sin becoming known. This supposes, in their case, a certain interval between the sin and its becoming known to them as such. But the omission of this statement when the priest is in question seems to suggest that the anointed priest would realise at once, intuitively, that he had done what he ought not. This implies a holy sensitiveness in the priest that one would covet. It implies such habitual nearness to God that if, in an unguarded moment, one has done what ought not to be done, it is felt at once, and the soul immediately turns to God about it. My impression is that the degree of a believer's holiness—the degree in which he has truly known what it is to be an anointed priest —can be measured by his sensitiveness as to sin.

When there have been actions or words or feelings that are of the flesh it is often some time before there is any true movement of self-judgment. This indicates that nearness has not been known or preserved, or the distance that sin produces would be more quickly and keenly felt. In such a case the believer has got away—as to the condition of his soul—from his place with God as an anointed priest, though he may have formerly known that holy and near position and character. If we are not habitually near to God we may go on a long time with what is really of the flesh, and not perceive it. It may need a sharp word to our consciences, or perhaps a sharp stroke of discipline, to bring it home to us. " Before I was afflicted I went astray, but now I keep thy word." Our true liberty is to judge what is of the flesh inwardly, so that, though it is fully discerned by us and we are humbled by discerning it, it does not come out to be a public reproach.

If a priest sins he cannot go on with the service of God, but to a sensitive priestly heart restoration is not necessarily a long process. It is indeed a grave fault for such a one to sin " according to the trespass of the people," but the scripture supposes that he is marked by the sensitiveness which properly belongs to the priestly anointing. It is very· sad if this sensitiveness is lacking ; such a condition really belies the character of the anointing.

The moment there is the consciousness of having sinned the divine provision is available. Christ is at once introduced in sin-offering character. Such is grace—the blessed grace of our God ! He does not say that the priest must repent deeply for three months, and then, when he has truly and deeply judged himself, he may bring a sin-offering ! That might be our way, but it is not God's. Deep and holy and divine self-judgment is not brought about by thinking of the sin, but by apprehending Christ in relation to it, and by taking up with God .what it has cost Him to deal with it and put it away. Christ is available through divine grace. Let us never forget that ! Let us turn to God at once when there has been a movement of the flesh, and avail ourselves of Christ in sin-offering character ! Let us beware of Satan's effort to keep sin before us, and darken our

souls by it, and hinder us from turning to God so that
we may learn the value of Christ in relation to it !

The first movement in regard to the sin of a believer
is on the part of Jesus Christ the righteous. We have
Him as " a patron with the Father " (1 John 2 : 1).
His advocacy results in suitable exercises being produced in the soul of the one who has sinned, and those
exercises are presented typically in Leviticus 4. We
take them up in the light of the grace that is in
" Jesus Christ the righteous," and it is really the
fruit of His present service in grace that we are able
to take them up. To be carried in that way through
the exercise of a chapter like this—humbling though
it surely is to us—leads to great growth in grace, and
in the knowledge of our Lord and Saviour Jesus Christ.
If I have sinned it is very humbling to me, but God
intends to make Christ better known and more appreciated in my heart, through that sin. It is the
exposure to me of what I am, but if I turn to God
about it He will use it to enlarge my knowledge and
appreciation of Christ. In the case of the priest a
large apprehension of Christ is suggested—" a young
bullock without blemish." The special seriousness of
sin in such a one has its answer in a specially large
apprehension of Christ in relation to it.

The sin-offering in each case is brought to the entrance of the tent of meeting, or to the place of the
burnt-offering. This seems to indicate a readiness to
be perfectly open and candid about the matter. If I
have really learned something more of the value of
Christ through my sin I can afford to be quite open
about it. I do not mean that it is necessary, or
desirable, to speak of one's wrong-doing to everybody,
but there is a preparedness to do so if any occasion for

it arises. It is just the opposite to the attempt to
cover up things that we may appear to be better than
we really are. If saints were more prepared to own
things which they know in their consciences to be
wrong it would greatly promote fellowship. Of course,
all must be " before Jehovah " to have true moral
value.

Think of the impression that would be made on all
Israel as the anointed priest was seen bringing his
sin-offering " to the entrance of the tent of meeting
before Jehovah " ! It is true that he has sinned, but
he has something greater before him than his sin.
He is " before Jehovah," and he is in possession,
typically, of a large apprehension of Christ. His soul
is filled with the apprehension of Christ in relation to
his sin. Do you not think that would take away the
fleshly reluctance to own the wrong that he had done ?
I do not think Peter minded his fault being put on
record for the church. As to Moses and David, it is
themselves who have told, in the most public way, the
story of their faults. This shows how completely they
were morally apart from the sin by self-judgment, so
that they had no thought of preserving their own
reputation.

If I became possessed before God of Christ in
sin-offering character I am sure it would give candour
and transparency. I should be ready to listen to
James, who says, " Confess therefore your offences to
one another, and pray for one another, that ye may
be healed," James 5 : 16. If we were more free to
make confession of faults it would lead to more
prayer for one another. The confessional is the devil's
travesty of this, designed to bring people under the
power of a false priesthood. James says, " Confess

. . . to one another." Those who go to "confession" are as much entitled to hear the confession
of the so-called "priest" as he is to hear theirs.

If I have done wrong there is moral elevation in
owning it, but the flesh regards it as degradation. If
I have apprehended Christ in sin-offering character in
relation to my sin it will deliver me from the pride of
the flesh that would refuse to acknowledge the wrong.

The priest laying his hand on the bullock's head and
slaughtering it expresses the sense that he has of the
necessity for Christ and His death in relation to the
sin committed. It is a deep exercise to have to own
to God that one has done something for which Christ
had to die—one has given place to the man He died
to remove. It may be I have spoken a hasty word
or allowed a wrong feeling ! Where did it come from ?
The man in Psalm 51 traces his sin to its root. "Behold,
in iniquity was I brought forth, and in sin did my
mother conceive me." My sin is the manifestation of
the fallen and sinful man whom Christ died to remove.
We are not right with God until we acknowledge this.

Christ has borne the judgment of sin ; He has died
to close the history sacrificially of the man who is only
evil continually. If I have allowed something of that
man to come into evidence, God would use the very
exercise occasioned by this to give me a new lesson
in the appreciation of Christ and His death. The
death of the bullock, the blood, the burning outside the camp signify the complete removal from
before God in sacrificial death and judgment of the
man after the flesh. In being brought to appreciate
the death of Christ we are brought into harmony with
God as to the sin, and as to the source from which it
proceeded, and as to the way God has dealt with it.

We learn to hate sin ; it becomes only a grief to us. Jabez prayed " that thou wouldest keep me from evil, that it may not grieve me ! And God brought about what he had requested," 1 Chron. 4 : 10. When evil is only a grief to us, because of what it cost Christ to remove it, we can return consciously to priestly nearness. Perhaps this is the reason why it is not said of the priest that is anointed, as it is of the other cases, that his offering makes atonement for him, or that his sin shall be forgiven. In bringing his offering the priest returns consciously to priestly relations with God. That involves atonement and forgiveness ; the greater includes the less. The priest takes up his holy service with a deepened spirituality, as having acquired an apprehension of Christ in relation to what is in himself which he had not before.

The priest brings the blood into the tent of meeting, and sprinkles it seven times " before Jehovah before the veil of the sanctuary." Not once or twice, but *seven* times ! Indicating how God would have the soul take up before Him a sense of the perfection of the efficacy of the blood of Christ to remove the stain from before Him of what has now come on the conscience. This is not being washed again in the blood, or a re-application of the blood to us, as some people unscripturally teach. As to justification, or the non-imputation of sins, the believer is " perfected in perpetuity " by the one offering of Christ ; his sins and his lawlessnesses God will never remember any more to lay them to his charge. See Hebrews 9 and 10. The efficacy of the blood never diminishes or changes on God's side, and the believer is in all its sin-cleansing efficacy in perpetuity. But when he sins he cannot go on with God apart from moral exercises by which he apprehends afresh with God the precious and holy value of the blood of Christ.

The blood put " on the horns of the altar of fragrant incense " would intimate that the offerer returns to liberty and confidence in prayer, which he could not do while his heart condemned him. He does not ignore his sin, but it has led—through grace—to an apprehension of Christ which sets him free with God.

I have heard that a broken bone when healed is stronger in that place than anywhere else, and this seems to be suggested as the fruit of a sin-offering exercise by David asking " that the bones which thou hast broken may rejoice," Psa. 51 : 8.

Then all the blood of the bullock being poured out " at the bottom of the altar of burnt-offering " seems to provide a basis, as it were, for the offering of the fat. The blood has so fully vindicated every righteous claim of the altar that the offerer can now get an apprehension of the excess. If CHRIST is known as the sin-offering, His value could not be limited to the removal of what is obnoxious to God. The very way it was done, and the excellence of Him who offered Himself, were such that infinite satisfaction and good pleasure were secured for God. That is the fat. It forms, in a certain sense, a link with the burnt-offering. Restoration to full liberty with God is not complete until there is an apprehension of how the offering of Christ for sin has brought in delight for God. Instead of the moral corruption of the man who has come into evidence in the sin, and who has been sacrificially ended in the death of Christ, there is the supreme excellence of One delightful to God, and its holy fragrance. The priest would resume his service in the blessed consciousness of this.

If we have sinned, the way to get right with God, and to please God, is to avail ourselves of Christ as the sin-offering. Sometimes a great deal of the regret which is felt is not really " grief according to God," but the mortification of wounded vanity. This may lead to a resolve to be more careful another time, but it does not lead to increased apprehension of Christ, and it does not put the soul right with God.

The complete consumption in holy judgment of what was offensive to God is seen typically in the burning of the whole bullock outside the camp. This implies a deep sense in the soul of God's entire rejection of the man from whom the sin proceeded. The wrong thing done is traced to the root, as we may see in Psalm 51, and the soul is brought into harmony with God as to the character of the man after the flesh, and as to the judgment which has come upon that man in the death and judgment-bearing of Christ. It is there that we really find " a clean place," for the man of sin and shame and defilement is ended in a holy sacrifice, and the " ashes " speak of judgment eternally exhausted.

The case of the priest comes before that of " the whole assembly," for priestly exercise and discernment would be needed to take right account of the sin of the whole assembly, so that the sin-offering as in view of priestly sensibilities and restoration of priestly service comes first. It remains for us to note the application of the same principles to the different cases which follow. ·

The sin of " the whole assembly " is a very serious matter, because, like the sin of the anointed priest, it interferes with the service of God. If the whole assembly sins against " any of all the commandments of Jehovah in things which should not be done," it must affect the service of God. The thing may be " hid from the eyes of the congregation," but it is not hid from the eyes of the Lord, and instead of that being before Him which is for His pleasure, there is that which is an offence to Him.

I doubt whether we are sufficiently exercised about the sin of " the whole assembly." Rev. 2 and 3 shows us the sin of the whole assembly. It is hid from the eyes of many, but it has really " become known " ; the Lord has made it known. Would any one venture to say that the present state of " the whole assembly " gives God pleasure ? No, it is an offence to Him. It has left its first love, it has ceased to be in subjection to Jesus as Lord, it does not hold Christ as Head, nor does it own in a practical way the blessed reality of the presence of the Holy Spirit. There is an order established generally which is of man and not of God. The mustard seed has become a great tree. All this is a very grave sin, and the Lord has made it known that there might be opportunity to repent. In the epistles to five of the assemblies (Rev. 2 and 3) there is a call to repent. " The elders of the assembly " have had the opportunity to come with the sin-offering and lay their hands on its head. If there is no repentance the Lord will assuredly remove the candlestick, and spue the assembly out of His mouth. Things are just on the eve of this being done.

Many will admit that things are not what they ought to be, but will excuse them on the ground of human infirmity, or errors in judgment, or want of light. The Lord Himself, in grace, takes account of the sin in Leviticus 4 as done " inadvertently." But the

plain fact is that all the things in the Christian profession of which the Lord disapproves are SIN. Place
is given everywhere to the man who was condemned
at the cross. Whatever is wrong in the Christian
profession, and contrary to the commandments of the
Lord, springs from man after the flesh. The one
who brings the sin-offering judges this in the light of
the fact that Christ bore the judgment of that man,
and died to bring him to an end before God. In the
recognition of this he can call on the Lord out of a
pure heart, as morally apart, by the death of Christ,
from that man. But this makes the sin of " the
whole assembly " a very grave matter, and when
we see it in this light we must take the path of
separation.

I would put it to any heart that loves the Lord
Jesus Christ in sincerity, Would you like to go on with
something of which He disapproves ? If the congregation and the elders of the assembly will not
bring the sin-offering of the congregation, the faithful
individual must. And how could we call on the
Lord out of a pure heart if we go on with things which
He has made known to us to be sin ?   Hence 2 Timothy
comes in. We are to withdraw from iniquity, to
separate from vessels to dishonour, and to turn away
from those who have a form of piety but deny its
power.

Those who own the sin of the whole assembly, and
avail themselves of Christ as the " sin-offering of the
congregation," can truly " call on the Lord out of a
pure heart " ; and I do not doubt that such can know
something of forgiveness in an assembly sense. If
the spiritual features of the assembly are found
amongst saints in some measure, and the service of

God, and the enjoyment of assembly privilege, it is blessed evidence of forgiveness and of restoring mercy. I think many have tasted something of the reality of this.

In the early part of the last century many godly persons felt deeply the sin of the assembly ; not merely their personal failures but that " the whole assembly " had departed from God's thoughts. Priestly exercise was brought about as to what was suitable to God, and much light was given as to His ways and purposes, and as to Christ and the assembly. This led to a judgment of things in the light of the death of Christ, and to a movement of separation, and the result has been a revival, in measure, of the true spiritual features of the assembly, and of the service of God, and of the enjoyment of assembly privilege.

There is such a thing as assembly exercise as well as individual exercise, and it is deeper than anything purely individual could be, because it is connected with what is suitable to God in His house. So that for saints who are professedly walking together as owning the truth and principles of the assembly to " do somewhat against any of all the commandments " of the Lord—however inadvertently done—is a serious matter. But grace has anticipated the possibility of such a thing, and has made provision for it. The sin-offering for the assembly corresponds with that for the anointed priest ; the exercise in these two cases seems to be measured by the divine estimate of the sin, and the apprehension of Christ which meets it is a very full one. In the following cases there is not with each the same degree of self-judgment, or of apprehension of Christ ; it is according to the measure and depth of exercise with each. But in the case of

the anointed priest and the assembly a divine measure
of exercise is called for, having its answer in a large
apprehension of Christ.

We cannot go on carelessly with the things of God.
There is a tendency to make light of things which
are really movements of the flesh, but if we make
light of such things God does not. " I will be hallowed
in them that come near me, and before all the people
I will be glorified," Lev. 10 : 3. We cannot do that
which should not be done, and go on with the service
of God as if nothing had happened. There must be
self-judgment, and the sin-offering brought. But
grace has provided that which will fully and divinely
adjust the whole matter, and grace would use even
the sin to deepen our self-knowledge, and to give us
enlarged apprehension of Christ.

* * * * *

" A prince " or " ruler " represents one prominent
in the congregation—one who has cared for the order
of the people of God. It is more serious for such to
sin than for " one of the people of the land," and
therefore it calls for a stronger and more energetic
apprehension of Christ in sin-offering character to
secure forgiveness and restoration. One who has been
in any way prominent amongst the people of God
must have got his place by having certain moral
qualities or spiritual formation. He would be a
greater man morally than " the people of the land " ;
otherwise his place would have been only fleshly
pretension. But I have no doubt this scripture contemplates a true " prince," not a fleshly pretender.
When the sin of such comes to his knowledge he gives
evidence that he is a " prince " by bringing a " male "
offering. He has a more vigorous apprehension of

Christ, and therefore a deeper self-judgment, than " one of the people of the land."

In the case of one who has been a " prince " this would be justly looked for in view of restoration of confidence and fellowship, when his sin had been such as to interfere with these. The offering must be in proportion to the offerer. In a " prince " God would look for such an apprehension of Christ as would give great energy to self-judgment. Such would not spare or screen himself in any way. The spiritual energy in which he would judge himself would go beyond anything that his brethren might require. His exercises would give *them* an insight into soul-experiences which would deepen God's work in their souls.

David is the great example in Scripture of a " prince " who sinned ; it is very instructive for us to observe the sin-offering exercises of David. They are fully detailed for us in what are called the penitential Psalms (Psalms 6, 32, 38, 51, 102, 130, 143). These Psalms are not only an encouragement to souls under exercise, but they give us an insight into experiences which are perhaps beyond our own moral depth. They minister to self-knowledge, and to the knowledge of God. We should carefully ponder them in connection with the sin-offering. Each one was written by a " prince."

Christ is always available as the sin-offering, and the sooner we avail ourselves of Him the better. It is good to be so established in grace that when we sin we avail ourselves at once of Christ as the sin-offering. God looks for an apprehension of Christ as sin-offering in proportion to the spiritual capacity of the individual. What is spoken of in Scripture as sinning wilfully is turning away from Christ—

deliberately turning away from the sin-offering as
apostates do. If a man does that there is no other
remedy available ; there is nothing left to bring him
to repentance.

Grace is the true power of holiness. Grace never
excuses sin or makes light of it, but it shows me the
holy One of God going to the cross and being made
sin. In His unutterable anguish and suffering I learn
what sin is before God, and that it has been judged in
Him that I might learn to judge it in myself.

If the sin of a believer is of such a nature as to
suspend the confidence and fellowship of his brethren,
that confidence cannot be restored without evidence
that he has judged himself. Two birds or a handful
of flour would not suffice, or be accepted, if a man
ought to bring a sheep ! A female goat is accepted
from " one of the people of the land," but a " prince "
must bring a male. The measure of one's self-judgment
is the measure in which we have apprehended Christ
as the sin-offering, and in a " prince " God looks for
this to be an energetic exercise. It is not saying
lightly, " I am sorry." What a profound depth of
self-judgment appears in the Psalms we have referred
to ! They are the exercises of a " prince " who
sinned, and they have become moral instruction for
all the people of God. We see there a character and
energy of self-judgment that is wonderful, and as we
look into greater depths of experimental self-knowledge
in another than we have sounded in ourselves, it
shows us what we are. We are thus morally deepened,
and we get a true sense of what Christ died for. When
a man really gets to the root of things, as David did,
he has done with making excuses.

The blood being put on the horns of the altar of

burnt-offering, and the fat burned on the altar, links
the sin-offering with the burnt-offering. I do not
think anyone would go truly through the exercise of
the sin-offering with God without reaching the burnt-
offering. Psalm 51 is a deep sin-offering exercise, but
it ends with the thought of the burnt-offering, and
God doing good to' Zion and building the walls of
Jerusalem. It would not be like God to leave us
merely with the negative thought of being relieved
of the sin. We do not leave God's presence without
getting a sense of the sweet odour of Christ in burnt-
offering character. We are not only in perfect
clearance from sin, but we are in divine acceptance.
And the thought of good being done to Zion, would
suggest that every sin-offering exercise contributes to
the strength and blessing of the assembly. The
experience of the one who brings his sin-offering—
what he has acquired of Christ in relation to his
exercise—results in a contribution to the good of the
assembly. And the mention of the peace-offering
(verses 26, 31) would seem to be suggestive of the
restoration of the privilege of fellowship with the
people of God. If a man is really right with God he
will be put right with his brethren also.

If a brother has sinned God would encourage him
to avail himself of Christ as the sin-offering. That
is the first thing to be concerned about. If he comes
into the apprehension of Christ and of His death
in relation to his sin he will judge himself. He will
then be a spiritually deepened man—a " converted "
or " restored " man (Luke 22 : 32)—and he will be
available, like Peter, for the comfort and strengthening
of his brethren. The power of God in grace is such
that one who has sinned can be fully restored to the

c

confidence of the brethren, and made a greater help
to them than he was before. This shows what God
is, and the better we know God the more qualified
we shall be to help in the restoration of those who
sin. But this is priestly work. It requires that we
should eat the sin-offering for our brethren (Lev. 6).
In this way we make the sin our own. Indeed
we can never think before God of the sin of a
brother or sister without realising that it is a mirror
in which we can see what we are ourselves. But in
eating the sin-offering we also realise what the sin
has cost Christ, and how His death alone could remove
it. Then we can take up advocacy and pray for our
brother. In 1 John Jesus Christ the righteous is the
Advocate, and at the end of the epistle the saints
are put in the place of advocacy : " If any one see
his brother sinning a sin not unto death, he shall ask,
and he shall give him life, for those that do not sin
unto death," 1 John 5 : 16. If you pray for a brother
you have a moral title to go to him, and to speak to
him as one who has made his sin your own. One who
has done so will have moral power.

*   *   *   *   *

Little needs to be added as to the sin-offering of
" one of the people of the land," save to note that the
offerer in this case brings typically a weaker apprehension of Christ than the " prince " ; he brings a
female goat or sheep. It is not that his sin is more
easily atoned for, or that anything less than the full
value of the death of Christ could atone for it. But
we are occupied in these chapters with Christ and
His death as known and apprehended by the faith
and affections of saints, and in this we cannot go
beyond our measure. Perhaps the three classes

spoken of in this chapter might answer in some way to John's three grades of babes, young men, and fathers. God would not look for the measure of exercise in a babe that He would rightly look for in a father. But things have to be taken up in truth according to our measure. The soul has to avail itself of Christ, and to apprehend the import of His death so that there may be a true judgment of the root from which the sin proceeded. If I sin I am entitled, through infinite grace, to lay my hand upon Christ, and He is never far away. The sin-offering always lies at the door, as God said to Cain. Everything has been reached and judged in the death of Christ ; it is for us to come into the apprehension of it. Then we not only judge ourselves rightly, but we get a blessed sense of forgiveness, and an enlarged appreciation of Christ.

CHAPTER 5

IT is noticeable that the section of this book referring to the sin-offering is longer than that referring to the other offerings ; it extends from chapter 4 : 1 to chapter 5 : 13. Then the trespass-offering is in chapter 5 : 14–26. That so much should have to be said on this subject is sad evidence of the existence of much amongst the people of God that calls for it. In verses 1–6 of this chapter we have three specific instances, which would probably cover in principle every kind of sin amongst the people of God. The first is failure in respect of *witness* ; the second is failure as to the maintenance of *separation* ; and the third is failure as to sobriety or *self-control*.

The first instance of guilt is that of one who refrains from uttering that of which he should bear witness. It shows that such a thing is likely to occur among the people of God. One has known instances of persons being in a position to bear witness of evil which should have been made known, who have failed to utter it. This is a serious matter, for it is said of such, " If he do not give information then he shall bear his iniquity."

But there is another side of things to which this would apply. We are left here in the place of witness for Christ, and there are times when we are directly challenged—when we " hear the voice of adjuration " —and if we fail to bear witness we are guilty. The Lord heard " the voice of adjuration " when before the High Priest (Matt. 26 : 63), and He witnessed a good confession. We are responsible to be con- fessors of the truth—confessors of Christ—but we often fail to utter what we should witness ; we shrink from the reproach which is connected with the Name of the Lord Jesus. Christ Jesus witnessed the good confession in the presence of the High Priest and of Pontius Pilate (1 Tim. 6 : 13), and this would show that " confession " is not amongst believers, but in the presence of the hostile world. It does not mean telling Christians that one believes in Jesus, but owning Him before unbelievers.

True confession is in answer to a challenge. At school, or in the office, or at the works, you are asked to do something, or to go somewhere, and you are obliged to decline because you know that it would not please the Lord Jesus. Then the challenge comes, Why not ? Now you have to utter what is in your heart ! Sometimes we evade the reproach—which is really a privilege and honour—by merely saying, I do not go to the pictures, or whatever it is. But tell them why ! The Lord Jesus has become great and precious to you. In the presence of those to whom He is nothing confess that He is great to you, He is Lord to you ! Such a confession involves cost, because it involves bearing the reproach of Christ ; that is really the greatest and truest honour.

Our witness is to be of what we have " seen or known " in Christ. If we have travelled along the moral road mapped out in this book, and learned Christ as the burnt-offering, the oblation, the peace-offering, and the sin-offering, He has acquired a great place in our affections, and we are to witness accordingly. We have " seen or known " something that is worth confessing. Then let us confess it ! Many hold back because they feel they will bungle over it. Perhaps you will bungle, but never mind, get it out ! There is tremendous power in just saying, Jesus is Lord to me. The man to whom you say it knows, at the bottom, that Jesus ought to be Lord to him, and his conscience will support your confession, whatever he may say with his lips, and the Holy Spirit will support it too. Some are kept back from witnessing of what they have " seen and known " by the fear that they will not be consistent. But the witness gets divine support ; all the power of the kingdom of God supports a confessor of the Lord Jesus. Satan would keep us back from being true witnesses so that we might not get the support of the kingdom. A man, who in a foreign land was ashamed of the British flag, could not expect to be supported by British power if he got into difficulties. You may depend upon it that in God's kingdom the flag will be

honoured and supported. Then let us not be ashamed
of it.

I suppose most of us know what it is to have sinned
by failing to utter what was in our hearts ! Why did
we not utter it ? Because we shrank from the cost,
and we missed an opportunity of bringing Christ into
evidence. It was for the moment a hiding of Christ
and a retaining of self. Every true confession brings
Christ into evidence in a positive way ; there is something aggressive about it ; it is additional to the
quiet and retiring life of one who does not want the
world or its things. One cannot but feel that there
is often a holding back of witness to what has been
" seen or known." And such a holding back, when
one is definitely challenged, is *sin*.

Then in verses 2 and 3 it is a question of touching
what is unclean. The world is full of many different
kinds and degrees of uncleanness, as we see in figure
in these verses. Large things and small things—
beast, cattle, or crawling thing. Unless we preserve
separation there is not only personal failure, but the
fellowship is compromised. " Wherefore come out
from the midst of them, and be separated, saith the
Lord, and touch not what is unclean, and I will receive
you ; and I will be to you for a Father, and ye shall be
to me for sons and daughters, saith the Lord Almighty,"
2 Cor. 6 : 17, 18. We cannot be on terms of intimacy
and friendship with the unconverted, or make companions of them and walk in their ways, without being
rendered unclean. The unclean creatures of verse 2
would perhaps typify things outside oneself—association
with unbelievers as referred to in 2 Corinthians 6.
While the "uncleanness of man" (verse 3) would perhaps
be more what we get in 2 Corinthians 7 : 1. " Having

therefore these promises, beloved, let us purify ourselves from every pollution of flesh and spirit, perfect-
ing holiness in God's fear." That is every uncleanness
which we find in ourselves ; we have to preserve
purity from it all.

The third form of specific sin (verse 4) is " talking
rashly with the lips, to do evil or to do good, in everything that a man shall say rashly with an oath." If
it was " to do evil " one ought never to have said it
at all ; if it was " to do good " one ought not to say
it without doing it. The sin here lies in the rashness of what is said, and the more rash a man is in
his speech the more likely is he to strengthen what
he says by an oath. See Matthew 26 : 74. Strong
asseveration is very often found identified with
rashness and sin. A man whose intents and
purposes are formed in the fear of God does not
speak rashly, nor does he need to use anything
in the nature of an oath. Our Lord has said,
" But let your word be Yea, yea ; Nay, nay ; but
what is more than these is from evil (or, the evil one),"
Matt. 5 : 37. Alas ! the unsubdued state of the
heart often discloses itself in the rashness of the lips !
Indeed James says, " If any one offend not in word,
he is a perfect man, able to bridle the whole body
too."

If one has sinned in any of the three ways here
spoken of, the moment comes " when he knoweth it."
The prophetic word comes home, either in secret or
through ministry, and there is the consciousness of
having allowed what is of the flesh. A cloud comes
over the joy ; there is not freedom in the service of
the Lord, or in prayer, or in fellowship with the
brethren. Then an upright soul turns to God in con-

fession, and brings his trespass-offering. Provision
is made for cleansing, and for learning in a new way
the value of Christ, as we have seen in chapter 4.

It is very encouraging to see the grace that makes
provision for one who is not able to bring a sheep or a
goat. The one contemplated in verses 7–10 is feebler
in his exercises, and in his apprehension of Christ.
But he gets cleansing and forgiveness though he can
only bring " two turtle-doves or two young pigeons."
God takes account of the actual conditions which are
found amongst His people, and in this the measures
of all are not alike. There is not with all the same
capacity for the apprehension of Christ, and therefore
not the same capacity for self-judgment. The cause
of these differences, and of some having less ability
than others, is not explained here, and we need not
attempt to account for it. It exists as a matter of
fact, and God recognises it, and we have to recognise
it. There are moral differences just as there are
mental and physical differences. In this chapter God
takes account in grace of different capacities in His
people. The man who brings two birds has a smaller
apprehension than the one who brings a sheep. But
even he is able to discern the difference between Christ
as the sin-offering and as the burnt-offering. The
second bird seems to take the place here of the fat in
the larger offerings, and brings in the thought of the
blessed acceptability—the positive excellence and
sweet fragrance—of Christ in the offering of Himself.
So that it indicates an apprehension in the offerer not
only of clearance, but of the excess that secures for
him through the death of Christ a return to the joy
of acceptance.

There is an even smaller measure in one who brings

" the tenth part of an ephah of fine flour." This represents the feeblest measure of exercise that is taken account of in this connection. There is no true perception in such an offerer that his sin necessitated the death of Christ. He does not measure it in its true gravity, nor realise that sin is such a solemn thing that death is its penalty. But he has a sense that he has done wrong, and he has also a sense of the perfectness of Christ. He could say of Him, like the thief, " This man has done nothing amiss." He judges himself in some measure—perhaps a small measure—in the light of what Christ was. And he has a conviction that only what was seen in Christ will do for God. He has the impression in his soul that Christ is needed, and he has to do with God about his sin in the consciousness of this, and in the grace of God he gets forgiveness.

It is wonderful how God accepts any measure of true exercise, and any measure in which a soul apprehends Christ and judges himself in the light of Christ, and this ought to have its answer in what we look for in one another. We must not expect to find the same depth of self-judgment in every one. If we have to do with a brother whose exercises are feeble we are apt to say that there is little in him. This is perhaps true, but it should not lead us to think little of him. There is more need for our priestly service for him, and that he should be cared for and helped. If I regard him as of no account, I show that I no more understand his divine value than he does himself !

These provisions made in grace do not in any way excuse carelessness or lightness as to sin. No one can say, It does not matter whether I judge myself deeply or not. God knows our ability, and if we ought

to bring a sheep He will not accept a handful of flour.
We may be assured that the priest would never accept
two birds from a man who was able to bring a goat!
But while remembering this as to ourselves, we should
remember as to others that all have not the same
apprehension of Christ in sin-offering character, and
therefore have not the same capacity for self-judgment.
And the provisions of this chapter meet very graciously
the exercises of many who have sinned, whose distress
is that they do not feel able to judge themselves as
deeply as they would like to do. Satan often uses
this to keep souls in bondage. If you are conscious
that you have sinned, and if you have had to do with
God about it in spiritual reality, and have availed
yourself of Christ as the sin-offering according to your
measure, you may be fully assured that the sin is
forgiven. And your moral capacity is really being
increased by the exercise; you are learning more
fully to distinguish " good and evil " (Heb. 5 : 14), and
to judge the latter in view of Christ and of His death.

*   *   *   *   *

We come to the trespass-offering in verses 14–26.
The difference between the sin-offering and the trespass-
offering would seem to be that in the sin-offering the
offence is viewed as a question of what is due to God
in His holy nature and to His dwelling-place in the
midst of His people. Hence *confession* of the sin,
and the holy exercise of self-judgment connected
with the apprehension of Christ in sin-offering character
are needed. But sin has very often to be looked at,
not only as grieving to God in His holy nature, but as
an offence against His government. It is in connection
with His government that restitution comes in. If
one has been unfaithful in the holy things of Jehovah

it is not enough that one should confess and bring a sin-offering. Restitution must be made for the wrong done; it must be put right. There was something due to God that was not rendered in its season, and things will not be right until it is rendered.

" If any one act unfaithfully and sin through inadvertence in the holy things of Jehovah." Such a one has failed to render what was due to God. The tithes are the last thing mentioned in this book, and they are " holy to Jehovah " Lev. 27 : 30–33. There was no prosperity in Israel when the tithes were not brought. See Malachi 3 : 8–12. Our lives are to be so ordered that there is something distinctly for God. When this is so, the way we act in our house-holds and in our business, ministers to our spiritual food, and helps us as Levites. See Deuteronomy 14 : 22, 23, 29 ; Numbers 18 : 21. If the tithes are rendered there is food in God's house (Mal. 3 : 10), and you may depend upon it that if you minister to the house, the house will minister to you ! Then the stranger, and the fatherless, and the widow, will have their share ; grace will flow out in every direction where there is need. If there is a lack of food and blessing it raises the question whether " the whole tithe " has been brought " into the treasure-house." If we considered more for God, and His portion, the result would be much food to be enjoyed when we come together (Deut. 14 : 22, 23). And what we are as dwelling in the land would minister to what we are as Levites.

One cannot doubt that there is much unfaithful acting " in the holy things of Jehovah." But a soul really conscious of having sinned in this way would be exercised to make up the deficiency, and even to go beyond. And it is noticeable that the principle

of " valuation " comes in here. This is not left to
the individual conscience, but to the valuation of
Moses. If there is a trespass in the " holy things "
none can estimate it but the One who is Son over
God's house. As to God's holy things Christ is the
only One who can justly estimate unfaithfulness, and
what is needed to put things right. There must be a
special having to do with Him. It is important to
see that there is such a thing as " the shekel of the
sanctuary." That is, a divine standard of moral
value. People do not think much of a trespass in
" holy things " to-day. It is appalling how holy
things are trifled with, and made the plaything of
the mind of man. God's redemption rights are ignored,
and the holiness of His sanctuary profaned, in innumerable ways. But there is One who rightly estimates
everything. We see this in Revelation 2 and 3.

If there has been unfaithfulness in ths " holy things "
one must get to the Lord about it, and get His valuation. This brings in a marked difference from the
sin-offering, in which the offering is according to the
capacity of the one who has sinned. In the trespass-
offering all is according to the valuation of Moses.
This brings in a divine estimate, and therefore in each
case the offering is a ram.

Moses is a type of Christ as Son over God's house ;
every trespass must be valued by Him. Verses 17–19
expressly refer to one who does not even know that
he has sinned. " Yet is he guilty, and shall bear his
iniquity . . . he hath certainly trespassed against
Jehovah." One should always remember the possibility of having sinned without knowing it. Paul
said, " I am conscious of nothing in myself ; but I
am not justified by this ; but he that examines me

is the Lord," 1 Cor. 4 : 4. I may not know that I have trespassed, but *Moses* may know! How important it is then really to have to do with the Lord, and get His valuation of things! I trust our souls feel the need of taking up the exercise of Psalm 139. "Search me, O God, and know my heart; prove me, and know my thought; and see if there be any grievous (or idolatrous) way in me; and lead me in the way everlasting." We shall get the Lord's valuation at the judgment-seat, but it would be better to get it beforehand. For the trespass-offering is available now, and it gives opportunity for increase in the knowledge of Christ. Believers are sometimes afraid of facing things with the Lord : they do not know how much gain there is in doing so.

Getting the valuation of Christ leads to bringing an offering of full maturity and strength, and this secures a corresponding energy of self-judgment. Christ values " by shekels of silver, according to the shekel of the sanctuary." He knows perfectly the divine rights which have been infringed, and the holiness of the sanctuary which has been offended. And the result of having to do with Him is that we are able to bring "the ram of the trespass-offering." A ram indicates maturity and energy; it is a very strong and distinctive apprehension of Christ as covering in the value of His death the sin which has been committed in the " holy things."

If we have sinned in regard to the " holy things " a wonderful measure of restoration is open to us through the grace of God. There is ability in the man who brings the trespass-offering to " make restitution," and even to " add the fifth part thereto." Thus God gets more in result than He would have had originally.

After Mark's failure and restoration Paul could say that he was "serviceable to me for ministry," and his Gospel indicates a very energetic appreciation of Christ. I have no doubt he got a divine valuation of things, and brought his trespass-offering, and made restitution with a fifth part added. We have all gained by his exercise. The soul that has brought the ram of the trespass-offering will be henceforth an enlarged contributor in the assembly.

If some divine principle has been ignored by the people of God, the trespass will not be put right until they accept that principle and act on it. And when such a trespass is rightly felt it will lead to a special care about that principle which would correspond with the "fifth part" added.

The trespass-offering involves restitution. Grace comes in to enable one to make full reparation. It is not merely that atonement is made, but whether in the case of what is due to God or to one's neighbour, it is fully rendered with an added fifth. I suppose that Mark in going to be with Paul in prison at Rome at the close of his life was really undertaking a more difficult and dangerous service than the one he had shrunk from in earlier days. He added the fifth part. It is not simply being forgiven, and going on with God as forgiven, but the failure is *made good* so that the one whose rights had been infringed is better off than he was before! If I have injured a brother— said something untrue of him or the like—and I have really brought the trespass-offering according to the valuation of the Lord, I shall restore in full. I shall not be afraid of letting myself down too much; I shall add the fifth part thereto. And the result will be that the brother I have injured will think more of

me than he ever did before, for he has now seen more
of the grace of God in me. Thus God has gained,
for He has had the Ram of the trespass-offering
brought to Him ; the one who was trespassed against
has gained, for all that was taken away has been
restored with twenty per cent interest ; and the
trespasser has gained, for he has learned to distinguish
good and evil in a truer way, and he has acquired an
apprehension of Christ which he had not before, so
that he can bring more of Christ to the assembly than
he ever did before. So that the whole assembly gains
also. How happy would it be if every wrong amongst
the people of God were righted in this way ! And
this is undoubtedly what the grace of God would
bring about. It is a fine finish to the exercises which
Leviticus 4 and 5 bring before us.

' An intrusted thing or a deposit ' (verse 21) may
suggest that we hold a good deal on trust for the
people of God, and it is a serious exercise as to whether
we are true to the trust, and discharging its obligations.
Whatever we have of Christ, and of the precious
truth of God, belongs to all our neighbours. We hold
it, in a sense, upon trust for all saints, and we are
under obligation to see that—so far as in us lies—
they get the good of it. One feels sometimes like
saying to believers, ' I have some very valuable
property of yours in my charge, and the sooner you
put in your claim for it the better pleased I shall
be.' All the precious truth in regard to Christ and
the assembly is a " good deposit entrusted," and we
have a holy responsibility to see that it does not
suffer any diminution or damage in our hands, but
that it is preserved in its full value, and held faithfully
for the whole church to whom it belongs. The gospel,

too, is a sacred trust. These things are not to be held as if they were our exclusive property; they belong to many others. Paul had the sense of having things enstrusted to him, and he was exercised not to be guilty in regard to them (Rom. 1 : 14, 15 ; 1 Cor. 9 : 16–23 ; 1 Tim. 1 : 11, etc.).

CHAPTER 6

THIS chapter, and the next, gives us *the law* of the offerings, and this is chiefly for " Aaron and his sons." That is, it views the offerings from the standpoint of *priestly* activities, and this exclusively until the peace-offering is brought in, when the range widens to " the children of Israel," and the thought of fellowship is the final note. " The law " indicates the fixed principle on which the service of God must be carried on. If there is not priestly exercise with regard to Christ in burnt-offering, oblation, and sin-offering character, the fellowship of God's people will be impaired. The general lack of priestly exercises at Corinth led to things which compromised the fellowship. But there was priestly activity on the part of some, and on the part of Paul, and the result was that the Lord gave a prophetic ministry which brought about self-judgment, and restored divine conditions of fellowship. A priest is a spiritual person who considers first what is due to God.

The first thing in " the law of the burnt-offering " is that " the burnt-offering shall be on the hearth on the altar all night unto the morning, and the fire of the altar shall be kept burning on it." The " night " indicates the character of the period which has followed the offering of Christ. The " morning " is coming, prefigured by Solomon dedicating the house (2 Chron. 5 to 7), when there will be universal gladness brought in on the ground of the burnt-offering, and the earth will be filled with divine glory. But in the meantime it is " night." Christ is disallowed and rejected ; it is still the time of His delivering up and sufferings.

It was by the eternal Spirit that Christ offered Himself without spot to God. His inward perfections were tested by all that God is as in holiness against sin. That testing brought out the sweet savour of infinite perfection. It will never be repeated. " The ashes " are the witness that that testing is past, and can never be gone through again. It was a " whole burnt-offering " ; all that Christ was wholly devoted to God in the place of sacrifice, and found infinitely perfect and fragrant. All was accomplished in the offering of Christ once for all.

But the " continual fire " on the altar speaks of how the fragrance of Christ is perpetuated before God in the praises of the saints. It is the priests' business to keep the fire burning. See verses 2, 5, 6. It is to burn " all night unto the morning." This is to go on continually as priestly service. Fervent affections are to be maintained in which the preciousness and per- fections of Christ are cherished by the Spirit in such wise that they ascend to God in continual praise. The Songs of degrees lead up to this point. " Behold, bless Jehovah, all ye servants of Jehovah, who *by night* stand in the house of Jehovah. Lift up your hands in the sanctuary, and bless Jehovah," Psa. 134. This is an " all night " priestly activity which is to go on until the last verse of the Psalm brings in " the morning."

The Spirit is fire to consume and set aside in judgment all that is of the flesh ; He is the " spirit of judgment and the spirit of burning," Isa. 4 : 4. But he loves to take another aspect, and to be the power by which the fragrance of Christ as the burnt-offering is caused to ascend in the praises of the holy priesthood—" a continual fire." In the oil for the candlestick (Exod. 27 : 20) we have seen a type of the Spirit as the One who maintains the light of Christ in ministry manward all through the night of His absence. But in the " continual fire " I think we see the Spirit as the power for the presentation of Christ Godward in praise. We " worship by the Spirit of God," Phil. 3 : 3. The priests stand by the altar " all night " to perpetuate in their intelligent praises the fragrance of the burnt-offering.

The " wood " in this connection might perhaps represent a condition of soul which is readily available for the action of the Spirit—spiritual affections which are quickly moved to intense activity when they are ordered in a priestly way before God for His service. The two on the way to Emmaus quickly responded to the priestly handling of the Lord, and their affections burst into flame. " Was not our heart burning in us as he spoke to us on the way, and as he opened the scriptures to us ? " (Luke 24). The Lord was really at that moment doing what was afterwards the Spirit's work, and there was that in them which soon caught fire. The priestly service brought before us in " the law of the burnt-offering " is no cold formality or religious routine ; it is marked by holy fervour such as the Spirit alone could create or maintain. The wood being " in order " would suggest intelligent and spiritually regulated affections such as Paul had in view when he said, " I will pray with the spirit, but I will pray also with the understanding ; I will sing with the spirit, but I will sing also with the understanding," 1 Cor. 14 : 15. Fervency in spirit and intelligent order must ever be found together in the service of God. But the fervency and order are under priestly charge ; all is spiritual in character ; there is no natural or fleshly element in the fervency or in the order ; they are such as could only be brought about by spiritual means and by spiritual persons.

In the priest dealing with " the ashes " we have an entirely different exercise before us, but one which perfectly corresponds with what we have been considering. The " ashes " speak of a sacrifice wholly consumed ; they speak of a dead Christ. I would put it to my own heart as to whether I know what it means to put on linen garments and take up the ashes ? If we are in His acceptance with God it is surely a righteous thing to be dead with Him here ! We take this up first *with God*. I understand that to be intimated by putting the ashes " beside the altar." From the altar the " continual fire " is causing the sweet odour to ascend, but " beside the altar " we confess that Christ is in " the place of the ashes "— He is a dead Christ here. We cannot in righteousness be identified with the one without being identified with the other. It is a matter of righteousness to identify ourselves with the place Christ has in this world. Paul makes this the basis of his appeal to the Colossians, " If ye have died with Christ," Col. 2 : 20. And in what is probably the most ancient " spiritual song " of Christian times—quoted in 2 Tim. 2 : 11–13—we read " For if we have died together with

him, we shall also live together." This is believed to
be part of a hymn ; at any rate it was current amongst
the saints, and it is most likely an example of the kind
of song in which the early Christians spoke to themselves and to one another !

Then, having taken our place in righteousness *with
God* as identified with a dead Christ here, we " put on
other garments." I think that suggests that we
deliberately prepare ourselves for the place of reproach
here. If we wear garments of righteousness with God
we must wear garments of reproach with men. The
ashes are to be carried forth " without the camp unto a
clean place." We must leave everything that has a
name, or a place, or religious sanction upon earth
to bear the reproach of One who has no place here at
all save in the hearts of those who love Him. See
Hebrews 13 : 13. The place of the reproach of Christ is
the only " clean place " here.

I think the action of Joseph of Arimathea and
Nicodemus may illustrate the teaching of this type.
They were true disciples but secretly. They had
never put on their linen garments ! But the death
of Christ brought things to an issue, and the claims of
righteousness could no longer be evaded. In identify-
ing themselves with the dead Christ, and claiming His
precious body, they put on their linen garments. He
was to them the Christ of God, but the place of death
was His in this world. And they carried the ashes
forth unto a clean place. Nothing marks the place
of Christ in relation to this world more definitely than
His burial. He has wholly disappeared from the
view of the world, and will not appear again until
His foes are made His footstool., Do you not think
those two hearts went out with Him from everything

here ? The council—the great assemblage of religious
leaders—had condemned Him to death, but they
identified themselves with Him. No one could think
that either of them ever took his seat in the council
again ! They came out in true priestly character.
The only " clean place " here is the place of identification with the death and burial of Christ. To be
identified with the acceptance of the burnt-offering,
and to be sustaining the fragrance of it before God
" all night," necessitates also that we should be
identified with the " ashes " and with the " clean
place " without the camp. " This is the law of the
burnt-offering."

*   *   *   *   *

In " the law of the oblation " we have the priests'
part in relation to that offering. The *offerer* represents
the saint in his exercises with regard to the acquisition
of Christ, and movements of heart Godward which
are typified by his coming with a " gift." It is a
contrast with man in his emptiness saying, ' Nothing
in my hand I bring ' ; it is the saint coming with
that in his heart which is delightful to God. In the
apprehension and appreciation of Christ we realise
that the time of God's grief as to man is past, and the
time of His good pleasure has come. A new kind of
humanity has come in in the Person of Jesus, perfect
in every detail, and suitable to be anointed by the
Holy Spirit. Indeed He was conceived by the Holy
Spirit, and every part of His humanity was invigorated
and strengthened by the Holy Spirit of God. No
leaven was there.

The *priest* represents the saints as having holy and
intelligent knowledge of how the offering is to be
dealt with for the service and pleasure of God. We

should covet to be true " sons of Aaron " as well as offerers.

The priest presents the oblation " before Jehovah, before the altar," and then burns upon the altar his handful of the fine flour and of the oil, and all the frankincense. God has His portion first. Then " the remainder thereof shall Aaron and his sons eat : unleavened shall it be eaten in a holy place." What we eat becomes part of ourselves ; it is assimilated into our being ; our constitution is formed and built up by it. The holy priesthood is nourished and strengthened, and formed in sensibilities and character, by feeding on Christ as the oblation. There is no feeding on Christ as the burnt-offering ; that all goes up to God on the altar. We can apprehend and appreciate it, but we do not appropriate it as food. But as the oblation, God gives Christ to the priesthood as food ; self-judged persons walking in the Spirit can feed on Him ; and the Christian viewed as a priest is marked by the appropriation of Christ in this character ; thus Christ becomes Substance in his affections. It is a great thing when Christ has become the hidden Man of the heart—when God can look into the hearts of His saints and see Christ there instead of self and the world.

God would have our inward thoughts and affections formed and nourished by feeding upon Christ, so that the way we think and feel about things might be according to Christ, and this would result in His being reproduced in us. Transformation according to Rom. 12 : 2 is not brought about by rules and regulations imposed from without as demand ; it is brought about from within, " by the renewing of your mind." The mind is renewed as we get it occupied and filled with the perfect way in which the will of God came into expression in the life of Jesus. What an insight we get into the " good and acceptable and perfect will of God " as we see it all, and feed on it all, as carried out in every detail in that holy life ! We see it there not as demand but as supply—as food for us. As we appropriate it, and are nourished by it, the will of God becomes blessed to us, and we learn increasingly to hate the action of our own will. We have a new way of thinking about everything then. If Christ has become food to me the pride, vanity, and fashion of the world are as dust under my feet. There is then spiritual vigour through what we feed on to be in accord with Christ, and to prove what is " the good and acceptable and perfect will of God."

In Ephesians saints are viewed as having learned the Christ, and heard Him, and as having been instructed in Him according as the truth is in Jesus. And there we get the thought of " being renewed in the spirit of your mind," Ephes. 4 : 20–24. This is an even deeper assimilation to Christ than Romans 12. It was a very good mind that wanted Christ to be received (Luke 9 : 54), but James and John needed to be renewed in the spirit of the minds ! We can only get that renewing by feeding on Christ " in a holy place." " The court of the tent of meeting " indicates that one is withdrawn in spirit from the sphere of human thoughts and activities, and even from what might be legitimately connected with one's own tent. It is where priestly exercises are taken up in relation to God's holy things. I suppose all believers have more or less of the exercises of piety in their own tents, but God would encourage us to take up exercises connected with the " holy place."

We can have " the court of the tent of meeting " at home, but it suggests something quite distinct from what would be connected with our own tents as in the wilderness. Saints have the privilege of taking up many exercises at home which do not stand in relation to their own personal things, but to " the tent of meeting." With some a very considerable part of their exercises has this character, and I think this indicates that they have priestly features. The general lack of strength for the service of God may be largely traced, I think, to the lack of priestly food.

The difference between the " manna " and the " oblation " as food is that manna is the supply of grace to enable the Israelite to meet all the exigencies of the wilderness pathway. This would answer more to what we have spoken of in Romans. But the oblation is food to nourish priests so that they may have spiritual vigour to carry on the service of God in prayer and praise, and in everything that pertains to the testimony. The two exercises go on side by side. We need manna for the wilderness path : we need to feed on the oblation for priestly strength in sanctuary service. Feeding on Christ as manna will give us renewal of mind, and strength to effect transformation of the responsible life. Feeding on Christ as the oblation will bring about renewal of the spirit of our mind, so that the very spirit of our minds will be formed in correspondence with Christ. There is great pleasure for God in that. The divine way of bringing it about is to give us Christ as food ; it is a blessed and satisfying way.

The oblation is to be preserved unleavened. No fleshly or inflating element is to come in. " It is most holy." And it requires, and I think we may say

produces, an intense degree of holiness in all who
come in contact with it. " Whatever toucheth these
shall be holy." There is nothing so sanctifying as
having to do with Christ. We get apart from the
world, and sin, and flesh when we are really engaged
with Christ. " The Imitation of Christ " will never
make any one like Him, but feeding on Him will, for
it nourishes the affections and gives power. What are
we nourishing our affections on ? Is it Christ, or the
worthless and passing trifles of the world ?

*   *   *   *   *

The offering on the day of the priest's anointing is a
" continual oblation." It is not like the voluntary gift
of Leviticus 2, but is obligatory. The anointed priest
must begin and end his day of holy service with an
offering which presents the sweet odour of Christ's
perfections to God. Only one day is contemplated,
but it is " an everlasting statute " ; each day of
priestly service must begin and end thus. In chapter 2
the oblation has oil poured on it, or is mingled or
anointed with oil, but here it is " saturated with oil "
—a more intensive thought. The priest begins his
day's service with a peculiarly strong apprehension of
how fully the Spirit had His way in every detail of
Christ's blessed pathway—all was in the energy and
grace of the Holy Spirit. And he returns at the end
of the day to take up the same apprehension with God
again. A " day " which begins and ends thus will be
filled with the fragrance of it for God's delight. The
priest would serve with his spirit, and be acceptable
in all that he did. And the offering is " wholly
burned to Jehovah " : it is a priestly apprehension
of Christ which is wholly for God's delight.

The " baken pieces of the oblation " might indicate

how God has been pleased that we should apprehend
Christ. He has not put all in one Gospel, but has
given us four. Matthew, Mark, Luke, and John each
had priestly apprehensions of Christ as the oblation,
but each had his own distinctive presentation. Men
have often tried to merge the four Gospels in one
account, but this sets aside the divine wisdom in which
the beauty and perfection of Christ have been set
before us, and substitutes for it a human compilation
in which there is no priestly intelligence, and in
which the true features of the oblation are obscured.
There is nothing in which priestly discernment
becomes more manifest than in the ability to perceive
the differences in the Gospels, and to apprehend their
significance. It is not the least part of God's favour
to the assembly in these last days that He has given
more priestly discrimination as to the different " pieces
of the oblation." The divine presentation of Christ in
the Gospels is wonderful. Everything that would
have been natural in the Evangelists is held in abey-
ance. Can you think of *men*—merely men—writing
an account of such matters in such few and simple
words ? Would not *men* have used abundance of
adjectives, and expatiated on the wonders they had
seen ? But all that is absent. Each of the Evangelists has, in the sovereignty of God, his own spiritual
apprehension of Christ, and presents it according to
the wisdom of God, so that every incident, and the
detail brought out in each incident, is contributory
to, and forms an essential part of, the particular view
of Christ which God would make prominent in each.
There is spiritual and priestly intelligence in the
presentation, and spiritual and priestly intelligence are
needed for the apprehension of these precious features

of Christ, and for their offering to God in the service
of holy affections such as anointed priests can render.

*   *   *   *   *

The first thing in "the law of the sin-offering"
is that "At the place where the burnt-offering is
slaughtered shall the sin-offering be slaughtered before
Jehovah." A sin-offering exercise comes in when
there has been some allowance of the man who had
to be removed in death, but the priest in taking it
up has behind it in his soul the sense of the excellence
of another Man, who has brought in everything that
God could delight in, and in whose death every perfection has gone up in sweet savour. It is as knowing
the perfect and eternal establishment of God's will in
a Man wholly devoted to Him in death that the
priest takes up exercise in regard to what has been
displeasing to God.

In no other offering is holiness so emphasized as in
this. Four times it is said about the sin-offering and
the trespass-offering, "It is most holy." We are now
brought to the abode of God's holiness, and we have
to think of sin in the light of that. Even worldly
people are shocked at certain things; the sense of
propriety is offended; but this is not holiness. God
requires holiness amongst His people; without it
"no one shall see the Lord" (Heb. 12 : 14).

The priest who offers the sin-offering has to eat it
in a holy place—" in the court of the tent of meeting."
He has a deep sense that something has come in of
the man whom Christ died to remove. He views the
sin from that standpoint, and makes it his own, and
gets a fresh apprehension of the death of Christ as
that in which the root of the sin has been dealt with.
In mind and spirit he is thus brought into accord with

God ; he feels about the sin as it ought to be felt
about. Priestly strength and intelligence are needed
for this. The priest who eats the sin-offering appropriates Christ in a way that puts him in real accord
with Christ as to the sin or trespass, and as to the
grace in which He took it up and made it His own.
So that there is no lightness about sin, but a deep
inward sense of what it cost Christ to deal with it ;
a sense, too, that it has been dealt with in divine
holiness, but in pure and perfect grace towards the
one who has sinned. The priest measures the sin by
what it cost Christ to bear its judgment, but he is
inwardly nourished upon the holy grace in which He
did so. This brings about that there is found in the
priest all that is morally suitable in regard to the sin,
and this enables God to go on with His people in
holiness and complacency.

Practically there is much amongst the people of
God that needs the sin-offering, but God would not
only give the sense of this, but He would have His
priests formed inwardly in spiritual feelings and sensibilities as to it. There is a sense in which priests who
eat the sin-offering make atonement. See Lev. 10 : 17.
Atonement means *a covering*. In the full sense of
atonement—the all-important sense—Christ is absolutely alone. In bearing the judgment of sin so as to
put it away sacrificially from before God none can
share with our precious Saviour, or have any part in
His holy work of sin-bearing. Hence there is no
eating of any sin-offering whose blood was brought
into the sanctuary (verse 23). We could not possibly
take up that side of things at all.

But if there has been sin amongst the people of God
it is due to Him that it should be rightly felt about.

Christ not only bore the judgment of sin and put it away, but He had every right and divine sensibility about the sin which He removed sacrificially. He loved righteousness and hated lawlessness. In this the holy priesthood can have part, and it comes in as one eats the sin-offering. We have also to remember that the sin which may have come to light in another is an exposure of what is in ourselves according to flesh. It holds up a mirror to me to let me see what I am. But the priest judges all in spiritual sensibilities which are the result of feeding on Christ as the sin-offering. The sin has been there, but it has been rightly felt about by a priest who has measured it inwardly by the death of Christ, and this covers it morally. So that God goes on with His people in holiness, not passing over any sin as a light matter, but securing, not only that it should have been judged once for all in the death of Christ, but also that it should be measured morally in the light of that death, and rightly felt about in priestly exercise before Him. One would earnestly desire that more priestly ability to take up things in this way were found amongst the people of God. It is often easier for us to *burn* the sin-offering than to *eat* it. See chapter 10 : 16–18. That is, to act in a judicial spirit rather than to make the sin our own before God, as did Ezra, Nehemiah, and Daniel. (See Ezra 9, Neh. 9, Dan. 9.) Eating brings about deep inward exercise, and it develops the sensibilities that we have spoken of, so that we do not think about sin merely as the world does, but according to God.

If there had been priestly sensibilities in the whole assembly at Corinth they would have been all down on their faces before God about the sin that was amongst them. But the exercises of Paul, and perhaps some few priests amongst themselves, saved the situation. One priest who eats the sin-offering might save many. One cannot but feel the deep importance of this in view of many things which come in amongst the people of God. If there were more priestly exercises there would be more power to deal with things, but this involves a breaking process, and much scouring and rinsing (verse 21). Paul went through this in a priestly way first, and ate the sin-offering for the Corinthians. Then they had their exercises ; priestly sensibilities were revived ; and things were dealt with so as to secure holy conditions.

Having to do with the sin-offering necessitates holiness. " Everything that toucheth the flesh thereof shall be holy." Contact with the sin-offering commits us to the refusal of man after the flesh, for in it that man, and all that pertains to him, was judged. One cannot be in contact with God's utter refusal of that man in the death of Christ, and go on with the allowance of him practically. The *garment* being washed on which the blood of the sin-offering is splashed would suggest an effect on the whole outward life— the deportment and ways—a moral cleansing and purification so that one appears as marked by purity and the beauty of holiness.

The " earthen vessel " would have reference to what man is naturally—to those things which might give him character, or place, or distinction as a man upon the earth. A man might be naturally eloquent, or have great mental powers, or some other natural gift which would give him a place as a man here. But if the sin-offering comes into contact with it, it results in the breaking of all that in the estimation of the man himself, so that he does not trust these things, but is cast upon God to be sustained by spiritual resources and power. "But we ourselves had the sentence of death in ourselves, that we should not have our trust in ourselves, but in God who raises the dead," 2 Cor. 1 : 9. "But we have this treasure in earthen vessels, that the surpassingness of the power may be of God, *and not from us*," 2 Cor. 4 : 7. Paul had been in contact with the sin-offering, and the " earthen vessel " was " broken " for him.

The " copper pot " might perhaps be suggestive of what saints are as begotten of God, or after the inward man. Viewed thus there is ability to endure testing, and to abide. " He that does the will of God abide for eternity," 1 John 2 : 17. When the sin-offering comes into contact with what the saint is as the subject of divine working there is no breaking, but an exercise is raised as to moral suitability. So the scouring and rinsing with water have their place.

CHAPTER 7

THOUGH the law of the trespass-offering (verses 1–7) contains certain details which are not mentioned in the law of the sin-offering—the sprinkling of the blood on the altar round about, and the presentation and burning of the fat—its provisions are similar. " As the sin-offering, so is the trespass-offering ; there shall be one law for them."

Then the priest's compensation for his service in connection with the three offerings is brought before us. As to the sin and trespass-offering " it shall be the priest's who maketh atonement therewith." The

priest who presents " any man's burnt-offering " has
the skin for himself. And every oblation baken in the
oven, or prepared in the cauldron and the pan, " shall
be the priest's who offereth it ; to him it shall belong."
There is always personal gain from taking up priestly
exercise or rendering priestly service. One could not
minister to the pleasure of God in relation to Christ
without getting great gain for oneself. The offering
priest acquires Christ for his own nourishment and
satisfaction, or, in the case of the burnt-offering, he
appropriates His outward blamelessness and beauty,
with a view, probably, to being found invested with
it. The skin would represent the outward moral
beauty of Christ as it could be discerned by saints.
Inwardly the priest is furnished with Christ as food,
so that his affections and spiritual intelligence are
nourished and strengthened in correspondence with
Christ. And provision is also made for him to be
marked by the possession of those *outward* features
which marked Christ, " who did no sin, neither was
guile found in his mouth ; who, when reviled, reviled
not again ; when suffering, threatened not ; but
gave himself over into the hands of him who judges
righteously," 1 Peter 2 : 21–23.

When the offering is typical of the perfection of
Christ viewed as under testing (verse 9) it is to be the
portion of the priest who offers it, but when His
perfection is viewed simply in itself (verse 10) He
becomes the food of " all the sons of Aaron . . . one as
the other." The appropriation of the perfection of
Christ *as under testing* requires special exercise. There
are special and personal exercises as well as those
which we take up with our brethren. We learn to
appreciate Christ in a peculiar way by our personal

experiences, and this gives a certain distinctiveness
to each saint. To offer that which speaks of Christ
as under testing would suggest that the offerer had
some reason to appreciate Him in that character. I
think it would suggest that the offerer had been
taught by his own experience under testing to value
and love Christ in that aspect. Take some of the
experiences of Christ as they are expressed in the
Psalms. They are not really appreciated until the
soul has had, in some tiny measure, similar experiences. I suppose most of us know how a deep trial
teaches us to see a sweetness and beauty in the scriptures that we have never seen before. God brings in
Christ in relation to the way in which we are being
tested, and we learn His perfection so as to become
offerers and offering priests. The priest who offers
takes up the product of such an exercise in a priestly
way with God, and is thus morally entitled to have
it as food for himself. But the oblation in a general
sense—all that Christ was in His Personal perfection,
and as wholly imbued with the Spirit—is common to
" all the sons of Aaron."

*   *   *   *   *

We have in chapters 6–7 : 10 a cluster of priestly
exercises which have to be taken up if the fellowship of
God's people is to be maintained on a proper footing.
The whole tone and character of Christian fellowship
is lowered if it is taken up—or attempted to be taken
up—without priestly conditions ; that is, apart from
the consideration of what is due to God. Priestly
conditions and exercises were lacking amongst many
at Corinth, and hence the fellowship was being compromised by unholy associations. " The law of the

sacrifice of peace-offering " has in view the fellowship of the people of God.

The sin- and trespass-offerings come before the peace-offering so that we may be quite free. The sin-offering would relieve one of any necessity for *self-occupation*, and the trespass-offering deals with every element in connection with which the rights of God may have been infringed, or which would hinder communion *with one another*. In the institution of the offerings (chapters 1–5) the sin- and trespass-offerings come last. The end reached there is self-judgment and the adjustment of all wrongs Godward or manward. But in the *law* of the offerings the peace-offering comes last. What is in view is the enjoyment of spiritual good in communion one with another. The law of the offerings is thus preparatory to our being intelligently partakers of the Lord's table. 1 Corinthians 10 stands in connection with the peace-offering. Christians " partake of the Lord's table " ; it is what is provided for us which we can enjoy together ; it is a well-furnished table, and it gives character to our fellowship here. If we are not true to the fellowship of the table according to 1 Corinthians 10 we shall not eat the supper according to 1 Corinthians 11. The fellowship is characterized by what we enjoy together in contrast to all that is in the idolatrous world. Partaking of the Lord's table is preparatory to the privilege of the Lord's supper. If a Christian goes in for the enjoyments of the world he practically gives up the happiness that belongs to him as a partaker of the Lord's table. The two things are so contrary to one another that it is impossible to enjoy both.

There is a festive character about the peace-offering. " And thou shalt sacrifice peace-offerings, and shalt

eat there, and rejoice before Jehovah thy God," Deut.
27 : 7. It suggests enjoyment in common ; no one
can be really festive alone ; even the world has the
idea of increasing happiness by sharing it ; that is
why they have parties, dinners, etc. " Bring the
fatted calf and kill it, and let us eat and make merry "
(Luke 15 : 23) has something of the thought of the
peace-offering in it. Even our private exercises and
discipline are in view of our enjoying more what we
have in common with our brethren, and in view of our
contribution to their joy. Paul and John knew what
it was to be outwardly isolated, but they did not lose
the gain of the fellowship, nor cease to contribute to it.

The first feature of the peace-offering is that it is
" for a thanksgiving " (verse 12). It might well be
so, seeing that we are set together in the presence of all
that God is as known in blessing through Christ and
through His death. When a man can say, " I thank
God, through Jesus Christ our Lord," he is free. He
has God before him instead of himself and his own
wretchedness. He is conscious of having received the
most wonderful good that was ever thought of. It has
come to him from the heart of the blessed God through
the death of the Lord Jesus. He can sit down with
his brethren in the fellowship of the peace-offering.
The better we know God through Christ the more
thanksgiving there will be. The young convert can
bring his peace-offering of thanksgiving, and he can
share—if clean—in what others bring, and every
advance he makes in the knowledge of Christ adds
something to his offering, and to the common joy.

Let us test our happiness by asking, Did it come
through the death of Christ ? If not, let us beware
lest there be an idolatrous element in it ! All those

things which we can enjoy together as the people of
God have reached us through death, and if two or any
number of hearts are enjoying those things, and the
holy love which gave them, they can thank God with
one accord. " The cup of blessing which we bless, is it
not the communion of the blood of the Christ ? "
(1 Cor. 10 : 16). Our souls drink together into that
infinite wealth of blessing—the revelation of God in
love !

Then with " the sacrifice of thanksgiving " the
offerer presents " unleavened cakes mingled with oil,
and unleavened wafers anointed with oil, and fine flour
saturated with oil, cakes mingled with oil," verse 12.
There is not only the thought of the death of Christ,
and of all that has come to us through that death, but
a blessed apprehension of *the kind of Man* it was who
died—One who knew no sin, and who was wholly in
the grace and power of the Holy Spirit. Only that
kind of Man will do for God ; every other kind of man
must be displaced, so that the moral universe may be
patterned after Christ. What an important element
this is of the fellowship of saints ! When Paul says
" We all partake of that one loaf," I think he has a
moral idea in his mind. It is the moral side that is
prominent in 1 Corinthians 10, not merely the outward
act of breaking bread, but what is morally involved in it.
The fact that we break bread together, and partake of
one loaf—which it supposes that all Christians do—
suggests that every one in the fellowship has partaken
morally of Christ. We have come to the apprehension
of an entirely new order of man in Christ, and we have
partaken of Him so as to be in the life of Christ morally.
What I mean by that is that the moral features of
Christ mark the saints as having His Spirit. For

example, Christ was marked by obedience, dependence, separation from the idolatrous world, and by delight in the saints, the excellent of the earth.   See Psalm 16.

Christian fellowship cannot be taken up in the flesh ; it can only be taken up by those who have partaken of Christ, and are morally in His life. A lawless or independent and self-sufficient person is not suitable to the fellowship. If one finds his happiness in the idolatrous world, or prefers the company of relatives and unconverted people to that of the saints, he is not in the fellowship. The way to promote fellowship is to give more place to the features of Christ. The partnership then becomes very real and spiritual. The saints become " one loaf, one body " (1 Cor. 10 : 17), as expressing together what is of Christ. In the light of this one can understand the important place which the unleavened cakes and wafers and fine flour and oil have in relation to the peace-offering.

But then there is also " his offering of leavened bread " (verse 13). This implies the recognition and acknowledgment of what we are in ourselves. If, on the one hand, the offerer is a partaker of Christ, he is, on the other, conscious that he is still in " mixed condition," and that the flesh is still in him. He cannot say that he has no sin (1 John 1 : 8). So he brings " his offering of leavened bread." This is essential to the peace-offering. It secures a spirit of lowliness and self-distrust, and leads one to walk softly. " Let him that thinks that he stands take heed lest he fall." And if a fault comes to light in another the spiritual are to restore him in a spirit of meekness " considering thyself lest thou also be tempted," Gal. 6 : 1. In relation to the fellowship one is never to lose sight of this. It keeps us sober as to ourselves, and considerate and forbearing as to others.

Then " the flesh of the sacrifice of his peace-offering of thanksgiving shall be eaten the same day that it is presented " (verse 15). The eating is not to be separated far from the offering. It is serious to consider that what began as a true offering of thanksgiving or a vow may degenerate into what is " an unclean thing " (verse 18). It shows the importance of maintaining a close link between what we enjoy together, and the consciousness of holding it in relation to God. The " peace-offering of thanksgiving " must be renewed each day if the daily eating or communion is to retain its holy character. This is not grievous to the spiritual mind, for the true sweetness and power of what we enjoy together lies in the fact that we have taken it up first *with God*. And it is a very sweet privilege to come afresh to the altar with our peace-offering each day, and renew *with God* for His pleasure our apprehensions and appreciations of Christ. If this is neglected we cannot wonder if the " fellowship with one another " loses its holy and spiritual character, and becomes formal, or even merely social. The true joy of the communion is lost. The love of God comes out in this, that He would not have us to go on enjoying together indefinitely that which we have once taken up at the altar with Him. He would have us daily to renew our apprehensions of Christ *with Him*, and to find in this a continually fresh starting-point for our communion with our brethren. Otherwise our enjoyments may be separated from their true Source, and their spiritual value lost.

In the case of a " vow or voluntary " offering (verse 16) the flesh may be eaten also on the next day. This supposes greater spiritual energy in the affections of the offerer, and therefore greater ability to sustain the communion. There may be not only different measures of apprehension of Christ as set forth in the different animals offered, but also a difference in the strength of motive which lies behind the offering.

We can only enjoy things with God at all as we are in the spirit of " thanksgiving." " In everything give thanks, for this is the will of God in Christ Jesus towards you." Thanksgiving is the response to the wealth of blessing which divine grace has brought us into. But when we come to the " vow," or what is " voluntary," it suggests spiritual power for dedication to God. It implies a more distinct subjective work in the soul. Hence communion can be more sustained. There is often true response to the grace of God in grateful affections without much spiritual energy, and therefore things may soon deteriorate into merely human sentiment which is " unclean." The remedy for this is to continually renew the apprehension of Christ in movements of heart Godward. If we do so it will inevitably carry us on from " thanksgiving " to " vow." We shall increase in spiritual capability, and be more efficient contributors to the fellowship.

God loves the definite dedication which is implied in a " vow," and spiritual power is found with those who bring an offering of this character. A true " vow " is in the power of the Spirit ; it is no mere resolution of the flesh or the legal man. It is the happy dedication of a spiritual man. Many saints do not go beyond the " peace-offering of thanksgiving," but God contemplates His people being so affected by His grace and love that there will be purpose of heart to bring about dedication to Him. God supports this, and the one who has it gets the gain of it. If there is a spirit of dedication it secures divine support. A truly dedicated man would not talk about his dedication ; it would be enough for him that his " vow " was acceptable to God, and that the grace of God supported him in it. The gain of a " vow " in relation to the peace-offering is that there is extended ability to continue participation in the fellowship without things becoming " unclean " from lack of conscious nearness to God.

" The law of the sacrifice of peace-offering " emphasises the necessity for cleanness on the part of those who eat. See verses 19–21. Later in this book we get much instruction as to the clean and the unclean, that we may know what to keep apart from. Holy things are profaned if there is not purity as to ourselves and our associations. " The soul that eateth the flesh of the sacrifice of peace-offering which is for Jehovah, having his uncleanness upon him, that soul shall be cut off from his peoples." The attempt to bring uncleanness and Christ together ends disastrously. God will not allow it.

The prohibition against eating fat and blood (verses 22–27) is very significant : both are reserved. The unique excellence which attaches to the Person of Christ is very jealously guarded by God, and also the unique value of His blood as making atonement. One would not hesitate a moment about severing one's links with any person or persons who did not maintain the truth as to the Person of Christ, or as to His atoning death. There is a reserved portion of delight —an excellence and richness attaching to Christ— which is exclusively for God. It is an essential feature of our communion that we should understand this. If a divine Person comes into Manhood and goes into death there must be an excellence disclosed that is beyond the creature to appropriate. But if it cannot be *eaten* it can be *offered* ; it becomes the subject of worship. The fat is twice spoken of in chapter 3 as the " food [or bread] of the offering " ; it is Jehovah's portion ; that which He alone can appropriate. The priest can send up the sweet odour to God of that which it is not for him to appropriate ; it is burnt " on the altar upon the burnt-offering." We can *contemplate* what is not given to us to *appropriate*. It does not diminish the joy to know this. God loves to participate in the joy of His people, and, indeed, to have the richest portion in that which is the Substance of their communion. It is an added joy to know that the blessed God has that in the Fatted Calf which is beyond what the returned sons get. It is killed for them, but the Father has His own peculiar portion in it.

The blood is reserved also, and chapter 17 tells us why. The life of the flesh is in the blood, and it is given upon the altar to make atonement, " for it is the blood that maketh atonement for the soul." That is the aspect of the blood generally in the Old Testament. But in the New Testament the Lord speaks of the cup in His supper as " the new covenant in my blood, which is poured out for you " (Luke 22 : 20), and He gives that cup to His saints to drink. The blood still retains all its blessed character and efficacy as having atoning value ; it is a perfect covering for sin ; but we know it also as bearing witness to all the blessing in the heart of God which has come to light through the revelation of God in the love of the new covenant. The word *atonement* occurs many times in the Old Testament, but it does not occur in the New.

" Atonement " in Rom. 5 : 11, A.V., should be " reconciliation." God revealing what is in His heart is more
than covering men's sin. In blessing the cup, and
drinking it, we are not occupied with the covering or
atoning value of the blood, but with what is witnessed
or revealed in it.

The closing section of this chapter requires of the
offerer that " his own hands shall bring Jehovah's
offerings by fire, *the fat with the breast* shall he bring "
(verse 30). God would have us to hold in a very
definite and personal way the apprehension of all that
excellence in Christ which is His own peculiar portion
and delight, but He would have us to hold it along
with a precious sense of the love of Christ. The more
definitely we hold the unfathomable depth and
preciousness of what there is in Christ for God, the
more shall we apprehend the love of Christ. The fat
and the breast are to be together in the offerer's hands.
The Person who is so delightful to God, and in whom
there are such inscrutable excellencies that God alone
can feed upon them, is known to us in His affections.
One can understand the Apostle, when praying that we
might know the love of the Christ, adding, " which
surpasses knowledge," Ephes. 3 : 19. He had in his
hands " the fat with the breast," and the surpassing
character of the love was connected with all the
intrinsic wealth and worth of that glorious Person as
known of the Father. To fail to hold the " fat " would
be to fail, correspondingly, to hold the " breast."
What " holy hands " are needed to hold such infinite
preciousness ! And emphasis seems to be laid on " his
own hands." This is not looking to enjoy what others
bring, or complaining of the lack in others ! What
are you bringing with your " own hands " to contribute

to the pleasure of God, and to priestly food, and to the common joy of the fellowship ?

The " breast " is waved before the priests eat it. They eat in the consciousness of how God delights in the love of Christ being known and appropriated by His saints. And the " breast " would speak of His love Godward as well as saintward and to the assembly. He loved His " master " as well as His " wife " and His " children," Exod. 21 : 5. " I love the Father, and as the Father has commanded me, thus I do," John 14 : 31. Indeed Christ loves His saints, and loves the assembly, because it is the Father's will that He should do so. Have you thought that it really pleases God that His Son should love you and give Himself for you ? The waving of the " breast " would mean that the love of Christ has been taken up by the saints in relation to all the pleasure that God has in it, and their affections move before God in the appreciation of it. It is because of His love to the Father that Christ has so devoted Himself to His saints. He was daily Jehovah's delight—" the nursling of his love "—but He was so as " rejoicing in the habitable part of his earth," and as having His " delights with the sons of men," Prov. 8 : 30, 31. It is a peculiar pleasure to God when the love of Christ is appreciated by the saints in relation to His delight in it. When that moves in their affections it answers to the waving of the " breast."

The " breast " is given as food to " Aaron and his sons." The love of Christ is the common portion of the priesthood ; it does not belong to one more than another. But as being food it becomes characteristic of the person who eats it ; it forms him spiritually. The divine thought is wonderful—that there should be

a priesthood so nourished upon the love of Christ that
they take character from it ! The effect of eating the
" breast " would be that we should love as Christ
loved, and God would have everything in priestly
service moved by that mighty mainspring. " A new
commandment I give to you, that ye love one another ;
as I have loved you, that ye also love one another,"
John 13 : 34. " This is my commandment, that ye
love one another, as I have loved you," John 15 : 12.
But one must really be nourished by the love of
Christ to do this. Paul knew what it was to eat the
" breast of the wave-offering," and he was marked by
the love of Christ ; it was the mainspring of all his
devoted service. He loved as Christ loved, and all his
service was of priestly character ; there was something
distinctively *for God* in it.

Then " the right shoulder " becomes the portion of
the priest who presents the peace-offering. It is thus
connected with a personal exercise like the oblation
baken in the oven, or prepared in the cauldron or the
pan (verse 9). It seems to indicate that the priestly
presentation of the peace-offering is an exercise which
secures a special personal knowledge of the character
of Christ's walk here. (" Shoulder " is really " leg " ;
it would refer to the strength of His walk.) The
offering priest not only has the " breast " in common
with his brethren, but he has a peculiar and personal
sense of how Christ walked here in the service of love.
And he gets the " shoulder " as food so that he may
have spiritual strength " even as *he* walked, himself
also so to walk," 1 John 2 : 6. So that what was
true in Christ may become true in him ; 1 John 2 : 8.
How could one walk as Christ walked except as
nourished and strengthened by feeding on " the

shoulder of the heave-offering " ?   He ever walked in
the blessed activity and service of love. How marvellous that He should become food for us that we
might, in some small measure, love as He loved, and
walk as He walked ! What broken and contrite hearts
we ought to have that we have so little entered upon
our priestly privilege of eating the breast and the
shoulder, and the result has been that we have so very,
very feebly, if at all, loved as He loved, and walked as
He walked !

There is a priestly side of the truth connected with
our fellowship, and if that priestly side is not taken
up the fellowship will not be maintained in its true
character, or in the spiritual energy which rightly
marks it. How sad that so many believers should
look at these types as belonging to a past dispensation,
and now past and done with ! The truth is they are
precious instruction for us, and divinely intended to be
so. They are instruction in Christ and in the knowledge of God. May the Lord enable us to consider these
things, and if we do so He will give us understanding !

CHAPTER 8

GOD would have all His people to be interested in
priesthood, and instructed in what pertains to it ; so
He tells Moses to " Take Aaron and his sons with him,
and . . . gather all the assembly together at the
entrance of the tent of meeting " (verse 3). Aaron
was called by God to the honour of priesthood (Heb.
5 : 4) ; his sons came into it as being kindred with him.
And " the Christ also has not glorified himself to be
made a high priest." The One who said to Him,

"Thou art my Son," said also, "Thou art a priest."
He has taken up the priestly office by God's appoint-
ment, and in Hebrews He is the only One who is called
a priest. The Spirit of God is drawing attention in
that part of Scripture to CHRIST as the "merciful and
faithful high priest in things relating to God" (Heb.
2 : 17), as the "High Priest of our confession" (chap.
3 : 1), as the "great high priest who has passed through
the heavens" (chap. 4 : 14), as the "priest for ever
according to the order of Melchisedec" (chap. 5 : 6, etc.),
as "high priest of the good things to come" (chap.
9 : 11), and as "a great priest over the house of God,"
chap. 10 : 21. But it is made clear that He has a
sanctified company of brethren who are "all of one"
with Him (chap. 2 : 11), and it is as being so that the
saints are "a spiritual house, a holy priesthood,"
1 Peter 2 : 5. Though *their* priesthood is not formally
taught in Hebrews it is implied in drawing nigh to God,
and approaching God, and in having boldness for
entering into the holy of holies, and in the offering of the
sacrifice of praise (Heb. 7 : 19, 25 ; chap. 10 : 19 ;
chap. 13 : 15).

There are those who are kindred with Christ. "Take
Aaron and his sons with him." It is not sons of Adam
that are seen here, but sons of Aaron. That is, it is the
saints viewed not according to what they are naturally,
but according to what they are spiritually as the result
of the working of God. I trust we know what it is to
have been attracted to Christ. We see the power of the
attraction of Christ in the Gospels, and how different
ones responded. The two disciples who heard John
speak, and Simon, and Philip, and Nathaniel, and many
others. When Christ was presented they were attracted ;
there was that in them which was kindred with Christ ;

a magnet only attracts what is kindred to itself. The disciples were attracted to Christ, and became attached to Him ; nothing would induce them to give Him up. In listening to Him, and following Him, they were doing the will of God, and He recognised them as His brethren. See Matt. 12 : 46–50 ; Mark 3 : 35 ; Luke 8 : 21. Such are bound up with Christ eternally. You may find flaws in the saints if you look for them, but they appreciate Christ, and that shows that they are kindred with Him.

" Aaron and *his sons with him*." Through infinite grace we are bound up with Christ, not only in God's purpose—though that lies behind all—but in affection which is the product of God's working in our souls. *Believing* in John's Gospel is the believing of affection ; the heart has found an Object in whom it can rest. When that is so every detail connected with Christ becomes of greatest interest to the heart. How the bride in Canticles delights to speak of every feature of the Bridegroom ! She loves to dwell on every detail. To such a heart the chapter before us would have profound interest.

The reader is referred to " An Outline of the Book of Exodus "—chapters 28, 29—for remarks on the priestly garments, and the consecration offerings. The chapters in Exodus give us Jehovah's command-ment as to what was to be done ; Leviticus 8 describes how Moses, as the one faithful in all God's house, carried it out. All leads to Aaron and his sons keeping the charge of Jehovah at the entrance of the tent of meeting as nourished on the flesh of the ram of consecration, and on the bread of consecration. This is typical of the assembly as the consecrated company. The consecration-offering comes as near to that aspect of the Lord's death which is before us in His supper as

anything in the Old Testament. His body devoted in
love to the will of God and for the assembly, so that
every thought of the divine pleasure might take effect
and be known in our hearts as the fruit of infinite
love. The result would be that we should " keep the
charge " during the seven days which are typical of
the whole period of priestly service ; everything would
be maintained that is due to the Lord's Name. It is
not here the privilege of *going in* with Him to share the
relationship in which He stands to His Father and
His God, now known as our Father and our God, but
rather the privilege and holy responsibility of keeping
the charge " at the entrance of the tent of meeting."
It is the maintenance in faithfulness here of what is
due to Him during the time of His rejection—having
part with Him in faithfulness to His interests here.
We eat the Lord's supper on the Lord's day in view of
complete identification with the interests and testimony
of Christ all through the week. John 13–17 contemplates Christ going to the Father, but leaving His
own here to " keep the charge "—to have part with
Him in that testimony which He brought here. The
Father made known, the love of Christ revealed, the
Comforter given, the intercession of Christ, and the
mutual affections and service of the saints, all come in
with relation to keeping the charge ! Keeping the
charge is " until he comes " !

<hr>

CHAPTER 9

THE " eighth day " is the beginning of a new period,
but looked at as in relation to the seven preceding
days. It has in view the appearing of Jehovah and

His glory (verses 4, 6, 23). All that goes on during
this present period has in view " the world to come,"
when the glory of God will appear publicly, and " all
the house of Israel " will come under priestly blessing.
The answer to the offerings in this chapter is the grace
that will be brought to the people of God at the revelation of Jesus Christ (1 Peter 1 : 13). All the blessing of
God is coming out in its fulness ; His glory will appear
publicly ; His acceptance of the offering of Christ will
be publicly known and delighted in.

The scene at the end of this chapter is, typically,
the public appearance in this world of the glory of
Jehovah, and His grace and blessing as founded on,
and as the adequate answer to, the sin-offering, the
burnt-offering, the oblation, and the peace-offering.
In the early chapters of this book we have seen in type
how God is exercising His saints, individually and
collectively, at the present time in the apprehension
and appreciation of Christ in these varied characters.
But what a joy to know that the value of Christ in all
these different aspects is to be publicly known in this
world, and is to have its public answer in blessing here,
and in the out-shining of all that God is in supreme
and infinite grace !

It is here that Aaron appears for the first time as an
offering priest. So that what is before us in this
chapter is Christ Himself as offering, and the wonderful
result of His offering in the appearance of the glory of
God. Indeed, we see here " the sufferings which
belonged to Christ, and the glories after these "
(1 Peter 1 : 11). The peculiar character of the present
moment lies in the fact that it anticipates spiritually,
and in the way of testimony, what will be publicly
known when Christ appears. To speak in the language

of this type, the sacrifices have been offered, and
Moses and Aaron have gone in, but they have not yet
come out. The time of the *public* blessing of the
house of Israel, and of men universally, has not yet
come. Christ has not yet come out, but another divine
Person, the Holy Spirit, *has* come out—though unseen
and unknown by men—to empower the priestly
company here to make known in the way of
testimony the glory of God in grace. The gospel
is the answer now to the precious value of the
sacrifice of Christ. It is the appearing in testimony
of all that God is as made known in grace and blessing
on the ground of the death of Christ. So that while
this chapter looks on to the time when the results of the
death of Christ will be known in public and universal
blessing, when Christ as King and Priest will appear
again, it also speaks of what is now here consequent
upon the coming of the Spirit. At the present time
the gospel is the fruit and answer to the offering of
Christ ; the glory of God in grace appears in it.

Aaron offers for himself and for the people (verse 7).
That indicates typically that Christ is with God now,
not only on the ground of His Personal title, but on
the ground of His death. On the ground of His
Personal title He could be there alone, but we could
not be with Him. But He is there on the ground that
He has been once offered ; He has died to put away
sin by the sacrifice of Himself, and to establish the will
of God ; He has brought all His infinite perfections
into the place of sin and death. " By his own blood "
He " has entered in once for all into the holy of holies,
having found an eternal redemption," Heb. 9 : 12.
That is, He has taken His place as Man with God on
the same ground as is available for all His people. If

He is with God as having offered Himself, it is the
same ground on which *we* can be with God. If He had
only entered in in His Personal perfection each one of
us would have to say, " I cannot be with Him." But
if He is there as having been offered I say, " Blessed be
God ! on that ground I can be there too." He loves,
as the true Aaron, to be with God on ground which is
available " for the people " also.

In this chapter Aaron presents all the offerings and
then he blesses the people. That was the attitude of
Christ when He rose from the dead. The sacrificial
work was over, and in resurrection He " lifted up his
hands toward the people and blessed them." He
went to heaven with hands uplifted in blessing (Luke
24 : 50, 51). The result of the offering and sacrifice
is widely extended blessing. We see that in Psalm 22
where we get first, " My brethren . . . the congregation "—the assembly as answering to Aaron's sons ;
then " the great congregation "—speaking of " the
whole house of Israel "; and finally " all the ends of
the earth."

It is of much interest to see how " the sons of
Aaron " appear in this chapter as presenting the blood
to Aaron, and delivering the burnt-offering to him.
They are sympathetic with all that he does, and, we
might say, co-operating with him in it. It suggests
the assembly as a company with understanding of the
necessity for Christ offering Himself, and who are
intelligent as to His offering, and as to the fruit of it.
Before the moment when the public result of that
offering will fill the world with blessing at the " appearing of the glory of our great God and Saviour Jesus
Christ " (Titus 2 : 13), the assembly is in accord with
Christ as to His offering work, and as to all that will

result from it in the blessing of Israel and of all the ends
of the earth. This makes the priestly company
evangelical to-day, as being in sympathetic accord
with the true Aaron. The glory of God in grace is
appearing now in the testimony of the glad tidings,
and the priestly company is in accord with it. The
offering of Christ has secured that the glory of God
can shine out in grace, and man can be blessed in a
way that is commensurate with that glory. It is a
marvellous thing to preach the gospel, for it is a setting
forth of the glory of God in grace. Many preachers
weaken their testimony by dwelling almost exclusively
on the benefit of man. The true evangelical testimony
is " Behold your God ! " (Isa. 35 : 4 ; chap. 40 : 9).
The true evangelist serves in a priestly spirit (see Rom.
15 : 16) ; he considers for God. If there were more
fidelity in keeping the charge (Lev. 8 : 35) there
would be a more powerful and spiritual setting forth
of the gospel. There would be more accord with
Christ as to the testimony of grace. What is the
present attitude of Christ ? It is set forth in verse 22.
The offering work is finished, and the true Aaron has
hands uplifted in blessing. All may come under those
priestly hands ; all may be blessed according to the
delight and glory of God as secured by the offering of
Christ in its varied aspects.

Then He has gone in as Lord and Priest. This
chapter says nothing of what He does within. That
is the assembly's secret as identified with Him within !
But another divine Person has come out to be the
power of the present testimony of grace. See 1 Peter
1 : 12. God's glory in blessing will shine forth in the
world to come to the ends of the earth : but it is
shining forth to-day in the testimony of His grace by

the Holy Spirit. Christ is the true Moses in Romans 5
—the Mediator through whom all God's blessing
comes to men ; He is the true Aaron in Hebrews 9—
the " high priest of the good things to come " ; things
which *have come* now spiritually. He will come forth
in manifested glory and blessing very soon.

> " We look for Thine appearing,
> Thy presence here to bless ! "

It will be publicly and universally known then that
His offering has been accepted, and that on the ground
of it the glory of God can appear and cover the earth
as the waters cover the sea. But in the meantime the
Holy Spirit has come down and rested on men as
cloven tongues of fire to give a powerful voice in this
world to the glory of God in grace. The blessing of
God for men to-day is according to the value of the
Person and offering of Christ.

These precious types are full of instruction, but
Christianity transcends even what is so wondrously
pictured here. For the consecrated company to-day
are not only entrusted with the holy " charge " at
the entrance of the tent—their testimony here to
what will soon be in display—but they are privileged
to go in even to the holy of holies, to know in the
greatest nearness to God the blessedness of Christ as
His Resource for the bringing to pass of His will and
glory in the whole moral universe.

CHAPTER 10

THIS chapter shows us the failure of priesthood in
Aaron's two elder sons, but it also shows in " his sons
that were left " how the priesthood was to be main-

tained in a remnant. So that we see here what answers to present conditions. There has been grievous public failure characterised by the introduction of " strange " elements which do not belong at all to the divine system. In that system, as we have seen in type in the tabernacle, every detail was to be " as Jehovah had commanded." But Nadab and Abihu " presented strange fire before Jehovah, which he had not commanded them."

It is significant that it had been said, " *And ye shall not go out* from the entrance of the tent of meeting seven days, until the day when the days of your consecration are at an end : for seven days shall ye be consecrated," chap 8 : 33. This is connected with keeping the charge. Everything that is of God, all that speaks of Christ and the Spirit, all that is the result of divine grace and working in the saints, is within the divine system. We have to keep the charge—to confess the sufficiency of what is within— and to see that no foreign element is introduced.

It seems evident that Nadab and Abihu went outside for their strange fire, and this has been the secret of all the failure. To bring in outside elements is ruinous. I understand that Nadab means " Liberal " ! He represents the popular liberal spirit that would regard restriction to the Lord's commandment, and to what is spiritual, as narrow-minded and bigoted. Abihu means " He is my father." This would suggest a claim to be in relationship with God, such as is often now found without the moral conditions which are essential to relationship. There is much said to-day about the Fatherhood of God, but very little thought of what is suitable to Him.

" Strange fire " is what is of the world or of the flesh

introduced into the service of God, where nothing
really has place but what is of the Spirit of God.
" Strange fire " would be a human imitation of what
is divine. There would be great danger of this if a man
were not saying " Lord " to Jesus. That does not
mean merely using the word " Lord," but being in the
truth and spirit of it ; it is the setting aside of man's
will and importance in presence of His supremacy.
Then, again, to be divinely preserved from what is
" strange " there must be the confession of " Jesus
Christ come in flesh." A divine Person come in Manhood to be the Beginning of everything for God ! This
involves the complete setting aside of man after the
flesh. These are God-given tests (see 1 Cor. 12 : 3 ;
1 John 4 : 1–3), and the action of the Spirit or what is
" strange " would be evidenced by the presence or
absence of these confessions.

The introduction of " strange fire " involves the
death of priesthood. In christendom generally priesthood is dead in a moral sense. I could not say
precisely when this took place historically, but very
early in the history of the church human elements
were introduced ; things were brought into the service
of God which were not according to divine institution,
but according to what pleased men.

The act of Nadab and Abihu—Aaron's two elder
sons—is a type of the public failure of the priesthood
as committed to man's responsibility. I think it can
be spiritually discerned that publicly the priesthood
has failed, and has come under the judgment of the
Lord. But notwithstanding this God would have the
full thought of priesthood to be maintained by the
two younger sons. Eleazar means " God is helper,"
and in him and his brother we see, typically, a

remnant in whom the priesthood is maintained by God's help.

The public failure would naturally discourage and dishearten, and lead to giving up divine thoughts. But we have to see to it that we do not uncover our heads nor rend our clothes (verse 6). The " high caps " speak of holy dignity, the clothes of moral suitability to God, and the anointing oil of power and competency in the Spirit. The thought of a remnant in Scripture is not a fag end of secondary value, but a bit of the original ; it includes all that is really for God. All saints constitute the remnant to-day, though all may not take up or maintain the priestly character which attaches to them according to the will of God. Verses 6 and 7 are encouragement to maintain true priestly exercises and conditions in spite of the public failure. It is right that " the whole house of Israel " should bewail what has happened, but neither the holy dignity nor the moral suitability of the priesthood is to be laid aside ; the anointing remains as power.

These two exercises are left to us in a day of most serious public failure ; *outside* we bewail the breakdown and the judgment ; but *within* we may, and must, maintain with God all that is priestly. As to the public position we can only bow in confession of the failure, but in relation to what is divine and spiritual the holy service of God is to be carried on ; there is to be no discouragement. It says in verse 7, " Lest ye die." The priesthood may die through the exercise of *will* as in Nadab and Abihu, or it may die by being given up through *weakness*. Naturally we might be so affected by the public failure that we surrender priestly conditions ourselves. The tendency might be to say, " It is all over ; things are in such a state that it is no good trying to maintain anything " ; and everything priestly for God might be let go. But God would have priestly conditions maintained by you and me and all saints. We are to be found spiritually superior to the natural effect of things, and thus true overcomers. Discouragement leads to uncovering the head and rending the clothes. To " bewail the burning " is a right exercise for the people of God, but at the same time priestly dignity and state, and the holy functions of the priesthood, are to be preserved, not surrendered. 2 Timothy was written by Paul after the public failure was fully manifested to encourage Timothy and ourselves to maintain things spiritually for God. The help of God remains, and is available for us.

" Lest wrath come on all the assembly " (verse 6). It would be a dreadful thing if priestly service ceased. But if a few saints maintain priestly conditions, and are found continually presenting the preciousness of Christ before God, and praying for all saints and all men, things are maintained for the good of " all the assembly."

Then two *everlasting statutes* come in which are of permanent importance. " Thou shalt not drink wine nor strong drink, thou, and thy sons with thee, when ye go into the tent of meeting, lest ye die " (verses 9–11). The first tendency in presence of public failure is to be discouraged and disheartened. Then, on the other hand, there may be a resorting to that which excites and stimulates in a natural way. There is often a sense of spiritual weakness, and an attempt to make up for it by some kind of natural stimulant. But the bringing in of such things clouds spiritual discernment, and leads to failure in distinguishing

" between the holy and the unholy, and between
unclean and clean." And if we cannot distinguish, we
cannot teach.

This section coming in here would suggest that
probably Nadab and Abihu had sinned while under the
influence of wine or strong drink. Religious excite-
ment, the exhilarating effect of music, eloquence, and
other influences which act on natural sensibilities, are
to be avoided if we would preserve spiritual conditions
which are suitable to God. Such things only cause
people to lose spiritual discernment. Do you think
that a person who went in for " Pleasant Sunday
Afternoons " and concerts would be able to distinguish
between strange fire and divine fire ? The priesthood
is entirely spiritual, and has to do with a spiritual
order of things. It can only be carried on outside the
sphere of natural discouragement and natural exhilaration. There are many things which excite nature that
would not do violence to the natural conscience, nor
even to the unenlightened conscience of a believer. We
have to seek divine instruction as to such things, and
beware of them, if we would keep ourselves in holy and
priestly condition.

The other " everlasting statute " (verse 15, refers to
what remains as a positive source of satisfaction and
strength for the priesthood, and the priestly family,
despite all the failure that has come in. There are
" sons " left to eat priestly food, and there is " the
oblation that is left " for them to eat (verse 12). " The
oblation " is typical, as we have already seen, of all
the blessedness and perfection of Christ as found here
in holy Manhood for the pleasure and glory of God.
If we consider Him we shall find that there was no
discouragement there by reason of man's failure, for

it is written, " He shall not faint nor be in haste (or
be crushed) till he have set justice in the earth : and
the isles shall wait for his law," Isa. 42 : 4. Neither
shall we find any natural exhilaration there ; He was
a true Nazarite to God. In the oblation all was unleavened ; there was no corrupting or inflating element
present. All that Christ was here for the delight of
God is " left " to be " most holy " food for the priesthood in a day of departure and ruin. It is to be eaten
" beside the altar," which suggests preparedness to
suffer ; for the altar would speak of a suffering Christ,
and of a sacrificial spirit in the priesthood as being
near to it. Manhood in the power and grace of the
Holy Spirit, as seen in Christ, is God's delight, but it
is not acceptable to men. It has the place of suffering
and reproach here. The oblation is to be eaten in " a
holy place."

Then " the breast of the wave-offering, and the
shoulder of the heave-offering shall ye eat in a clean
place, thou, and thy sons, and thy daughters with
thee " (verse 14). This is the priestly part of the
peace-offerings, and it is shared by all the priestly
family—daughters as well as sons. The " daughters "
would represent those who are spiritually weaker than
" sons " ; the female is a weaker vessel (1 Peter 3 : 7).
But this does not debar them from feeding on the love
of Christ, or appropriating His grace for strength of
walk. The " holy place," where the oblation is to be
eaten, would have a sanctuary reference, but the
" clean place " would refer to the purity of our associa-
ions as in the fellowship. And the households of the
,aints would be a " clean place " from which the contaminating influences of the world are excluded.
Personally, and in our households, we have to main-

tain separation from all that is idolatrous and unclean, so that there may be a " clean place " where the wave-breast and the heave-shoulder can be eaten.

All this remains as an " everlasting statute " in spite of the public breakdown of the priesthood. There is a remnant " left " to maintain things by the help of God. The anointing remains ; Christ remains in all His perfection as set forth in the oblation ; the fellowship remains, too, with its precious sources of satisfaction and strength in the love and power of Christ. As we avail ourselves of these things the priesthood, and all the conditions suitable to the service of God, will be maintained in the vigour of life. So that this chapter, solemn and exercising as it is, is really most encouraging as showing how divine resources are " left " to us in the day of failure, and that priestly service may be continued for the pleasure of God. May we be enabled to take it up, by God's grace, in faith and love, and with all the spiritual exercise that is becoming !

But there is another important lesson ere this section of the book closes ! The goat of the sin-offering should have been eaten by " the sons of Aaron that were left," but instead of that it had been burnt ! This is not the first and public failure, as seen in the Christian profession generally, but it is failure in the reserved and preserved remnant. This has a serious voice for us as indicating a failure that is very likely to be found in a preserved remnant. I think it indicates where we *do* very often fail.

Moses " diligently sought the goat of the sin-offering." It was a matter of great concern to him to know how it had been dealt with. " The people " (chap. 9 : 15), " the assembly " (chap. 10 : 17), had a great place in Moses' heart ; he was one who had known what it was to bear their iniquity on his spirit before Jehovah—precious type of Him who took it all upon Himself not only in priestly affection and solicitude, but as the actual sin-offering. If we are in sympathy with the thoughts of Christ we shall feel the state of the people of God, and shall realise the necessity that exists for the sin-offering. And we shall not only have a divine estimate of the departure and failure, but we shall eat the sin-offering. We shall identify ourselves with the sin of the people in the grace of Him who has been in the truest and fullest way the Sin-offering for them. This is priestly privilege of a " most holy " character. What spirituality—what nearness to Christ—what freedom from self-occupation and self-consideration does it demand ! Alas ! must we not own that we are much like Aaron and his sons in this matter ? We fail to meet the mind of the Lord, and to be in sympathy with the heart of Christ, as to the state and sin of the assembly at large, and as to the grace which would do in spirit what Christ did actually and sacrificially— that is, make the sin of the people our own. I believe that one result of our not feeling the state of the assembly in priestly sensibilities, and in accord with the sin-offering aspect of Christ's death, is that we have to be made to feel it personally, and the sorrow and suffering of it, by coming into contact with it in those with whom we walk. It is sometimes as though the Lord said, " If you do not feel the failure of the assembly sympathetically with Me, you shall feel it, and know the sorrow of it, in your own associations."

It is easier to *burn* the sin-offering that to *eat* it. There may be righteous indignation against evil, and a dealing with it in a judicial spirit, which wholly fails in this priestly element which so honours God, and which brings the priesthood into such intimate accord with the death of Christ. We may judge evil, and withdraw from it, without ever making it our own in a priestly way. The maintenance of what is due to the Lord is most important. Things that are evil must be dealt with according to the holiness that becomes God's house. But in what spirit is discipline to be exercised in whatever form it becomes necessary ? It is to be exercised in the spirit of those who have made the sin their own in confession before God. We may judge with a legal severity and hardness which is not in keeping with a dispensation pre-eminently marked by priestly grace, and under which the restoration of the offender is always the end in view. But to eat the sin-offering would be to estimate the sin according to God, and according to the death of Christ which was necessary to put it away, but so to make it our own that our spirits are entirely free from harshness or hardness, but are in accord with the grace in which Christ became the Sin-offering.

Aaron was under the pressure of his own exercises, and of the severe discipline of God upon himself; he was not sufficiently at leisure from himself to eat the sin-offering. He had so much trouble and sorrow of his own that he was not free to take up the exercise that the whole state of Israel called for. Is it not often so with ourselves ? " Such things have befallen me." Aaron did not excuse himself; he owned his weakness and inability, and when he did so " Moses heard it ; and it was good in his sight."

It is part of priestly responsibility and privilege to take up the exercise of eating the sin-offering for the people of God—the assembly. " He has given it to you that ye might bear the iniquity of the assembly, to make atonement for them before Jehovah." It is much to the Lord to be able to look down and see even a few hearts that feel about the sin of the assembly as it ought to be felt about, and in accord with His own death for that sin. But Aaron here represents those who have a sense of what ought to be, and of what is suitable to God, but who have to confess inability to take it up. I would not speak for others, but personally I think this is about as far as one could go. If so, it is better to own it. The Lord can bear with confessed weakness and failure ; He cannot support pretension. It is a beautiful touch of tender grace that when Moses heard it, " it was good in his sight." The Lord has often to be satisfied, if one may so say, with a measure of exercise and spirituality that comes short of what His heart desires. He would have us to be sympathetic with Him as to " the iniquity of the assembly," and to bear it in our spirits. He looks for this. May He give us grace to eat the sin-offering ! Or, at any rate, to own how becoming it is that we should do so, and to confess with lowly hearts how little spiritual ability we have for this function of the holy priesthood !

It is striking and suggestive that this very comprehensive section of the book—dealing with the priesthood in its original institution, in its normal characteristics, in its failure, in its continuance through God's help in a remnant after the public failure—should end on the note that is struck in the closing verses of the chapter ! May its lesson not be overlooked or forgotten !

CHAPTER 11

WE come in this chapter to what concerns " the children of Israel " generally. They were to hallow themselves and be holy because Jehovah was holy. " I am Jehovah who brought you up out of the land of Egypt, to be your God : ye shall therefore be holy, for I am holy " (verses 44, 45). Do we value the privilege of having God—of possessing Him as *our God* ? The instruction of this chapter is given so that nothing may interfere with this. The corresponding passage in Deuteronomy 14 begins by saying, " Ye are sons of Jehovah your God." Therefore we must be careful not to eat anything, in a moral sense, that would give us a character inconsistent with the place and relationship which we have with God.

If we are not practically holy we cannot enjoy what God is for His people, nor shall we answer to His pleasure. The two things go together : " I will be to him God, and he shall be to me son." If we have God as our inheritance and portion, it is in view of His having His portion in us. But if we feed on what is unclean we cannot enjoy God, for He is holy ; neither can He have pleasure in us.

Our discrimination as to clean and unclean is not to be according to human standards, but according to God's holiness. This is a very high standard, but the children of God would not wish it to be lowered a hair's breadth. They would like to be taught to discriminate between clean and unclean, and to refuse everything that does not suit the holiness of God. A worldly standard of clean and unclean might have done for Egypt, but the fact that we have been brought out of Egypt, and are now set in relation to God's sanctuary, brings in a divinely elevated standard of practical holiness.

The priests were to " put difference between the holy and the unholy, and between unclean and clean," and they were to teach the children of Israel (chapter 10 : 10, 11). We have to hallow ourselves in the light of the instruction of this chapter. It applies to every day of the week, and to every hour of the day, because there are ten thousand things around us here—and in our own flesh—which are unclean, and we have to see that we do not assimilate them, or come into moral contact with them.

Eating would typify the inward appropriation of certain features into our moral being. It would specially apply to what we read or give place to in our minds and thoughts. The world's literature contains much that is unclean ; if we assimilate it, and take character from it, we cannot be hallowed for God. *Eating* is more serious than *touching* because the inward constitution is built up by what we feed on. But *touching* renders unclean, and Paul applies this very scripture when he says, " Wherefore come out from the midst of them, and be separated, saith the Lord, and *touch not what is unclean*, and I will receive you ; and I will be to you for a Father, and ye shall be to me for sons and daughters, saith the Lord Almighty," 2 Cor. 6 : 17, 18.

This chapter is a divine guide-book as to what is clean and unclean. The character of walk is the first test of a clean creature, but it must be accompanied by inward rumination. " Whatever hath cloven hoofs, and feet quite split open, and cheweth the cud, among the beasts—that shall ye eat " (verse 3). The cloven hoof indicates separation from the world and its

E

principles ; it speaks of a pious walk. We read of " the truth which is according to piety " (Titus 1 : 1) ; piety becomes a practical test for anything which may be presented to us as the truth. We are entitled to ask, Will it give God a greater place in relation to the practical life and walk of His people ? If not, it may be doubted whether it is the truth at all.

But then a separate walk must be accompanied by inward occupation of heart and mind with what is of God. This is chewing the cud. Jeremiah said, " I sat not in the assembly of the mockers, nor exulted : I sat alone because of thy hand " ; this would answer to the cloven hoof. But the preceding verse says, " Thy words were found, and I did eat them, and thy words were unto me the joy and rejoicing of my heart," Jer. 15 : 16, 17. This would be chewing the cud. Paul says to Timothy, " *Think* of what I say, for the Lord will give thee understanding in all things," and he speaks in the same chapter of withdrawing from iniquity and, of separating from vessels to dishonour (2 Timothy 2 : 7, 19, 21). This gives us the same thing in principle.

Meditation is most important. " Mary kept all these things in her mind, pondering them in her heart," Luke 2 : 19. We do not get spiritual gain so much by hearing and reading as by meditation. Many read their daily chapter, but get little from it because they do not meditate. But then, on the other hand, some are like the camel that " cheweth the cud, but hath not cloven hoofs." He represents one occupied with truth, but not exercised to walk according to it. It is possible to take up divine things in a mental way—to be occupied with doctrines and points, without the practical life being affected in the way of separation. Such are unclean.

Then the swine has the right kind of walk—" for it hath cloven hoofs, and feet quite split open "—but there is no inward assimilation of the mind or grace of God ; " it cheweth not the cud." That is like the Pharisee, who is punctilious as to his outward walk, but has not a thought in common with God. The Lord described such as making clean the outside of the cup and the dish while within they are full of rapine and intemperance ; and, again, as being " like whited sepulchres, which appear beautiful outwardly, but within are full of dead men's bones and all uncleanness," Matt. 23 : 25–33.

God would have His people habituated to the distinguishing of good and evil. " Full-grown men, who, on account of habit, have their senses exercised for distinguishing both good and evil," Heb. 5 : 14. God has given us the perfect exemplification of all that is clean in the life of Jesus, and that is what we are to take character from. It is a daily, hourly, constant exercise.

The first section (verses 1–8) of the chapter refers to " all the beasts which are on the earth." On the earth a careful walk is needed, a walk which is the result of exercise and deliberation and of considering how things stand in relation to God. But it may be noted that the unclean beasts on the earth are not said to be " an abomination," while those in the waters, and the fowls and the creeping things, are. We might learn from this that there are certain things which we are not to take character from, nor even to touch, that have not quite the character before God of " abomination." There may be that which is merely natural, which is not the result of consideration in the fear of God, and which does not carry the mark of piety in the walk, which could hardly be looked upon as an abomination. Still it is unclean because it is not the outcome of exercise toward God. We are not to take character from it. In that which is an " abomination " I think elements of positive and active evil will be found. The refusal of it has to be more pronounced and definite.

The next section (verses 9–12) refers to " all that are in the waters." " The waters " represent the world as an element closely surrounding, through which we have to pass. The clean creatures there have " fins and scales." " Fins " would represent the ability to take a definite course without being at the mercy of the currents and tides which are ever moving this way and that in a world of lawlessness. The blessed Lord passed through all the influences here without being in the smallest degree deflected from His course. " I do always the things that are pleasing to him," John 8 : 29. " I have kept my Father's commandments and abide in his love," John 15 : 10. Following Christ gives definiteness to the course, and so does the leading of the Spirit. Those who walk by the Spirit will not be carried by the currents of lawlessness which are all around us. Lot going down to Sodom is an illustration of what it is to be without " fins." He had " scales " which kept out the corruption of Sodom, for he had a " righteous soul," and he is called " righteous Lot," but he suffered greatly from the lack of " fins." There was nothing definitely for God in his course, though he was a true believer.

" Scales " keep out the surrounding influences. The word is used of Goliath's coat of mail (1 Sam. 17 : 5). They suggest the protective character of the divine nature in the saints. Peter speaks of the saints becoming " partakers of the divine nature, having escaped the corruption that is in the world through lust," 2 Peter 1 : 4. The Lord could say, " The ruler of the world comes, and in me he has nothing," John 14 : 30. There was nothing there which the enemy could touch at all. But then John says also, " He that has been begotten of God keeps himself, and the wicked one does not touch him," 1 John 5 : 18. One can understand the Lord saying, " I am not of the world." There was nothing in Him in common with the world. All that is in the world is " the lust of the flesh, and the lust of the eyes, and the pride of life " (1 John 2 : 16), but in Him there was divine love spending itself for others, divine light shedding forth its holy beams to illuminate the hearts of men, and divine lowliness rebuking the pride of life in man. But how wonderful that He should say of His saints, " They are not of the world, as I am not of the world " ! All that which separated Him so completely from the world is true also in the divine nature of which His saints are partakers.

Our stature in the divine nature is measured by our knowledge of God. " In the desert God will teach thee, What the God that thou hast found." He has brought us out of Egypt, the place of human resource, that we might learn Him, and have Him as our Resource, and as we do so we are formed in the divine nature. It is through the knowledge of God that " the greatest and precious promises " are given to us. We might say that God Himself becomes the great Promise—the Pledge of every good—and it is through the appropriation of all that God is in this way that we " become partakers of the divine nature." (See 2 Peter 1 : 3, 4.) We become well furnished with " scales " to keep out " the corruption that is in the world through lust." Whatever is of the world morally is not only unclean, but it is " an abomination."

No clean fowls are mentioned either here or in Deuteronomy 14. The latter Scripture speaks of " all clean birds " and " all clean fowls," but they are not specified. The chief intent seems to be to warn against the unclean and the abominable. It would appear that the unclean fowls represent spiritual influences of evil. The Lord spoke of the fowls as catching away the good seed, and as roosting in the branches of the mustard tree (Matt. 13). Some of these birds are high-fliers, but they are nearly all destructive and birds of prey. They represent higher critics, religious infidels, teachers of every kind of false doctrine. People who deny the fall of man, and talk about the universal Fatherhood of God and the universal brotherhood of man, who question in various ways the inspiration of the Holy Scriptures, who set aside the Deity of our Lord Jesus Christ, and the atoning value of His sufferings and death, who say that the punishment of the lost will not be eternal, and so on. Some of them pass as being very fine birds, but they are destructive ; they are soul-destroyers.

The world is full of destructive spiritual influences, and all such influences are to be " an abomination " to us. A Christian spoke to me of a religious teacher who denied the Deity of Christ as " a very good man." I asked him if he could call a man " good " who robbed him of his Saviour ? Such men are evil-doers, whatever may be their pretensions (see 2 John 10, 11), and their teachings are to be held in abomination. One would make a difference between those who are misled and those who are active agents of evil. If one has been deceived by evil teaching it would be right to feel compassion for him, and seek his deliverance from the snare of the devil. But if people do not judge these evil influences, and keep wholly apart from them, they fall under their power. No false charity or mistaken kindness should lead us to regard evil teaching as other than abominable.

Then winged crawling things are in general an abomination. But if they have " legs above their feet with which to leap upon the earth " they may be eaten. These represent those who are of a lowly order, but who have power to "leap." They may appear pretty much like other crawling things, but when you look at them particularly you see something quite different. They have a God-given power to leave crawling and to leap. It suggests how God has given to those who would naturally be crawlers a power to leap. It speaks of an energy of life by which the soul can rise superior to the earth, and to all that would naturally hold it here. The impotent man in Acts 3 got the ability by divine power to leap up, and to walk and leap and praise God. He appeared in an entirely new character in the power of God's salvation. That is a great indication of moral cleanness ; we may safely take character from that kind of thing. " These shall ye eat."

Then " whatever goeth on its paws, among all manner of beasts that go upon all four, those are unclean unto you " (verse 27). They are marked by a soft tread, but a destructive purpose. " Such are false apostles, deceitful workers, transforming themselves into apostles of Christ. And it is not wonderful, for Satan himself transforms himself into an angel of light. It is no great thing, therefore, if his ministers also transform

themselves as ministers of righteousness ; whose end
shall be according to their works," 2 Cor. 11 : 13–15.
Jude speaks of men who " crept in unawares " ; they
came in with a sly, soft tread, but with an evil intent.

There is much about crawling things in this chapter,
and no doubt there are many things that answer to that
description morally. Then it speaks of " whatever
goeth on the belly " (verse 42). Those whose God is
their belly and who mind earthly things (Phil. 3) are
crawling things. The Apostle warns us with tears not
to take character from such, but to be imitators of him,
and of those who have their commonwealth in the
heavens.

Moles and field-mice do great harm to growing crops.
They suggest influences that would check the prosperity
of the people of God viewed as His husbandry under
divine tillage. There are many things which check
the prosperity and growth of the saints. Moles work
underground and disturb the soil about the roots, and
the field-mice nibble at the very vitals of tender plants.
We all remember the warning about the foxes—*little*
foxes—which spoil the grapes ! But moles and mice
are equally dangerous, and more difficult to catch, for
they work underground. If there is not spiritual
prosperity and vigour it is well to look for the moles
and mice !

Then the lizard in all his different kinds is unclean.
The lizard is not very destructive, so far as I know, but
the different characteristics mentioned would lead one
to think of various ways in which men delight to call
attention to themselves. " The groaning lizard "
might represent one who is morbidly occupied with
his own badness, or his trials, or who reveals his self-
importance by complaining of how badly other people

treat him. " The great red lizard " would give the idea of a person given to self-display. " The climbing lizard " would suggest the desire to get into an elevated position—loving " the chief place in feasts, and the first seats in the synagogues, and salutations in the market-places, and to be called of men, Rabbi, Rabbi." " The chameleon " changes its colour, like the man who is one thing with the brethren, and quite another when he is with worldly people.

These different unclean creatures set forth moral features which once characterised us all. It might well be said, " Such were some of you." But in the great sheet which Peter saw, " in which were all the quadrupeds and creeping things of the earth, and the fowls of the heaven," they were all seen as cleansed by God. Divine cleansing having come in, and hearts being purified by faith, God's people no longer take character from what is unclean. We have to see to it that as a holy people we exercise watchfulness to keep ourselves apart from the moral features set forth in these unclean creatures.

To touch the carcases of these things renders one " unclean until the even." There is a beautiful touch of grace about that, for it seems to suggest that every such defilement will be taken up and cleansed from the heart and conscience the same day that it is contracted. There is the same principle in " Let not the sun set upon your wrath," Ephes. 4 : 26. You are not to carry an angry feeling over to another day. Our individual path is made up of days, and God would have every question of anger or defilement settled before " even." How often we let defilement cling to us for days, weeks, months, perhaps sometimes years ! But God's way is to have the moral stain

removed at " the even " of the day in which it was
contracted. It is well that there should be a self-
review in holy exercise at the close of each day, and a
judging of every touch of what is unclean—that is,
every contact with what is of the flesh. In judging it
with God there is moral cleansing from it. Each day's
accounts are to be settled at " even," not carried over
to another day. If things have been had out with
God you can lay your head on your pillow without
guile. Get under the fig-tree and lay all bare before
God, so that there is nothing in reserve, and the Lord
can then say of you, " Behold one truly an Israelite,
in whom there is no guile," John 1 : 47. Then there
are sometimes differences between brothers and sisters
which leave a stain of uncleanness on the spirit.
Would it not be good to settle them before " even " ?
The longer things are allowed to run on the more
difficult it is to face them.

There is another side to this. If one has touched
what is unclean the evil effect cannot be thrown off at
once. It abides " until the even." It leaves its mark
for the whole of that day. It would have been a
serious thing for the unclean Israelite to eat a peace-
offering that day as if nothing had happened (chapter
7 : 20, 21). This serves to emphasise the necessity
for jealous care as to touching what is unclean. I have
no doubt that a great deal of time is lost spiritually
through unwatchfulness as to this. That is, believers
lose much happiness with God which they might
otherwise enjoy.

" All vessels of wood . . . every vessel wherewith
work is done " (verse 32) is defiled by an unclean
creature falling on it, and has to be " put into water,
and be unclean until the even ; then shall it be clean."

I understand such vessels to represent believers as vessels of service. If that which is unclean gets place with such, they have to come under the exercising power of the word which brings the death of Christ to bear upon them, and the result of this is that at even they are clean. But " every earthen vessel into which any of them falleth—whatever is in it shall be unclean : and ye shall break it " (verse 33). The " earthen vessel " represents what we are naturally. Contaminating influences find place with us because of what we are naturally, and all that in our nature which leaves us open to these defilements has to be corrected by discipline, which is really the breaking of the earthen. vessel. The result of the breaking of the earthen vessel is that the " vessel wherewith work is done " becomes more holy and serviceable. The believer as a vessel of service is helped by the discipline which breaks the earthen vessel. The " vessel to honour, sanctified, serviceable to the Master" prepared for every good work " (2 Tim. 2 : 21) is one who has kept himself in holy separateness from all that is dishonouring and defiling.

The provision of verse 36 is very sweet. " A spring or a well, a quantity of water, shall be clean." The only way to keep free from defilement in a world like this is to be in the energy of the Spirit. " A spring " suggests the energy of the Spirit in the individual giving direction to the exercises and affections of the soul. " The water which I shall give him shall become in him a fountain of water, springing up into eternal life," John 4 : 14. " A well " is a source of supply from which saints can draw ; it would speak of the ministry of Christ in the power of the Spirit. While " a quantity of water " would be realised in the assembly, where the Spirit can distribute gifts, and bring things out in a fulness that goes beyond what is individual.

The secret of immunity from defilement lies in the presence and living activities of the Spirit of God. There is a vital and divine power in the Spirit which enables saints to repel and throw off every defiling influence. "They shall take up serpents ; and if they should drink any deadly thing it shall not injure them." Paul shook off the viper that fastened on his hand, and felt no harm. This supposes such an energy of life by the Spirit that unclean things cannot affect us or leave any trace of their influence. "If, by the Spirit, ye put to death the deeds of the body, ye shall live," Rom. 8 : 13. "Walk in the Spirit, and ye shall no way fulfil flesh's lust," Gal. 5 : 16.

CHAPTER 12

THIS chapter conveys the thought of a more prolonged exercise than anything that has gone before in the book. Exercise connected with the sin-offering and the trespass-offering was gone through on the day when the sin or trespass came on the conscience of the offender. The uncleanness occasioned by touching what was defiling terminated at "even." But here there are seven or fourteen days of uncleanness, and a prolonged period of cleansing afterwards. This indicates that we have before us here a very deep and grave lesson.

In the previous chapter we have seen a variety of unclean animals from which character was not to be taken, and which were not to be touched if the children of Israel were to be a holy people for God. But now the lesson is brought home that the greatest uncleanness came by the birth of a human child after the flesh. Every increase of the people was to be marked by this prolonged exercise. The uncleanness of the *mother* is emphasised; the lesson of the chapter is that *the source* is unclean. This goes to the very root of things. "Who can bring a clean man out of the unclean? Not one!" (Job 14 : 4). And Bildad asks, "How should he be clean that is born of a woman?" (Job 25 : 4). God would have us to recognise the moral character which attaches to us as born into this world. Before an act is done, or a word spoken, or a thought conceived in the mind, there is that brought into the world which is marked by sin. "Behold, in iniquity was I brought forth, and in sin did my mother conceive me," Psa. 51 : 5.

Every mother in Israel had to take up the exercise of this. God was teaching His people, and is teaching us, that that which is born of the flesh is flesh, and the best bit of the flesh is unclean. There is no increase for the Israel of God apart from the recognition of this. No lesson is more needed to-day, even by those who profess to be the people of God. For it is widely held that man only needs suitable environment, education, and good moral influences brought to bear upon him, and he will be all right! But if the source is unclean, and that which is born of the flesh is flesh, how is that to be remedied?

Nothing is brought forth for God in this world apart from taking up this exercise. The double period for a female child is doubtless a reminder that "the woman, having been deceived, was in transgression" (1 Tim. 2 : 14), but it may also suggest that when Christ is not

distinctly in view, nor His death in its circumcision
aspect, the exercises connected with learning the true
character of the flesh are more prolonged. But in
either case the exercise has to be gone through in its
completeness. There is no cutting it short.

What is brought out in this chapter is the uncleanness of the mother, not of the child. That every child
born in the natural course would be unclean is obvious ;
but I believe that the male child here has a typical
reference to Christ. This chapter is directly linked by
the Spirit of God with the incidents recorded in Luke 2
—incidents which are indelibly engraved on the
affections of the saints. And there can be no doubt
that circumcision on the eighth day is a figure of the
death of Christ in which the flesh has been cut off
under the eye of God. It is because everything connected with the order of man after the flesh is unclean
that it has had to be cut off in the death of Christ.
" The circumcision of the Christ " (Col. 2 : 11) is His
death.

The immaculate conception of the virgin is disproved
by the fact that she fulfilled the days of purifying, and
brought a sin-offering according to this chapter. But
of her Son it was said by the angel Gabriel, " *The holy
thing* also which shall be born shall be called Son of
God," Luke 1 : 35. Of Him alone it could be truly
and fully said, that He was " holy to the Lord." The
Child was begotten in her of the Holy Spirit (Matt.
1 : 18, 20), and the body in which He came was prepared
of God (Heb. 10 : 5), wholly apart from any taint of sin.
He was " the holy one of God," John 6 : 69. Three
things are said of Him in words taught by the Holy
Spirit :   " Who did no sin," (1 Peter 2 : 22), " Him who
knew not sin " (2 Cor. 5 : 21), " In him sin is not "

1 John 3 : 5. I have no doubt that it is because the sinless humanity of the Lord Jesus was in the view of the Spirit of God that the uncleanness of the mother is spoken of in Leviticus 12 and not the uncleanness of the child. It is " she shall be unclean . . . and the priest shall make atonement for her ; and she shall be clean."

This chapter is, in type, Israel having to learn her own uncleanness, even though, in the wisdom of God's ways and according to His promise, she gave birth to Christ, the sinless One. And if Israel is unclean humanity is unclean. It was the coming in of Christ that made manifest all the uncleanness that was there. It raised the whole question of Israel's state and brought it to light, and she was manifested to be unclean—unfit to touch holy things, or to come into the sanctuary. The coming here of Christ made manifest as nothing had done before that His death was a necessity. " He was in the world, and the world had its being through him, and the world knew him not. He came to his own, and his own received him not," John 1 : 10, 11. There could be no greater evidence than this of the uncleanness of man : the world did not know Him, and Israel—with the light of promises, law, and covenants—did not receive Him ! The full testimony of divine goodness, relieving men of every need and pressure, had its answer at Calvary ! God revealing Himself in the perfection of grace and truth brought out all the deep-rooted enmity of the human heart. There is no room for divine love or holiness in the unclean heart of man.

" And on the eighth day shall the flesh of his foreskin be circumcised." This is a figure of the death of Christ as that in which the flesh is absolutely cut off

for God.   (See " An Outline of Genesis," chapter 17.)
" The eighth day " coming in after the " seven days "
of uncleanness suggests how God has taken account of
the uncleanness of the flesh, and has provided for " the
putting off of the body of the flesh, in the circumcision
of the Christ," Col. 2 : 11.   The eighth day stands in
relation to the preceding seven, but it has in view the
bringing in for God of that which is wholly apart from
the uncleanness of the flesh.

The death of the sinless Son of God made resurrection a necessity " inasmuch as it was not possible
that he should be held by its power."   He could not be
left in death.   The flesh, with all its uncleanness, has
been cut off in His death, but the very fact that it was
done in *His* death has rendered resurrection inevitable.
Man—in the Person of Jesus—lives apart from all the
uncleanness of the flesh, which was judged and cut off
vicariously in His death, and He is now for ever beyond
death.   The circumcision of His death—necessary on
account of what flesh was—necessitates resurrection
because of what He was.   If we think of the uncleanness of the flesh being cut off in His death, through
grace, we are reminded at the same moment of the
unsullied purity in which He lives to God as the Risen
One.   The eighth day covers both in type : it gives us
the circumcision aspect of the death of Christ, but it
teaches us also that the death of *Christ* involves
resurrection.   It involves that man shall be with God
eternally apart from uncleanness, apart from sin and
death, in suitability to all that God is, and that for
His pleasure.

The " seven days " give us the uncleanness of
humanity as demonstrated by the coming in of Christ.
The " eighth " day gives us, in type, the cutting off of

unclean flesh in the death of Christ, and an entirely
new place for man in the eternal purity of resurrection.
It speaks of something for God, as we see in type in
Exodus 22 : 30. " Seven days shall it be with its dam :
on the eighth day thou shalt give it me." The eighth
day is the day of completed cleansing for the leper
(Lev. 14), for the one who has a flux (Lev. 15), and
for the defiled Nazarite (Num. 6). Attention has
often been called to the fact that the numerical value
of the letters of the Name JESUS is 888. It is the
intensification of all that the number eight stands for
in Scripture. It is in relation to the previous seven in
two senses. Seven may be viewed—as in the woman's
seven days of uncleanness—as the perfect disclosure
of the fallen state of humanity. This has been met
and cut off in the death of Jesus for the glory of God,
so that men may be blessed according to the holy
worth of Jesus—Jehovah the Saviour. Or the seven
days may be viewed as the complete manifestation of
the personal perfection of Jesus in all His moral glory
and beauty as the Holy One of God brought out in life
and in death. There could be but one answer to that
—resurrection. Man in the Person of Jesus is now for
ever apart from sin, and beyond death, for God's
eternal satisfaction and delight, and the blessing of
God for men is according to what He is. Everything
for God is thus placed on the footing of what Christ
is, and nothing depends on what man is according to
the flesh.

But though God has reached this absolutely in all
its completeness and value so that nothing can be
added to it, nor anything taken from it, it is a very
deep and serious lesson for man to learn. Hence the
thirty-three or sixty-six days come in—a prolonged

exercise on the human side. It is for us, of course, not measured by days or weeks but by soul exercise. The prolonged period is spoken of here as " the days of her cleansing " ; it is thus morally contrasted with the days of uncleanness.

We learn the uncleanness of the flesh by its entire lack of appreciation of Christ, by its utter refusal of Him. I find that my flesh does not want Christ ; it prefers every vanity of this world to Christ ; and if brought face to face with Him so as to be tested fully it hates Him. This is a very searching and humbling lesson. Then we learn that in His death unclean flesh was cut off in holy judgment ; He bore its just condemnation. Thus in the light of Christ and of His death one learns to judge oneself. We see that what we are by nature and according to flesh is morally corrupt ; it is to be judged, refused, and hated, not gratified. The soul in this exercise is learning to be morally separate from what is of the flesh ; it is going through the days of cleansing.

The latter part of Romans 7 shows a process of self-discovery *under law*, but self-discovery in presence of *Christ* is an even deeper lesson ; it is an intensified exercise. But it is accompanied by a precious and subduing sense of grace, for the One in whose presence all my uncleanness is exposed is my Saviour ; He has died for me, and in Him God's thoughts of infinite grace toward me are set forth. If *I* am all wrong, *He* is all that is precious and acceptable to God, and all that He is, is for me.

There is a difference between being crucified with Christ and being circumcised in Him. Being crucified with Him refers to the place which we take up in the world—a place of reproach and contempt. But circumcision is what the world cannot take account of at all ; it is the death of Christ as known in the heart and spirit of the believer, and taken account of by God. The believer who has come to it has no confidence in the flesh ; he is morally clear of it in his spirit with God.

If souls are not in the light of Christ, and of what has been effected in His death, their exercises in relation to self-discovery will be prolonged and intensely painful. This is intimated, perhaps, in the much longer period of cleansing for a female child. There is something wrought of God subjectively—the female would typify this—but Christ is not clearly and fully in the soul's view. This probably sets forth typically the exercises of the remnant of Israel when God begins to work in them. They will fear God and love His law, and follow after righteousness, without having—at any rate in the early stages of their exercise —any clear light as to Christ, or as to what is connected with the eighth day. Their deep and prolonged exercise appears in many of the Psalms and in the Prophets—a sense of sin and an earnest looking to God for His salvation, but no clear light, as yet, with regard to Christ. The latter-day exercises of the remnant will be bitter and prolonged, but they will learn thereby that " all flesh is grass." They will be humbled by the consideration of their individual and national history—the law broken, the promises despised, the idolatry, the rejection of their Messiah, the refusal of Him who spoke from heaven. But the moment will come when they will see that all this, which is the evidence of their state in flesh, has been dealt with and judged in the death of their Messiah. He has made it all His own in wondrous grace that they might be relieved of it, and be able to bless themselves in Him (Ps. 72 : 17). When their exercises have reached a suitable point the light of Christ and of His death will break in upon their souls through the prophetic word, and they will learn to take their place with God on the ground of what He is, and of His death. The days of their cleansing will then be fulfilled. They will learn to part company with all that they are in their natural uncleanness, and to be with God on the ground of the Lamb of the burnt-offering, and the Turtle-dove of the sin-offering.

Something analogous to this is often found in souls to-day. They have exercises which are the fruit of mercy and of divine working in them. They have desires Godward, and they learn painfully their uncleanness bit by bit, first at one point and then at another, and go on for years without getting clear. Such prolonged exercises are very common under defective teaching, and where souls have not the ministry of Christ, or, at any rate, not what might be called an " eighth day " ministry. They are not cleansed from their uncleanness, though learning it, and learning to abhor themselves. They are not in liberty with God, and are not really in the truth and blessing of Christ.

It is important to see that " the fulness of the time " has come (Gal. 4 : 4). It is really the time of the Male Child and the " eighth day." Simeon received the holy Child into his arms and blessed God (Luke 2 : 28). He realised the exercise the Child's mother would have to go through, and how the Child would be " for a sign spoken against," and that " even a sword shall go through thine own soul ; so that the thoughts may be revealed from many hearts." All this was connected with the laying bare of man's uncleanness. But to Simeon He was God's salvation, " prepared before the face of all peoples ; a light for revelation of the Gentiles and the glory of thy people Israel." Everything was there in Him for God's pleasure and man's blessing. We have individually to learn this. None of us can touch holy things or come into the sanctuary until we have learned it.

The fulfilment of the period of cleansing is marked by bringing " a yearling lamb for a burnt-offering, and a young pigeon or a turtle-dove for a sin-offering." The soul takes its place consciously with God apart from the uncleanness of the flesh, on the ground of Christ, and of His death in burnt-offering and sin-offering character. It is worth while to go through much exercise to reach that—to see in any measure the marvellous triumph that has been effected by God's salvation through grace. We have to learn the necessity for severance from all that we were morally as of natural generation, but God's salvation has transferred us from the uncleanness of nature to the perfection and blessedness of Christ, and has given us capacity, by the renewing of the Holy Spirit, to touch holy things and to enter the sanctuary. We can be with God in holy freedom, apart from the uncleanness of nature. Is it not a " great salvation " ? Let us take heed that we do not neglect it, for the people of God may neglect the great salvation as well as the openly ungodly.

If we truly take up the exercise of Leviticus 12 we shall be preserved from leprosy as seen in chapters 13, 14. A man judging himself in the light of Christ would never become a leper. Leprosy is constitutional, and comes of what is unclean ; but if the unclean source is judged, and that judgment is spiritually maintained, there will be no leprosy. If the lesson of chapter 12 is not learned with God there may be an outbreak of the will of the flesh which exposes what the fallen nature really is, and it may for a time become characteristic of one of the people of God.

The answer to every exercise is Christ. Israel will find it to be so, and we have to learn it also. The more distinctly our souls are in the light of Christ the more easily and quickly we learn our lessons. Anything brought forth which is true increase in the Israel of God will be accompanied by such exercises as are indicated here.

CHAPTER 13

WE have something here much more serious than the sin of inadvertence, or the trespass, of chapters 4 and 5. It is not simply that there is sin in the flesh, and no good there, and that the mind of the flesh is enmity against God. That is true of the flesh in each one of us, and it has to be judged in secret with God. But leprosy is the breaking out of the lawlessness of the flesh in acts or words so as to call for the priestly discernment and pronounced judgment of the saints. It renders one unfit to occupy one's tent, or to partake in the privileges of the congregation of God.

The fact that such a condition is set before us in type with so much detailed instruction shows that it is likely to be met with amongst the people of God. It also shows that He would have His priests skilled in ability to discern it, faithful in dealing with it, and also qualified to render all the service needed for cleansing when His mercy has brought in healing. One cannot doubt that the instruction of these two long chapters has an important present application.

All unrighteousness is sin, but it is not always leprosy. Leprosy is a sore betraying the existence of a deep-seated constitutional taint, which becomes for the time characteristic of the person affected. It represents the coming into evidence in a pronounced way of the will of the flesh, so that for the time being the individual is characterised by it. This is a terrible thing, for the will of the flesh is unclean and abhorrent to God. It is like the presumptuous sin of Psalm 19 : 13, which David prayed to be kept from. One really characterised by it is unsuitable for the companionship of God's people. " He shall dwell apart ; outside the camp shall his dwelling be " (verse 46).

Miriam spoke against Moses ; Gehazi in his covetousness spoiled the witness of free grace to the Gentile ; and Uzziah presumed to exercise priesthood without divine title. All three were smitten with leprosy, and are examples of moral conditions which in the government of God result in leprosy. This shows how important it is to judge a corrupt and wilful state of soul, for if it is not judged in secret it will, sooner or later, come into evidence in the body by word or deed.

These chapters (13, 14) are wonderful instruction in grace, for if they emphasise the seriousness of leprosy they also intimate very clearly the possibility of the leper being healed and cleansed. The healing of a leper is entirely of God ; it is not the priest's work to *heal* him, though when he is healed the priest has a good deal to do with his *cleansing*. When there is pronounced activity of the will of the flesh God alone can bring a man to judge it. When self-judgment

comes in the leper is healed. He must be healed
before anything can be done for his cleansing. If the
priest went outside the camp and looked at the leper
and found him healed he knew that the power of God
had been in operation. When a man in whom will
has been active says, as Isaiah did, " Woe unto me !
for I am undone ; for I am a man of unclean lips, and
I dwell in the midst of a people of unclean lips : for
mine eyes have seen the King, Jehovah of hosts," the
leprosy is healed. In that chapter (Isaiah 6) we see
how by the touch of the glowing coal from the altar
his iniquity was taken away, and his sin expiated.
His lips were cleansed so that he spoke of the glory of
Christ. " These things said Esaias because he saw his
glory and spoke of him." See Isaiah 6 : 1–7 ; John
12 : 41. How wonderful the grace of it ! The deeper
the lesson of self-knowledge and self-judgment the
more profound the sense of grace. We have to do
with the God of all grace.

There may be sores which look like leprosy, but
which are not really leprous, and hence priestly discernment and care become most important. In
doubtful cases nothing is to be done in a hurry. There
are certain symptoms which have to be carefully noted.
The hair in the sore turned white is a serious indication.
It suggests definite signs of spiritual decline and decay.
The neglect of the private reading of the Scriptures
and of prayer cannot be seen by others, but when
persons lose their interest in the meetings and in the
people of God, and begin fault-finding and taking up
worldly interests and associations, these are obvious
and suspicious signs. Viewed along with other things
they serve to guide the priest in his judgment.

Then " the sore looketh deeper than the skin of his

flesh." This settles the question ; " it is the sore of leprosy." It is not merely an infirmity of manner, or a manifestation of irritability, but a settled and determined working of the will of the flesh. The man's mind and spirit are really characterised by what is displeasing to God ; the " sore " is " deeper than the skin." Such a one can only be pronounced " unclean." He is, for the time being, unfit to enjoy the privilege of the sanctuary, or of the fellowship to which saints are called.

There is a more doubtful case in verses 4–6, and it requires patience for the discernment of its true character. The man with a " sore " has to be shut up for seven days, and possibly another seven, before it can be determined whether it is leprosy or not. In such a case the man is not definitely pronounced " unclean," but he is " shut up." There is enough in his case to cause considerable exercise and waiting upon God, and the restriction of his liberty, until the true nature of what is working can be determined. The shutting up is really in the patience of grace ; it is because the priest has noted certain favourable indications (verse 4), and he is hopeful that no necessity may arise to pronounce the man unclean. But the case is sufficiently grave to demand care, and the man cannot be regarded as free from question, or as one who can move in and out freely as having the confidence of his brethren.

If at the end of the first seven days " the sore remaineth as it was, the sore hath not spread in the skin," it is another favourable indication, and gives further hope that it is not a case of leprosy. And he is shut up " seven days a second time." If things remain as they are and do not increase, it is, so far, favourable.

When any evil spreads it is a bad sign ; it shows that there is an active energy about it. A root of bitterness springing up may trouble the saints, and many be defiled by it. But if *will* is not persistently active— if it is not really leprosy—under the normal working of grace sores " become pale " ; they die down, and the virulence disappears. A bad feeling between saints, or on the part of one towards others, is a " sore," but there is always a secret and persistent working of grace which tends to heal such things. All ministry, and mutual spiritual activities amongst saints, and pastoral care, tend to healing.

You may feel very angry with a brother or sister, but as the days pass grace begins to assert its power in your soul, and the result is that you feel inclined to make a little more allowance than you did at first. Then it occurs to you that perhaps you were not so wise and gracious yourself as you might have been. Now if these exercises are being produced in your soul under the influence of grace you may be assured that the same process is going on in your brother or sister. The " sore " is becoming " pale " ! It is always so with the people of God if they judge the activity of their own wills. And as this is seen it is the happy indication that the " sore " is not leprosy.

Under grace there is always a working towards healing. So that if a sore spreads and becomes more virulent it is very serious. It indicates that, for the time, the will of the flesh is more in evidence than the power of divine grace in the soul. If sores do not become " pale," and if they spread, it indicates some positive working of the will of the flesh.

There may be much that is trying in a brother or a sister, but we must not be in a hurry to pronounce it leprosy. Perhaps if we got spiritually near to them we should find that those things were more trying to them than they are to us. The conscience is sensitive as to them, and the heart mourns them. In such a case there may be much the soul has to be humbled about, but there is not leprosy. The priest knows how to distinguish between infirmities of manner and habits of speech which may be a trial, but which are not "deeper than the skin," and those manifestations which indicate a positive and active working of the will.

In verses 9–11 we have a more definite case. "Behold, there is a white rising in the skin, and it hath turned the hair white, and a trace of raw flesh is in the rising : it is an old leprosy in the skin of his flesh." In this case things are so manifest that there is no need for delay in pronouncing upon it. There is clear evidence. "It is an old leprosy." There has been something there unjudged, perhaps for years, but it has now come to light. If things are gone on with in secret—perhaps allowed to work in the mind unjudged —there comes a time when, in the governmental ways of God, they are exposed. There is often a long secret history behind an open outbreak of leprosy.

What is seen in verses 12, 13, is in marked contrast to "an old leprosy " that has been long working in secret. Here the leprosy covers "all the skin of him that hath the sore, from his head even to his foot, wherever the eyes of the priest look." In this case all is out. It speaks of full confession. The priest pronounces him clean, and it is emphatically added, "he is clean." There is no guile in such a man ; truth is in his inward parts. There is not the slightest pretension to be other than what he is ; not a single

spot " wherever the eyes of the priest look " where
there is any hypocrisy or dissimulation.   He is leprous,
but he is, in type, upright with God and with his
brethren about it.   " He is clean."

But with such a one there may be again the appearance of " raw flesh," and on the day when this appears
" he shall be unclean."   There is the sad possibility,
even after an upright and open acknowledgment of
what has worked in one's flesh, that there may be
again an activity of that flesh.   How humbling is the
thought of this !·   What watchfulness and prayerful-
ness does it necessitate !   We need to be at all times
in absolute dependence upon God, " kept guarded by
the power of God through faith," 1 Peter 1 : 5.   To
those of us who have known by experience how " raw
flesh " can come into evidence, perhaps again and
again, it is a comfort to see that this paragraph does
not end without a suggestion of the " raw flesh "
changing again and becoming white, so that the man
can come to the priest, and be once more pronounced
clean because " he is clean."   How wondrous is the
grace and mercy of God that can bring about restoration even in such a case as is typified here !

Then " a boil " (verses 18–23) or " a burning inflam-
mation " (verses 24–28) are suspicious signs, and are
very apt to be starting points of leprosy.   I think
these things would refer to outbreaks of natural heat
and irritability and bad temper.   Probably such things
are found with most of us at times, though some may
be specially liable to them.   There can be no doubt
that such things often lead to prolonged ill-feeling.
An immense amount of blessing and joy is hindered by
personal feelings coming in amongst the people of God.
Such things interfere with the activity of the Spirit,

and are a great restraint upon spiritual freedom when saints come together. We have to be careful that what begins in personal infirmity does not end in a positive and persistent activity of the will of the flesh.

If wrong feelings come in, to speak of them to others is only spreading the sore. It is better to have " seven days " alone with God. That would check the springing up and spreading of roots of bitterness. It is because we lack the grace of God that these things come in ; if that grace continually acted on our spirits it would set them aside ; they would go like the morning mists before the sun.

It is striking that only in connection with leprosy in the head is the man pronounced " utterly unclean." I think this shows that the will of the flesh taking form in thoughts and teaching is the most serious form of leprosy. It might be said of every teacher of evil doctrine that " his sore is in his head." If a man has wrong thoughts of God or of Christ he is " utterly unclean." There was probably never more head leprosy than there is to-day—the proud will of the flesh manifesting itself in all kinds of evil thought and teaching. There is much that is not merely the fruit of human infirmity or ignorance but which is Satanic in origin and antichristian in character, and which has in it all the elements of apostasy.

Holding Christ as Head, and deriving from Him, is the divine preservative from this kind of leprosy. There are no pure and holy thoughts apart from Christ and the Holy Spirit. A saint of 300 years ago had some sense of this when he said :

> " Profaneness in my head,
> Defects and darkness in my breast."

But he could also add :

> " Only another Head
> I have, another Heart and Breast.
>
> .   .   .   .   .
>
> " Christ is my only Head,
> My alone only Heart and Breast.
>
> .   .   .   .   .
>
> " My doctrine tuned by Christ, Who is not dead
> But lives in me while I do rest."   (*George Herbert.*)

To have by His Spirit the intelligence and affections of Christ would preserve us from every form of leprosy.

The leper with garments rent and head uncovered, and with the cry, " Unclean, unclean ! " upon his lips, had to " dwell apart ;   outside the camp shall his dwelling be."   He had to realise his condition, and to own it publicly, and to accept the fact that he was unsuitable for companionship with the people of God, or for the enjoyment of their holy privileges.   He found himself, like the wicked person at Corinth, removed from amongst the people of God, but not to be forgotten by them.   He was still to be the subject of priestly solicitude and care.   " His tent " would ever be a reminder that he was of Israel, and in the light of these two chapters there would ever be the desire that he might be healed and cleansed, and brought back to his tent and his privileges.

The closing part of the chapter refers to leprosy in a garment, which would represent something not exactly personal, but closely identified with the person, such as one's occupation or habits or associations.   In this case the *man* is not leprous, but his *garment* lies under suspicion and must be " shown unto the priest."   Some callings are unclean, and a believer could not abide in them with God.   In such a case the whole garment is infected, and must be burned with fire. The *spreading* of the sore is an important indication, as it was in the person, and would prove it to be " a corroding leprosy."

If something which there is reason to suspect to be evil increases, and makes its character more apparent, it must be dealt with unsparingly. The first indication may not be sufficient to decide the matter, but as soon as it is seen to be extending it is known as " a corroding leprosy." If the sore has not spread after seven days the garment is washed and shut up a second seven days. The word, bringing in the moral cleansing power of the death of Christ, is applied to the existing conditions, and space given for the effect to be made manifest. If after the washing the sore has not changed its appearance, this is sufficient to prove it unclean even if the sore has not spread. There has been no effect from the application of the word, and this is serious. It is in this case " a fretting sore " ; not so virulent, perhaps, as the " corroding leprosy " of verses 51, 52, but decidedly " unclean," and the garment in which it is must be burned with fire. There are certain habits or associations which give indications that there is something about them which is not of God, and when the word is brought in and applied to them, and no change is produced, it makes apparent that they are unclean.

But if the sore becomes pale after washing it may be possible that the whole garment is not unclean, but only the piece where the sore is, which has to be rent from it. Sometimes it is not the whole of a certain association that is unclean, but only a part of it, in which case the unclean part only is to be got rid of. But if, after doing this, the sore appears again, it is evident that the whole is infected and must be burned. But if after washing the sore departs, " it shall be washed a second time, and it is clean." There are certain conditions which only need the application of the word of cleansing to bring them into moral suitability : in this case there is no leprosy. But there are other conditions which are in themselves so unclean that there is no remedy but unsparing judgment, and getting rid of all that is connected with them.

The people of God are to cleanse themselves from every pollution of flesh and spirit, and to perfect holiness in His fear. They are to hate the garment spotted by the flesh, and to keep themselves unspotted from the world. If any occupation, or habit, or association is found to hinder one's liberty with God, or the enjoyment of spiritual things, or happy fellowship with one's brethren, or power in service, it is to be suspected that there is some " sore of leprosy " about it, and it should be subjected at once to priestly scrutiny and care. Do not go on with anything that you cannot connect with God. If it cannot be done to His glory it is better to tear it out, or to burn the whole garment.

CHAPTER 14

WE may note that chapter 13 is addressed to Moses and Aaron ; chapter 14 : 1–32 to Moses only ; then chapter 14 : 33–53 is to Moses and Aaron. Priestly discernment is called for in the sections where Aaron is addressed, but chapter 14 : 1–32 is the setting forth of the mind of Jehovah as to the cleansing of the leper ;

it is a wondrous unfolding of Jehovah's grace through the mediator.

The leper must be " healed " before the priest can do anything. When *will* is active only God can deal with it. A course of persistent self-will must end disastrously if God does not come in in the sovereignty of His mercy. Paul delivered Hymenæus and Alexander to Satan that they might be taught by discipline not to blaspheme. In their case we may see an instance of how God can put a check on the action of man's will for the good of His saints without necessarily healing the leper. In another case, " An heretical man after a first and second admonition have done with, knowing that such a one is perverted, and sins, being self-condemned," Titus 3 : 10, 11. Such a man is a leper whose " sore is in his head " ; he has to be left with God after being twice admonished. Then there are cases where those who oppose are to be set right in meekness, " if God perhaps may sometime give them repentance to acknowledgment of the truth, and that they may awake up out of the snare of the devil, who are taken by him, for *his* will," 2 Tim. 2 : 25, 26. It is sovereign mercy if a man who has pursued a course of self-will wakes up out of it to be for God's will.

The Lord puts the cleansing of the leper entirely on the ground of sovereignty in Luke 4, for He says, " There were many lepers in Israel in the time of Elisha the prophet, and none of them was cleansed but Naaman the Syrian." It seems as though the leper in Luke 5 had understood that, for he said, " Lord, if thou wilt, thou art able to cleanse me." He submitted himself to divine sovereignty.

In the case of a self-willed believer the advocacy of

Christ might be answered by a discipline which would bring him to submission. Then God would use the attitude of the brethren towards him as a very deep exercise. It is brought home to him that the priest has pronounced him unclean, and that his dwelling is outside the camp. He has to take up all the exercise of this—to rend his garments, and uncover his head, and cry, " Unclean, unclean ! " He has to acknowledge his condition, and to realise that he is unfit to be a companion of God's people.

But all this has healing and cleansing in view. This chapter would encourage us to look for the healing of lepers. Indeed it is very clear evidence that God is with His people when healing comes about ; one of His Names is Jehovah-Rophi—Jehovah that healeth thee. It is a serious exercise if the state of God's Israel is such that He cannot manifest His healing power amongst them. The Lord's service in Israel was marked by healing, feeding, and teaching ; healing must come first, for an unhealed person cannot enjoy spiritual food or take in divine teaching.

For the cleansing of the leper the priest commands two clean living birds to be taken, and cedar-wood and scarlet and hyssop. The " two clean living birds " as typical of Christ would suggest what He was as coming down from heaven. It was characteristic of Him that He came down from heaven not to do His own will but the will of Him who sent Him (John 6 : 38). He was of the things that are above, and the whole principle of His moral being was obedience. God presents to the healed leper, and to every one of us, a new and heavenly kind of Man in Christ. As marked by activity of will the leper has manifested that he was " of those things which are beneath " (see note to

John 8 : 23 in New Translation), but he is now to learn Christ as " of those things which are above "— the perfect contrast to all that has been active in himself. His self-judgment is to be according to an estimate formed in the light of what was true in Christ.

The " cedar-wood and scarlet and hyssop " would, I think, intimate things which had their antitype in Christ. If the cedar speaks of " the loftiness of man," as it does in Isaiah 2, and the scarlet of anything that would give him distinction, and the hyssop of his low estate, I think these things may be also suggestive of what Christ was in the days of His flesh. It is said of Him, " His bearing as Lebanon, excellent as the cedars," Song of Songs 5 : 15. Wherever we look at Him—in the home at Nazareth, in the temple at twelve years of age, at the baptismal water of Jordan, in the temptation, with His disciples, with the multitudes, with His adversaries—His bearing had at all times the excellency of the cedar.

Then " scarlet " is a *distinguishing* colour, as we may see in Gen. 38 : 28 ; Joshua 2 : 18 ; 2 Sam. 1 : 24. " A cloth of scarlet " over the dishes, cups, bowls and goblets of the drink-offering and the continual bread on the table (Numbers 4 : 8) seems to speak of the distinction which God will put upon Israel when they have their administrative place as sustained by Christ for God's pleasure, and they become vessels of drink-offering as gladly devoted to Him. So the " scarlet " would set forth those features in Christ which in a marked way distinguished Him from all others as having the true glory of Man in contrast with every kind of vain-glory.

Then the " hyssop " would typify the lowliness in which He took a bondman's form, and was ever found amongst His own, and in the world, as the One who served. The lowliness of perfect obedience and sub- jection to the will of God ever marked Him.

The priest is to command that these things are to be taken for the healed leper. It is not the leper who brings them ; they are taken for him along with the two clean living birds. He is to learn in Christ all that is truly excellent and distinctive of man as having honour from God, and the lowliness in which it was all sustained so that He never sought His own glory or pleasure but the glory of God and the good of men. What a contrast is all this to that of which leprosy speaks ! What a humbling lesson does it all mean for the healed leper ! And yet what a blessed instruction in Christ !

Then one bird is to be killed in an earthen vessel over running (or living) water. This would seem to suggest the death of Christ as that of which the witness is preserved for application to the soul in the power of the Spirit. The living bird, the cedar-wood, the scarlet, and the hyssop are all dipped in the blood of the killed bird, and the one who is to be cleansed is sprinkled seven times by the priest, and pronounced clean. Christ is seen here as the Living One, but as having become dead on account of that state which had characterised the leper. If all that in Him which was so excellent and distinctive, so morally suitable to God, had to go into death it gives a profound sense of the cost at which cleansing has been made possible for the leper. If Christ after the flesh, with all His supreme moral excellence, had to go in death, what does it make of man's greatness or glory, or even of his voluntary humility ? It is seen to be vanity, and to be subject to death, but a death into which

Christ came in wondrous grace for the glory of God and to make cleansing possible for men. What powerful influence is this to bring to bear on the healed leper in seven-fold sprinkling ! Christ has been into death to bring to an end the man after the flesh, with all the activities of his lawless will, so that those who believe on Him might be henceforth characterised by the living activities of the Spirit. Both the living water and the oil in this chapter are typical of the Holy Spirit. " Living water " would suggest inward refreshment which meets the thirst of the soul and puts it on the line of true satisfaction. The " oil " would refer to the Spirit as giving capability to hear and to serve and to walk in spiritual intelligence and power.

Then the living bird let loose into the open field would suggest that Christ is known as having returned from death to heavenly associations. He has died to sin, and has done with it, and He now lives to God. It is good to get an apprehension of Christ as living to God, for if He lives to God it is that we may take account of ourselves as alive to God in Christ Jesus. There is something very attractive to an exercised soul in the thought of living to God ; that is, for God's pleasure. There is One blessed Man who does so absolutely, but He lives to God that we also may live to God in Him, no longer on the line of what we are as in the flesh, but in a new order of man—in Christ Jesus.

Up to this point all has been done for the man who is to be cleansed, but now he has to do something for himself. He has to wash his garments, shave all his hair, and bathe in water. In the light of Christ as having died to sin and living to God the healed leper brings his garments—all his outward associations and habits—under a process of moral cleansing. He has to overhaul himself, and to bring everything about him into suitability for the camp. One in whom there has been a leprous working of will is sure to have defiled his garments. Everything about him has been affected by his wilful state, and now that he is healed and self-judged he has to adjust and cleanse everything before he can resume the normal life of a saint as living to God. This is an exercise which can only be gone through with feelings of shame, but there is also an encouraging sense that one's exercises are now on the line of obedience and righteousness, and not on the line of one's own will.

The leper is not, typically, an unconverted man, but one of the people of God who has got into a wilful state. The exercises of such, in view of recovery, are deeper and more humbling than those of a convicted sinner, because the believer has known grace, has valued Christ, and has received the Spirit. And all this adds to the depth of his self-abhorrence when mercy grants him repentance and heals his leprosy.

Such a one has to " shave all his hair, and bathe in water." He feels the necessity for bringing under judgment everything about him that has been the outcome of his unclean state, or identified with it. He must resume his place in the camp as one who has obviously set aside, by the sharp razor of self-judgment, everything that has been affected by, or that has taken character from, his leprous state. He comes back to be wholly on the ground of Christ, and in the Spirit not in the flesh. All that he was naturally had come under the taint of the terrible moral disease which had worked in him, and he is now set to refuse it all, and to be on the line of the spiritual.

" And afterwards shall he come into the camp, and shall abide outside his tent seven days." He is now morally suited to the congregation of God, but he has a further exercise before he can be really at home as to his affections amongst the saints. Many have known what it is to be clear in conscience without being yet in perfect freedom of heart. This is reached on the eighth day, but not without passing through another exercise on the seventh day which is more searching as to every detail than the former one. He is now to shave " his head, and his beard, and his eyebrows, even all his hair shall he shave, and he shall wash his garments, and shall bathe his flesh in water, and he is clean."

What a comprehensive and particular process of exercise does this suggest ! Every detail of what had stood connected with his leprous state is thoroughly dealt with in unsparing practical separation. It is not merely a general self-judgment, but a sharp and decisive refusal in detail of all that has grown out of that state of uncleanness in which he has been involved. Do not let us pass lightly over this, or think that it can be dispensed with. The exercises typified here are essential to cleansing where there has been a persistent action of self-will.

" The eighth day " completes the cleansing, and all is now " before Jehovah, at the entrance of the tent of meeting." The eighth day, it will be remembered, is in another connection the circumcision day—typically the day when the flesh is seen to be cut off in the death of Christ. Here it is the day when the healed and cleansed leper is restored to the full privilege of an Israelite ; it answers to 2 Cor. 2 : 8. He is now to learn Christ and the Spirit in a very blessed way after having learned himself in a very humbling way. He is now to be brought into line with his brethren in their apprehensions and appreciations of Christ. But in relation to all this he is the subject of priestly service. Indeed, the amount of care and service that God makes available for the healed leper is a striking feature of this chapter. As we give more place to the truth of the assembly I am persuaded that priestly service will come more into evidence. There will be more spiritual ability to discern leprosy, but also to do all that is necessary for the cleansing of the healed leper. The leper cannot cleanse himself ; he cannot take up his spiritual privileges without coming under priestly service. Sometimes we hear of a man who has been naughty and wilful pronouncing himself to be healed and cleansed, and being quite hurt when his brethren do not at once accept his testimony. I think God would have such a one to recognise that he needs priestly service, and that he is dependent upon the priestly element in his brethren. But this raises a very real exercise as to how far we are competent to render priestly service. It requires the conditions set forth in type in the garments and consecration of the priesthood.

The first thing which the priest presents is the he-lamb for a trespass-offering. The priest and the healed leper are together in the recognition that what has come in needed the death of Christ to make atonement for it. There has been specific violation of some commandment of the Lord. The tendency is to be too general—to admit general failure, but not to own frankly what one has done wrong. Priestly service would help as to this. When we are really self-judged we are prepared to call things by their right names.

It is striking to see that the trespass-offering and the log of oil are presented and waved together. The man is led to see as before God that he has trespassed, and what his trespass meant to Christ who bore it in love, but I think there may be a suggestion here that he is also led to see what it meant to the Holy Spirit who was grieved by it. Indeed " the log of oil " might teach us to recognise that what answers to leprosy in a believer comes about by ignoring the Spirit of God. I should not fulfil the lust of the flesh if I walked in the Spirit, much less should I maintain it in *will*.

But " the log of oil " is more than the reminder of this. It intimates that the healed leper is henceforth to be a spiritual man. What is before God is the ability of Christ to bear the judgment of the trespass, but also that the one who trespassed is now to take character from the presence of the Spirit.

The priest has spiritual intelligence as to all this. And he has exercises in spiritual affections and sensibilities and sympathies also. The trespass-offering is *his* ; he has to eat it. He makes the trespass his own. One would desire so to walk with one's brethren that if a brother had been leprous and had been healed he might be able to count upon one doing this for him.

Then the ear, the hand, and the foot of the healed man have to carry the blood of the trespass-offering and the oil. What is first before God has then to leave its mark on the man. The blood claims him for the will of God. If the memorial of the trespass-offering is on his ear, hand and foot, those members can be no longer surrendered to the will of the flesh. Then there is the Spirit to give character to his hearing, action and walk. His members are to be held as dead in regard to his own will, but the Spirit comes in as life

to control them for God. He is to be characterised by
spiritual hearing, action and walk. It suggests, too,
in a blessed way how the Lord went through this scene
entirely under the Spirit's control. The priest has a
great sense of the place the Spirit has before God ;
he sprinkles the oil seven times before Jehovah. This
indicates how the perfection of divine pleasure is only
to be brought about in the power of the Spirit.

" The remainder of the oil that is in the priest's
hand he shall put upon the head of him that is to be
cleansed." Such is the wonderful grace of God that
the one who had been a leper gets something that he
never had before as an ordinary Israelite. He gets
an anointing which speaks of spiritual intelligence and
dignity such as he had not before. We may see something like this in the Corinthians and Galatians, who
had turned away from what was of the Spirit of God,
but who got through divine healing and the priestly
service of Paul more than they had had before. What
a thought it gives us of grace !

Naturally we might feel doubtful whether one who
has manifested the will of the flesh in such a way as to
be pronounced unclean would ever again be quite what
he was before. But this chapter would teach us the
immensity of a mercy and grace that can not only
heal and cleanse a leper, but can give him more than
he had before. It shows that whenever we go through
a real exercise with God, however humbling the
occasion of it may be, we get spiritual enlargement and
enrichment. Some might be inclined to say that this
puts a premium on departure and self-will ! Nothing
of the kind ! It puts a premium on having to do with
God ! If we went on steadily with God we should
learn the same lessons in a deeper and better way,

and our exercises would have more of a priestly character all through. One feels assured that the priest who cleansed the leper learned all that the leper learned, and learned it more deeply because of his greater nearness to God. Paul got for his own soul all that he passed on to the Corinthians and Galatians, but he got it in a priestly way ; that is, by spiritual exercise without the experience of having failed in the same way himself.

The sin-offering is more general in character ; it comes in here with reference to the man's uncleanness. And there is also the oblation and the burnt-offering. The whole state of man in the flesh, with all his uncleanness, has been judged and removed sacrificially in the death of Christ as the sin-offering. This clears the ground. Then the burnt-offering is the sweet savour of the death of Christ as the basis for the bringing in of everything that is for divine pleasure. And the oblation gives the preciousness of Christ as Man in the power of the Holy Spirit. That is the character of Man which will eventually fill all things for the pleasure of God. The man with oil upon his head can appreciate all this in a spiritual way.

What is priestly always helps in the direction of self-judgment, truer and more enlarged apprehension and appreciation of Christ, and a better knowledge of what is connected with the Spirit. One is impressed by the prominence given in this chapter to the priestly service rendered towards the healed leper. There is first discernment as to his being healed, and then ability to do all that is necessary for his cleansing and reinstatement in complete clearance, freedom and dignity in relation to the tent of meeting.

In verses 21–32 we have gracious provision for the

one who is poor, and whose hand is " not able to get "
the normal offerings. This reminds us that God
considers, and His priests consider, the spiritual means
and ability of those who need cleansing. " What is
regularly prescribed " may not be obtainable in all
cases. In such cases one lamb and two turtle-doves
take the place of the three lambs in the normal offering ; and one tenth part of fine flour mingled with oil
is accepted for the oblation instead of three tenth parts
in the normal offering. The same apprehensions of
Christ have to be there, with their corresponding self-
judgment, but a smaller measure is accepted when one
is poor. There is a compassionate taking account of
the means of the one concerned. The precious and
tender grace disclosed in this is " good to the feeblest
heart."

*   *   *   *   *

The " leprous plague in a house of the land of your
possession " (verse 34) would refer to an assembly
character of things. It is something which affects the
way in which saints are set together. And this not
looked at as in wilderness conditions, but in relation
to their enjoyment together of what is over Jordan.
The normal privilege of the assembly is to enjoy in
" house " conditions what is beyond death, and what
is heavenly in character. If something comes in to
disturb those " house " conditions, and to interfere
with the comfort and restfulness of the saints together,
it is easy to see that the mutual enjoyment of the land
of their possession will be suspended. If roots of
bitterness and envyings and jealousies come in they
interfere with peaceful " house " conditions. Principles
begin to work which are not suited to divine holiness,
nor in accord with the truth of the house of God.

When such things come in the first thing is to recognise that God has allowed it. Indeed it says, " And *I* put a leprous plague," etc. It is an exercise the Lord has brought upon us to bring to light the true state of things, and to teach His saints needed lessons, and to make manifest those whom He approves (1 Cor. 11 : 19). When difficulties arise we are apt to get occupied with facts and persons, and not to take sufficient account of what the Lord may have to say in connection with it. But we should first of all ask, What is the Lord calling attention to by this state of things ?

We find here a responsible person—" he whose house it is." " The angel of the assembly " in the New Testament (Rev. 2, 3) would answer to this. I doubt if there is anything of assembly character without an " angel." The " angel " is that element which is conscious of responsibility to the Lord, and which takes up exercises that arise in the light of that responsibility. We ought all to feel that we have a responsibility as to the " house " ; something of " angel " character ought to be in every saint. We can all see defects ; that does not need spiritual vision. But to feel that responsibility attaches to one before the Lord as to the house and its conditions is another matter. If there is no " angel " one would hardly expect to find the priest there. For a due sense of responsibility taken up in sobriety with God would be essential to priestly conditions being present. The priestly element is that which considers for God, and has spiritual discernment. " He whose house it is shall come and tell the priest." The one who feels responsibility calls what is priestly into activity. Both brothers and sisters who have a care for the

" house " are distressed if anything comes in which
is not of God ; they feel the seriousness of it, and cry
to God about it. It was from the house of a sister
(Chloe) that Paul heard of the disorder at Corinth.
No doubt there was something of " angel " character
about Chloe! Her name means " Tender verdure,"
which would be suggestive of the fact that being in
spiritual freshness and vitality herself she and her
house were sensitive as to the unhappy local conditions, and they seem to have told the " priest "
by communicating with Paul. It is not only that
those who love the Lord feel that His honour is affected,
but they love the brethren, and they want the brethren
to enjoy together the land of their possession. Leprosy
in the house hinders the enjoyment of the land, and
if we love the saints we cannot bear that they should
be deprived of the spiritual joy of their possession.
Every one of us should take a real and serious interest
in the " house."

Then the priest is to command that the house be
emptied before he goes into it. The principle seems
to be that the uncleanness shall be limited as much
as possible. The priest is not concerned to hold as
much as possible unclean, but rather the contrary.
He is anxious that everything that can be preserved
from defilement shall be preserved.

The priest knows what the right colour of the house
is ; he knows the holiness, truth, grace and love
which rightly mark " house " conditions. He knows
the meekness and lowliness and forbearance in which
saints can walk together in mutuality, and enjoy the
land of their possession. So that when he goes into
the house and sees " greenish or reddish hollows, and
their look is deeper than the surface of the wall," he

knows it is something quite different from the normal colour. It is something that is of the flesh working either on carnal or legal or mental lines. The priest knows it to be contrary to the true character of the house.

Now the question arises as to whether it is active, and as to how deeply things may be affected by it ? It may possibly be the outcome of infirmity or ignorance, and not exactly will. Where *will* is working energetically the shutting up of the house seven days will make more manifest that it is so. But if grace is in the ascendent it will be exerting its sway all the time to set aside through righteous self-judgment what is of the flesh. So that at the end of " seven days " the suspicious indications will be arrested or reduced. Patience is often needed to give time for the grace of the Lord to do its blessed work.

If the suspicious symptoms spread it is a bad sign. To see an evil principle spreading and getting a firmer hold gives the gravest concern to every one who cares for the well-being of the house. It shows that there is something that has to be positively rejected as unsuitable to the house. " The stones in which the plague is " are to be cast out in an unclean place. I take it that these stones represent principles that are not of God. They have to be absolutely rejected. If individuals identify themselves with such principles and seek to make them an integral part of the " house," and maintain this in face of instruction and admonition, they can only be regarded, for the time at any rate, as identified with the principles they espouse.

If we seek to maintain suitable " house " conditions we shall be called upon to exercise priestly discernment as to the character of the stones which go to make up the house. Can we accept that human order and clerical rule, or anything that is in principle sectarian, are suitable stones for the " house " ? Can we believe that it is of God that Christian fellowship should continue with one who teaches false doctrine as to the Person or work of our Lord Jesus Christ, or who questions the inspiration of the Holy Scriptures ? Can we admit the principle of independency into our " house " conditions if we have learned that there is one body and one spirit, and but one divine and spiritual order universally ? Can neutrality be pleasing to the Lord when questions arise with reference to what is vital ? Can anything be really suitable to God without moral conditions and spiritual vitality ? Can anything be really clean that sets aside any part of the truth concerning Christ and the assembly ?

" Overthrowing reasonings and every high thing that lifts itself up against the knowledge of God, and leading captive every thought into the obedience of the Christ " (2 Cor. 10 : 5) would get rid of every leprous stone, and would secure suitable " house " conditions so that saints might enjoy together the land of their possession. In rejecting leprous stones the thought is that we disallow that which is contrary to the true character and blessing of all saints. If we refuse a wrong and unclean principle to which some of our brethren adhere, our refusing it is really a kind and true service to them. In refusing it we are acting on their behalf, and for their good. Because what is unsuitable to divine " house " conditions is unsuitable to *all* those who by divine grace and calling are entitled to participate in those conditions ; that is, all saints. It is in love to all saints that every principle is to be refused which priestly examination has proved to be unclean. Such action will probably very often be misunderstood, but we must be content to leave this to be cleared up in the day when all things are manifested.

If true believers will identify themselves with principles which are not of God we cannot put them right, but we can pray for them, and for ourselves that we may more clearly discern what is suitable to " house " conditions, and how indispensable those conditions are to the enjoyment of the land of our possession.

After the leprous stones have been cast out the house is to be scraped, and the dust poured out in an unclean place. The seriousness of having been associated with what is unclean has to be felt throughout the house ; there is no going on as if nothing had happened. People say sometimes, after serious " house " exercises have been raised, We are just going on the same as we were before. But this cannot be if the Lord has been calling attention to something that ought to be removed. The scraping of the house brings home to all the gravity of the issue raised, and the necessity for complete purification.

But things do not stop there. " And they shall take other stones, and put them in the place of those stones ; and they shall take other mortar, and shall plaster the house." It is not only that human and corrupting principles are to be judged and refused, but there is to be positive gain by replacing them by principles which are according to truth and holiness, and the very face of things—the plaster of the house —has to be brought into keeping therewith. If saints discover that they have been associated with some principle that was not of God, and they cast it out, and replace it with what they have learned to be according to the commandments of the Lord, they will find it necessary to renew the " plaster " also. The very face of things in the house—the way things are done, and all that comes into view—will take a changed character.

But this scripture suggests that there may be cases where not even the removal of leprous stones and the introduction of new ones, and the replastering of the house, will put matters right. " And if the plague come again . . . it is a corroding leprosy in the house ; it is unclean." There is no remedy for such a state of things. " They shall break down the house, the stones of it, and the timber thereof, and all the mortar of the house, and shall carry them forth out of the city to an unclean place." In this case it becomes manifest that things cannot be divinely corrected or adjusted. There is something radically wrong with the whole principle of the house. It is not that certain features have had place which are not of God and which may be dealt with under priestly direction so that the " house " is preserved in suitable condition. But in such a case as is typified here the whole principle of association is contrary to God's mind, and has to be rejected altogether. One cannot doubt that there are houses of this kind to-day. Houses which are leprous because the whole principle of their constitution carries the impress of the mind and will of man rather than the impress of the mind and will of God.

If the plague does not spread in the house " after the house hath been plastered, the priest shall pronounce the house clean ; for the plague is healed." The leprous stones having been rejected, and new ones put in, and the house plastered, it is now found after priestly examination that the plague is arrested. But another exercise remains to be taken up even after the plague is healed, and the house pronounced clean. It has still to be purged from the defilement (verse 49), and this by bringing in positive apprehensions and appreciations of Christ, as set forth in type in verses 49–53. If these were not present, wrong principles might be rejected, and right ones accepted, without the fellowship being really spiritual. The way we are set together must take character from our appreciation of Christ, or we cannot enjoy together in an undefiled way our "house" conditions, or the land of our possession.

In the case of leprosy in a house I have no doubt we see typified an action of human will in the principles on which the people of God walk together. There is purification from the defilement of that in the appreciation of Christ, for in Him we see an entirely different principle of moral being. He came into the world saying, "Lo, I come (in the roll of the book it is written of me) to do, O God, thy will," Heb. 10 : 7. In considering Him we come under the influence of what will cleanse us from the hidden, subtle root of all that is unclean.

The cedar-wood, scarlet and hyssop are put along with the blood and the running water and the living bird for the purging of the house (verse 52). Everything truly great and glorious is seen in Christ joined with a lowliness that made Him the Servant of all. God has taken us in hand so that we may get, through our affections being engaged with Christ, an entirely new thought of greatness. The will of man always works along the line of making something of himself,

or pleasing himself. But " the Christ also did not
please himself," Rom. 15 : 3. Gabriel said of Him
to the virgin, " He shall be great," but it was the
greatness of One who was to lie in a manger, and not
to have where to lay His head. If we are truly great
it will put us in the lowliest place here. When the
disciples wanted to learn who was the greatest in the
kingdom of the heavens, Jesus called a little child to
Him, and said, " Whoever therefore shall humble
himself as this little child, he is the greatest in the
kingdom of the heavens," Matt. 18 : 1–4.

The " hyssop " suggests the lowliness of Christ.
Solomon's wisdom embraced all the trees " from the
cedar-tree that is on Lebanon even to the hyssop that
springs out of the wall," 1 Kings 4 : 33. Christ
expressed the whole range of moral perfection and
beauty. The excellent bearing and dignity of the
cedar was there, and the lowliness of the hyssop. He
could truly say, " My heart is not haughty, nor mine
eyes lofty," Psa. 131 : 1. And all the " scarlet "
in Him—everything that distinguished Him from
others—was of God ; there was no element of man's
will in it. When Peter and those who were with him
on the holy mount fully woke up they saw His glory,
but it was glory that shone in a praying Man, who
received all from God the Father in absolute dependence, and took no glory from Satan or from men. He
is the One who says, " Come to me . ... learn from
me ; for I am meek and lowly *in heart*," Matt. 11 : 28–
30. We cannot entertain the thought of that in
our affections without being purified from everything
that is of the nature of leprosy. If I am truly a little
child in the arms of Jesus I shall not readily take
offence, and when offended I shall be very ready to

forgive. (See Matthew 18.) This brings in a spirit which provides good " house " conditions.

If there have been leprous stones—which speak of elements coming in characterised by the will of the flesh—they have to be replaced by such features as were characteristic of Christ. Any greatness or glory or even voluntary humility that is of the will of man has to go out. Perhaps this is suggested in the cedar and scarlet and hyssop being cast by the priest into the burning of the red heifer (Num. 19). The cedar and scarlet and hyssop go into the fire, there to be consumed— never to come out again. But in Leviticus 14 the cedar and scarlet and hyssop are dipped in the blood ; they go into death in type ; but they come out again for the purifying of the man or the house. All the excellent bearing, and distinction, and humility of Christ were devoted to the will and glory of God in death, but God has approved them all by resurrection. There was nothing morally in Christ that could remain in death, or be held there. If *I* went into death there is a good deal that would never appear again, and I can say, Thank God, that it will not. But with Him where was nothing that death could hold ; every moral feature that was seen in Him has come out of death to appear and be perpetuated in the saints as having the Spirit of Christ ; to appear in a healed and purified Israel in a future day ; and indeed to give character to the moral universe, purifying it from every taint of creature will. Before the day of public purifying the blood, the running water, the living bird, the cedar-wood, the hyssop and the scarlet are the spiritual means by which the defilement of creature will can be cleansed either in an individual, or in what pertains to the " house " conditions in which God sets

His saints together. But *cleansing* only takes place after *healing*. If self-will has been active there must be first God-given repentance.

If everything great and glorious and suitable to God, and attractive to my heart as taught of God, has gone into death here, what does it make of any greatness or distinction that I could attach to myself as in the flesh ? The silver cord has been loosed, and the golden bowl broken ! Can I want to assert my will, or to be distinguished in any way, in the place where Christ died ? If I wish to retain what is of the will of the flesh I cannot have a true appreciation of Christ, for in Him there is nothing but what is of the will of God. For Christians not to judge what is evil in their associations is very serious. " Cease to do evil : learn to do well " is an important word in this connection. Whatever the conditions of weakness may be the Lord will always help faithful ones to disown evil principles, and give evidence that they are calling on Him out of a pure heart.

These chapters (Lev. 13, 14) have no doubt an application to Israel as well as a present bearing. The sin of Miriam and of Gehazi and of Uzziah are typical of the guilt into which Israel has fallen, and the leprosy with which they were smitten is a figure of Israel's state to-day. Israel's house, too, is leprous to-day, but it will yet be healed in the sovereignty of God's mercy, and will be purged and made clean by the application of all that is typified in Leviticus 14 : 51, 52, and Israel will dwell in holy and happy conditions in the land of their possession.

CHAPTER 15

THE " flux " which according to this chapter renders unclean would, I think, represent those defiling things which are the outcome of what we are naturally. We have seen in chapter 11 most careful directions as to clean and unclean in what might be eaten. It was there a question, in type, of what we receive into our moral being. But chapter 15 gives us the converse of this ; it refers to defiling things which come out of us. Peter could say, " Common or unclean has never entered into my mouth " (Acts 11 : 8), but he could not have said that nothing common or unclean had ever come out of his mouth ! This chapter suggests the possibility of that coming out of a man or woman which would render unclean. It teaches us that if we would preserve the moral purity that is suited to God's tabernacle (verse 31) there must be restraint on manifestations of what we are naturally.

The cases brought before us here are obviously less serious than those contemplated in chapters 13, 14. There is no exclusion from the camp here, but there is a distinct call for exercise and moral cleansing. There is a great deal about washing, bathing, and rinsing, and it is not until these exercises have been gone through, and cleansing effected, that the person who has had a " flux " can take up holy privilege in relation to God's tabernacle.

There are many things which are not exactly actions of sinful will, but which are the outcome of what a man is naturally. The outflow of that which should be kept under restraint is defiling. When Paul said to the high priest, " God will smite thee, whited wall," it was probably true, and an expression of righteous

indignation, but it was very different from the calm
dignity with which the Lord spoke when smitten on
the face. Paul appeared to feel at once, when his
attention was called to it, that there had been a lack
of self-restraint. How quickly he washed himself!

A thing may be true, but it may not be at all of the
Spirit of God that it should be expressed. To express
it might just be the unchecked outflow of what is
natural to one. We have to learn that if we would
retain liberty in what is spiritual there must be
restraint on what is natural. That is a simple statement, but it is a vital one. Normal Christian walk is
" according to Spirit " (Rom. 8 : 4), and it is well to
challenge what comes out of us sometimes by asking
whether it is of the Spirit of God ? If we do not
exercise restraint on what we might give expression to
naturally we shall find ourselves defiled, and out of
condition for the holy relations in which we stand to
God's tabernacle.

Paul could say, " By God's grace I am what I am,"
1 Cor. 15 : 10. That is in contrast to what he was
naturally. All our deportment, whether with one
another or in presence of the world, should be by the
grace of God. " For our boasting is this, the testimony
of our conscience, that in simplicity and sincerity
before God (not in fleshly wisdom but in God's grace),
we have had our conversation in the world, and more
abundantly towards you," 2 Cor. 1 : 12. If all is by
the grace of God there will be no " flux " to bring
defilement. The Christian walking normally speaks
and acts by the grace of God, and according to the
Spirit. " See that no one render to any evil for evil,
but pursue always what is good towards one another
and towards all ; rejoice always ; pray unceasingly ;

in everything give thanks, for this is the will of God in Christ Jesus towards you," 1 Thess. 5 : 15–19. Such a walk is to the spiritual man holy and blessed liberty.

If we wish to be preserved from what answers to the " flux " of Leviticus 15 we must cultivate what is spiritual and according to Christ, so that what comes out of us is according to God. The grace which carries with it salvation teaches us to " live soberly, and justly, and piously in the present course of things," Titus 2 : 11, 12. There will then be no " flux " to defile. A humorous tendency, or any unchecked manifestation of one's natural temperament, might become a " flux."

The washing, bathing, and rinsing of this chapter suggest a purification which is according to God, and suited to His tabernacle. The New Testmant, in speaking of the assembly being purified " by the washing of water by the word " (Ephes. 5 : 26), gives us the thought of a moral purification brought about by the word. The word brings what is of Christ to bear upon us to the setting aside of that which is unclean. In John 15 : 3 the Lord says, " Ye are already clean by reason of the word which I have spoken to you." His word had made Him known in their hearts, and they were clean as having Him in their affections. The " word " as in Ephesians 5 : 26 cleanses by bringing home to us the way which His love took in delivering Himself up for the assembly. All that was involved in His death is applied to us for purification in a moral way by the word.

In Leviticus 15 the person who has been defiled, or who has come into contact with defilement, has to wash and bathe. He has, in figure, to apply the word to himself as one exercised in the fear of God.

He subjects himself and his manner of life to the moral
action and purifying of the word. We see the principle
of this in Psalm 119 : 9. " Wherewithal shall a young
man cleanse his path ? by taking heed according to
thy word." It is an inestimable favour from God
that the word is available for cleansing. There is an
abundant supply of water—of what is divinely suitable for application in the way of cleansing to any one
who has been defiled, but who wishes to be clean.
The " word " has positive purifying power, for it
brings what is of God, and what has been set forth
in Christ, to bear upon that which has occasioned
defilement. We see how unsuitable to God and to
Christ are the unrestrained manifestations of what we
are naturally. They are set aside by that which is
more excellent getting place with us through the word.

I do not really use the " word " thus apart from
considering and weighing what it communicates, and
forming an estimate in my renewed mind of its excellency. There is often too much superficiality about
the way Scripture is read. Nothing profits me that
does not come to my soul as a divine communication,
leading me to judge and disapprove what is evil
because I " judge of and approve the things that are
more excellent." This would lead to being " pure and
without offence for Christ's day, being complete as
regards the fruit of righteousness, which is by Jesus
Christ, to God's glory and praise," Phil. 1 : 9–11.
Such would be truly clean.

The seven days of cleansing in this chapter, and the
sin-offering and burnt-offering of the eighth day, are
features the typical import of which corresponds with
what we have considered in connection with the
cleansing of the leper in chapter 14.

CHAPTER 16

It will be observed that this chapter reverts to chapter 10 in referring to the two sons of Aaron who " came near before Jehovah and died." It comes in after the failure of the priesthood, in which we may see an intimation of the breakdown of the whole system as having been set up in connection with man after the flesh. Even Aaron himself was not to come " at all times into the sanctuary inside the veil . . . *that he die not.*" If coming into the immediate presence of God meant death for the greatest personage in the system it was clear proof that man after that order— man in the flesh—could not draw near. Typically the whole system of the tabernacle and its sacrifices spoke of Christ and of His death, but it was actually set up in connection with failing and mortal men. Hence there was a complete breakdown on man's side on the first day of their service. Instead of being capable of serving God and approaching God, man in the flesh is a complete failure, and is under the judgment of death.

The tabernacle and its ordinances indicated that it was God's pleasure to dwell in the midst of a redeemed people, and to be approached by men, but it also indicated just as plainly that what God desired could only be brought about in a spiritual order of things. " The Holy Spirit showing this, that the way of the holy of holies has not yet been made manifest while as yet the first tabernacle has its standing," Heb. 9 : 8.

Then in this chapter it is not only that Aaron's sons have died, and that Aaron himself is forbidden to come inside the veil at all times on pain of death, but the children of Israel generally as set in relation to the

sanctuary and the tent of meeting are seen to be
marked by uncleanness, iniquities, transgressions and
sins, from which the sanctuary and the tent of meeting
needs to be cleansed. Atonement needs to be made for
Aaron and for his house, and for the whole congregation. It is not now, as in former chapters of this
book, what relates to the sin, trespass, or defilement
of an individual Israelite, or even one specific sin of
the whole assembly. The question raised is a far
deeper and wider one. It is a question of the
footing on which the priestly house and the whole
congregation can be with God as having His dwelling
amongst them in holiness. This question was typically
raised and settled " once a year " for Israel, but the
continual repetition of it year by year served to show
that the question was not really settled. " For blood
of bulls and goats is incapable of taking away sins,"
Heb. 10 : 4. It was a yearly reminder that this
question needed to be settled, and a prophetic intimation that it would be settled fully and eternally by the
offering of Christ. Read Hebrews 9 and 10, and see
how the Spirit of God contrasts the repeated offerings
of the yearly day of atonement with the manifestation
of Christ " once in the consummation of the ages . . .
for the putting away of sin by his sacrifice." He
emphasises that Christ has " been once offered to bear
the sins of many," and that by God's will " we have
been sanctified through the offering of the body of
Jesus Christ once for all." " But *he*, having offered
one sacrifice for sins, sat down in perpetuity at the
right hand of God. . . . For by one offering he has
perfected in perpetuity the sanctified." He " by his
own blood has entered in once for all into the holy
of holies, having found an eternal redemption."

It may be well to note the difference between the death of Christ as set forth in the Passover and in the sin-offering of the day of atonement. The Passover is necessary on our side, if we are to escape judgment and to have a place in the kingdom of God ; it will be "fulfilled in the kingdom of God" (Luke 22 : 16), when men will be relieved of judgment, and be brought into unity as under the sway of God known in righteous grace and blessing. But the sin-offering of the day of atonement deals with the question of sin from the standpoint of how it affects God in the abode of His holiness. It stands in reference to "the holy sanctuary," and "the tent of meeting," and "the altar." It has in view God dwelling in holiness, and the thought of man's approach to Him. Every moral stain must be removed so that there may be suitability to God in the place where He dwells in unsullied light and holiness. The sin-offering of the day of atonement goes to the very root of the question of sin as it affects the glory of God, and shows how God has glorified Himself in holiness with reference to sin so that He can have His once-sinful creatures near Him without a single spot or stain of unsuitability to the place where He displays all His brightness.

The Passover will be fulfilled in the kingdom of God, but the sin-offering of the day of atonement—while its value is known to-day, and will be known in the world to come—stands in relation to what is eternal. It is one of the greatest and most far-reaching types that Scripture presents to us.

"I will appear in the cloud upon the mercy-seat" (verse 2). The two sons of Aaron had died, Aaron was forbidden to come at all times inside the veil "that he die not," and the people as a whole were marked, as we have said, by uncleanness and iniquities. But God would retain His dwelling among them, and appear in the cloud upon the mercy-seat. On what ground could this be ? Only on the ground of the sin-offering, and the blood as sprinkled on the mercy-seat.

The state common to all the children of Adam was found in Israel also. Their peculiar privileges in having the law, and having God's sanctuary in their midst, only added the guilt of positive transgression, and brought out their uncleanness in a way of which the Gentile was unconscious. So that when the people of Israel truly and spiritually observe the day of atonement they will discover that, instead of being better than the Gentiles, their guilt was only intensified by the place of nearness to God into which they were brought. In principle this is true of those who are outwardly brought near to God in the Christian profession to-day.

Then on what ground can blessing be ? It can only be on the ground of mercy and atonement on God's side, and on man's side affliction of soul—repentance—and the recognition of the fact that he can do nothing. " Ye shall afflict your souls, and do no work at all " (verse 29). But this is a ground of blessing which, if God pleases to have it so, is available for all men. So that " the stranger " is expressly included (verse 29), and we know now that " the righteousness of God by faith of Jesus Christ " is " towards all, and upon all those who believe : for there is no difference ; for all have sinned, and come short of the glory of God ; being justified freely by his grace through the redemption which is in Christ Jesus ; whom God has set forth a mercy-seat, through faith in his blood," Rom. 3 : 21–26.

This gives the mercy-seat, and the blood put upon it on the day of atonement, a very wide bearing, and justifies us in regarding Leviticus 16 in the light of the gospel. A very wide scope of blessing has come in, consequent upon the complete breakdown of everything connected with man in the flesh, which has been specially set forth in Israel. The atonement for Aaron and his house has special typical reference to those who have the Spirit to-day, and constitute the priestly house. The atonement as made for the whole congregation would have a bearing towards the whole Christian profession. But Romans 3 gives the mercy-seat and the blood upon it a universal aspect which shows that in the mind of God the scope of what was typified on the day of atonement is not less than all men, or as Paul says in Col. 1 : 23, " the whole creation which is under heaven." God's righteousness being made known in grace through atonement, in view of the blessing of the assembly to-day and of Israel in a coming day, really makes known what He is in His nature, and in the disposition of His heart towards men. It is the shining out of what God is in His nature and in His holy glory. Eventually the moral universe—of which the tabernacle is a figure— will be reconciled in the value of what is typified here, and evil will be eternally confined to its own place in the lake of fire.

Aaron does not go into the sanctuary to make atonement in his garments " for glory and for ornament " described in Exodus 28. They set forth what Christ is as the living Priest who ever appears before the face of God for those who believe on Him. But *here* it is not glory and ornament, but righteousness and holiness. " A holy linen vest . . .

linen trousers . . . a linen girdle . . . the linen mitre
. . . these are holy garments." They speak of the
personal holiness of Christ as the One who knew no
sin. " The holy one of God," as Peter confessed Him
(John 6 : 69). The One of whom it is written, " Thou
wilt not leave my soul to Sheol, neither wilt thou allow
thy Holy One to see corruption," Psa. 16 : 10. " Jesus
Christ the righteous . . . is the propitiation for our
sins ; but not for ours alone, but also for the whole
world," 1 John 2 : 1, 2. No other could take up the
question of sin, and meet the glory of God about it so
as to make atonement.

There is a marked distinction throughout this
chapter between what is for Aaron and his house, and
what is " for the people." The one gives the ground
of blessing for the priestly family—typically the
assembly as associated with Christ ; the other the
ground of Israel's blessing in the world to come, but
the value of which is also known by believers to-day,
though it is not the distinctive portion of saints of the
assembly. The distinction is thus clearly made
between the heavenly company, represented by Aaron
and his house, and Israel as called to inherit blessing
on earth. There is also a distinction between Aaron
and his sons (Exod. 28) and Aaron and his house.
His " house " is a wider thought ; it is more the family
idea, and would take in daughters also. Atonement
in this chapter is for his " house." It is the priestly
family and its privileges that is in view rather than the
exercise of priestly functions.

For Aaron and his house there is " a young bullock
for a sin-offering, and a ram for a burnt-offering."
For the assembly of the children of Israel there are
" two bucks of the goats for a sin-offering, and one

ram for a burnt-offering." Aaron is first to present
the bullock of the sin-offering which is for himself, and
then he is to take the two goats for the people. Verses
6–10 seem to be a general statement ; the detail
follows.

The offering of the bullock for the priestly family
comes before the offering of the goats for Israel. The
blessing of Israel will come in after the blessing of the
assembly, and indeed their blessing will be dependent
upon ours. I suppose Abraham had some sense of
this when " he waited for the city which has founda-
tions, of which God is the artificer and constructor,"
Heb. 11 : 10. He understood that the time of blessing
on earth would be dependent on the appearance of
God's heavenly city. " God having foreseen some
better thing for us, that they should not be made
perfect without us," Heb. 11 : 40. Whether it be the
heavenly place and portion of the assembly, or blessing
on earth as known by millennial Israel, all is secured
according to divine righteousness and holiness by the
complete glorifying of God as to the whole question
of sin and sins.

The assembly takes precedence of Israel, and with
a larger offering. No redeemed family will know the
greatness of Christ sacrificially in the same measure
as the assembly knows it. " For himself, and for his
house " shows how Christ identifies Himself with the
assembly, and the assembly with Him. Believers do
not need to be told that no atonement for Him was
needed in the sense of dealing with anything personal.
But He identified Himself with the sin of His own on
the cross, and He has gone in to God on the ground
of His own blood. That is, He is not there simply on
the ground of His personal title, but on the ground of

having died. He is with God on the same ground
that we can be with God. Our Aaron loves to be with
God on ground where He can be identified with His
saints and His saints with Him. See Heb. 9 : 11, 12.

The bullock of the sin-offering for Aaron and his
house is first presented and slaughtered. This precedes
the going of Aaron inside the veil with the censer, and
both his hands full of fragrant incense. God presents
to us in the type the death of Christ before He directs our
attention to the fragrant incense. It is necessary that
we should have a large apprehension of Christ as
having gone into death as the sin-offering to set us
free to contemplate the cloud of incense that covers
the mercy-seat.

The first thing that has place " inside the veil " is
the censer full of burning coals of fire from off the
altar before Jehovah, and Aaron with " both his
hands full of fragrant incense beaten small. . . . And
he shall put the incense upon the fire before Jehovah,
that the cloud of the incense may cover the mercy-
seat." Outside is the slaughtered bullock, speaking
of Christ in death for the glory of God as the sin-
offering ; but " inside the veil " are the censer, the
burning coals, and the cloud of incense covering the
mercy-seat. It gives us a wondrous thought of what
has the first place with God in relation to the sin-
offering.

Scripture leads us to connect the thought of prayer
with incense. " Let my prayer be set forth before
thee as incense," Psa. 141 : 2. " All the multitude of
the people were praying without at the hour of
incense," Luke 1 : 10. See also Rev. 8 : 3, 4. This
leads me to conclude that the cloud of incense which
covers the mercy-seat represents the perfect answer in

confidence of heart which was given by Christ to God
when tested to the utmost possible degree by the holy
fire. Perhaps we do not give this the place that is due.
We think of His death as maintaining divine glory in
the highest as to sin. We can never think too much
of this ; it will be the theme of eternal wonder and
praise. We think of the precious blood in its infinite
efficacy and atoning power. We can never think too
much of it. But let us not forget that the mercy-seat
has been covered by the cloud of incense ! One has
been found in the place of supreme testing who has
expressed in that place what was most fragrant to
God.

How little can we enter into, or speak of, the sorrows
and sufferings of our Saviour and Lord ! They will be
for ever a fathomless depth. How could the creature
ever know what it was to the Holy One to be made sin ?
or what it was to the One who had ever delighted to do
the will of God to be forsaken by Him ? Or what it
was to the Prince of Life to taste death ? Or what it
meant to the Lord Jesus to feel the unutterable and
manifold grief and anguish which were inseparable
from passing through man's hour and the power of
darkness ? His was the loneliness of a sorrow which
none could share, and with which none could sym-
pathise for none could understand.

But what did it bring out Godward ? The cloud
of fragrant incense ! And if we enter at all into what
that hour involved, and what it meant to Him, we
have learned it from that cloud of incense. Under
the action of the holy fire the fragrance came out.
The sorrow Psalms of the suffering Messiah bring it
before us. The affections and sensibilities of the Lord
were supremely tested, but the testing brought out

infinite fragrance. We need to be in the holy of holies to know what that incense means ; it can only be contemplated in a spirit of adoration.

In Psalm 22 He is the forsaken One, but in that darkest of all hours He confides in God, and He says, " Thou art holy." Four times He says, " My God " ; once He appeals to Jehovah as " My strength." " Thou art he that took me out of the womb ; thou didst make me trust, upon my mother's breasts. I was cast upon thee from the womb ; thou art my God from my mother's belly." Such was the unspeakable perfection of the holy Sufferer ! His trust had been always absolutely in God, and it was still there though tested as never before. He looked to God alone amid the anguish, darkness and forsaking of the cross. He had no other help, no other confidence ; He stayed Himself upon His God—upon the One who in holiness had forsaken Him, and laid Him in the dust of death. The intense heat of the altar fire brought out this incense. We are not thinking, for the moment, of atonement, but of what the atoning sufferings and sorrows brought out—the holy perfection of His affections and sensibilities, and the confidence of His heart in God. This, if I apprehend it aright, was the cloud of incense that covered the mercy-seat.

Let us pass for a moment to Psalm 40, where He puts Himself in the place of all those sacrifices and oblations, burnt-offerings and sin-offerings which had failed to meet the desire or the demand of God. Coming into the world to do God's good pleasure, and to make known God's righteousness, faithfulness, salvation, loving-kindness and truth, it involves that innumerable evils compass Him about. He has to say, " Mine iniquities (or punishments) have taken hold upon me . . . they are more than the hairs of my head." The iniquities, or punishments, which He made His own were ours, for we well know He had none personally.

> " Our sins, our guilt, in love divine,
> Confessed and borne by Thee."

In taking all this up He must needs experience " the pit of destruction " and " the miry clay." But what was the attitude of His spirit Godward in it all ? " I waited patiently for Jehovah." He " made Jehovah his confidence." The spirit of obedience was there, for *His* God had prepared ears for Him ; His body was entirely for God's will, even in being devoted to death. The will of God was His delight, and in His affections. Amidst all that the sin-offering involved the consideration of His heart was for God, and that God's innumerable thoughts toward men might be brought into effect. The fragrance of all that has covered the mercy-seat.

Psalm 69 presents that Blessed One to us as sinking in " deep mire, where there is no standing," and as having to say, " They that hate me without a cause are more than the hairs of my head." Reproach has broken His heart ; He is overwhelmed. " I looked for sympathy, but there was none ; and for comforters, but I found none. Yea, they gave me gall for my food, and in my thirst they gave me vinegar to drink." But what is the attitude of His spirit ? He waits for His God (verse 3) ; He restores that which He took not away (verse 4) ; it is for God's sake that He bears reproach (verse 7) ; the zeal of God's house devours Him (verse 9). And in the midst of all the reproach and the grief and the weeping, He says, " But as for me, my prayer is unto thee, Jehovah, in an acceptable time " (verse 13). He counts upon Jehovah to answer Him (verse 16). All this has its place in the cloud of incense. It covers the mercy-seat. Man has failed to answer rightly to God in innocence, without law, or under law. But this glorious and holy One, the Son of God, the Christ of God, has answered perfectly to Him in the place of sin and death.

Not only is atonement made, but God has been glorified in the highest by all that was found in the spirit of the holy One who made atonement. In the sufferings and sorrows of atonement, and in all that was connected with that dread hour in which atone-ment was made—man's wickedness and Satan's power in full strength as well as the forsaking of God —what came out in Him was fragrant to God. The mercy-seat is covered by the cloud of incense. All that God is, in what divine glory claims with regard to sin, has found its perfect answer in a Man. It is not only that everything that needed to be removed has been removed in the efficacy of the blood which has satisfied every claim of God's holy glory in respect of sin. But one would desire to think with ever-growing appreciation of what came out in the spirit and sensibilities and affections of that Blessed One when in the place of making atonement. The infinite fragrance of that, I think we may say with absolute truth, gave God more delight than all the sin of man had given Him grief. It was the complete disclosure of the perfection of His beloved Son in manhood.

One can understand, I trust, in measure how that cloud of incense preserved Aaron from death. The man after the flesh, even as represented in Israel's high priest, is under death. He cannot live in the presence of divine glory. But Aaron disappears—may we not say ?—from the view of the mercy-seat as the cloud of incense covers it. The man after the flesh is not taken account of in the holiest. He is displaced by Another whose positive perfection renders infinite satisfaction and delight to God's attributes and nature. He answered perfectly to God even when His soul was being made an offering for sin. He answered perfectly to all that God is in mercy, and in holy glory that cannot tolerate sin. I am sure that it would deeply affect us if we meditated more on that incense. In this great type it comes before the blood. The blood is essential for us, and for God's glory too, but God loves that we should cherish in our hearts what was so fragrant to Him.

Then Aaron was to " take of the blood of the bullock, and sprinkle with his finger upon the front of the mercy-seat eastward ; and before the mercy-seat shall he sprinkle of the blood seven times with his finger " (verse 14). It is a striking fact in these types that the blood of the sin-offering alone was brought into the sanctuary. The blood of the burnt-offering or the peace-offering did not go beyond the brazen altar, which I think would suggest that the burnt-offering has reference to the acceptance in favour in which we stand in the very place where we were under God's judgment, and the peace-offering is the basis of the fellowship to which we are called as here on earth. But the blood of the sin-offering goes into the sanctuary " inside the veil." It does not go out to the brazen altar. The altar in verse 18 is the golden altar —the place of priestly approach and intercession. See Exod. 30 : 10. The altar in verse 25 is the brazen altar where the burnt-offering is offered, and the fat of the sin-offering burned. This would represent the place of Israel's approach and acceptance in a coming day, which they will not come to until they have seen the Scapegoat go away, and really kept *their* day of atonement. Aaron has to " go forth " to the brazen altar when he has ended all that is done within, and after the scapegoat has been sent away. But the true and distinctive blessing of the present time is what is taken up within by the assembly as typified by the sons and house of Aaron. It is our privilege to go in with the true Aaron, not only to serve in the holy place, but to be with Him in the sanctuary—the holiest of all.

The blood of the bullock for the priestly house, and the blood of " the goat of the sin-offering which is for the people," are both put on and before the mercy-seat. There could be neither heavenly nor earthly blessing if the poured-out life of Christ as sin-offering had not glorified God in the highest. The blood is on the gold. Indeed, there could be no mercy-seat at all without the blood being on it, so that this chapter is needed to complete the type. Christ is both the Ark and the Mercy-seat. He came to bring in and establish the will of God ; that is the Ark. But in a universe defiled by sin the will of God could only come in for blessing in the way of sovereign mercy. So that for the throne of God to take the character of a mercy-seat indicates that He wills to be known, and to bless, in spite of the moral stain that has come in. It tells what God is, who acts from Himself and for Himself in a universe that has become defiled by sin. The form of the phrase in Romans 3 : 25, " Christ Jesus, whom God has set forth a mercy-seat," indicates that He has done it on His own behalf. He has provided for His own glory, but in the way of mercy to the fallen creature.

But then this could not be apart from the vindication and manifestation of His righteousness in dealing judicially with that which was an offence to Him. The necessitates the death of Christ—the most stupendous fact in the moral universe. And now the blood is on the mercy-seat. God can be favourable to all men. He can justify and forgive sinners ; He can place those who were sinful before Him in perfect suitability to Himself. He can have a people before Him in favour and blessing on the earth, or He can have a company of heavenly sons in association with a glorified and heavenly Christ. Christ Jesus is the Mercy-seat, and He is a risen and glorified Man in heaven. All the value of His death and blood-shedding subsists eternally in Himself. He is " set forth a mercy-seat, through faith in his blood."

God can come out to men as having freed Himself by the death of Christ from man's sin and uncleanness. He comes out as a Saviour God in all the value of Christ, and of His death for sin. It is the character of this " day of salvation " that all that God is as revealed in Christ is available for sinful men on the ground of what was accomplished when Christ suffered and died. In the holiest spot in the universe the sin of man is not to be seen. The mercy-seat and the blood are there.

The blood being sprinkled seven times before the mercy-seat witnesses that all that is in the view of the mercy-seat—the things on the earth and the things in the heavens—will eventually be reconciled to the Godhead on the ground of peace being made by the blood of the cross (Col. 1 : 20). The things on the earth and the things in the heavens will be brought into correspondence with the holy nature of God. And at the present time the world is provisionally in reconciliation (Rom. 11 : 15). That is, God regards the world from the standpoint of Christ and of His death ; He is favourable to all men, for the death of Christ has come in on behalf of all ; and Christ is " the propitiation for our sins, but not for ours alone, but also for the whole world," 1 John 2 : 2. Scripture does not say that He bore the sins of all, but He has done a work which has glorified God in relation to sins, and He is available, as having done that work " for the whole world."

God has secured His own glory through the death of Christ so that all that is of Himself might remain in presence of the uncleanness of man. " He shall make atonement for the sanctuary, to cleanse it from the uncleanness of the children of Israel, and from their transgressions in all their sins ; and so shall he do for the tent of meeting which dwelleth among them in the midst of their uncleanness " (verse 16). It is on the ground of the atonement made by the Sin-offering that God's holy things remain among men. The camp of Israel represents those who are, in profession at any rate, the people of God. That there is much in the sphere of Christian profession that is displeasing to God, few would deny. But on God's part His holy things remain, and are available for men. God can be near to men with a free hand and a free heart to bless. The sins of men do not hinder God from being near to them in blessing, for He views all according to His appreciation of the blood on the mercy-seat. All may come, if they will, into the value of the death of Christ with God.

Then the Spirit of God is here dwelling in the saints ; the " true tabernacle " remains with all its holy furnishings ; " the testimony of the Christ " is still here. And the fact that these things are known as spiritual realities by many, and that they are remarkable features in the present ways of God, and that such things subsist notwithstanding all the evil that is in man and the iniquity that is in the Christian profession, is a great and powerful witness to the value of the death of Christ as before God.

Making atonement for the altar (verses 18, 19) refers to the place of priestly approach and service within, for it is the golden altar. See Exodus 30 : 10. The blood of the bullock and of the goat are put upon it as well as on and before the mercy-seat. The blessing of the assembly (represented by Aaron's house), and the blessing of Israel (represented by " the people "), are both bound up with the fact that Christ has entered " into heaven itself, now to appear before the face of God for us." He appears there in all the value of the blood of the Sin-offering. He is there for the priestly house who are " partakers of the heavenly calling," and when the assembly is removed at the rapture to its own heavenly place He will be there for the remnant of Israel. Indeed Israel has a memorial " before Jehovah " in that blessed Priest all through the time of His being in heaven. " God has not cast away his people whom he foreknew," for " the gifts and calling of God are not subject to repentance." Christ in heaven is the sure Pledge that " all Israel shall be saved," and will come into " their fulness " for the wealth of the world and the nations. (See Romans 11.) Israel does not know it, alas ! for " blindness in part has happened " to them, but saints of the assembly know well that Israel's blessing, as well as their own, is bound up with the place that Christ has taken " before the face of God."

What we have here typically is what the New Testament speaks of as the purification of the heavenly things (Heb. 9 : 23, 24.) It is most important for us to understand this, for the whole character of our blessing and approach to God hangs upon it, and it also determines the place which we take up in relation to religious things on earth. I suppose all Christians have the conviction that if they went to heaven they would find themselves in a place where there was no sin, and where all the conditions were suitable to God, and therefore where there was no cloud or sense of distance ! But how many Christians have taken into consideration that there is a system of heavenly things into which we can come now, and in the blessedness of which we can approach God—a system so divinely purified by the blood of the Sin-offering that there is not a trace of sin in it ? But this is what the epistle to the Hebrews opens up to us. We learn there that God has spoken to us in the Person of the Son, and He would have us to approach Him in the light of all that He has spoken. He has provided in the Sin-offering for the removal of everything that would have hindered this. The Son has " made by himself the purification of sins," Heb. 1 : 3. That means not merely that they are removed from the sinner, but they are removed from before God. They are no longer in His presence to defile His tabernacle.

" Propitiation for the sins of the people " (Heb. 2 : 17) would refer to the Sin-offering as meeting the glory of God about those sins in such a way that Christ has a righteous ground on which He can " be a merciful and faithful high priest," and can "help those that are being tempted." The question of sins has been so dealt with that it does not remain to hinder the service of the Priest on behalf of His people, who are viewed in Hebrews 2 : 18 as being still in the place of temptation.

Christ having "been manifested for the putting away of sin by his sacrifice " (Heb. 9 : 26), the heavenly things are purified. We can come into the region of heavenly things, and find that there is not a trace of sin there. This is simply a question of the value and efficacy of the blood of the Sin-offering. But then that blood has also furnished what purifies the conscience of believers " from dead works to worship the living God," Heb. 9 : 14. We have to do now with a sacrifice which not only purifies the heavenly things, but perfects those who approach. Such is the value of the Sin-offering that it perfects as to conscience. " The worshippers once purged having no longer any conscience of sins." We know that we have sinned, but Christ has " offered one sacrifice for sins," and " by one offering he has perfected in perpetuity the sanctified." Heb. 10 : 12, 14. It is entirely what has been effected by the Sin-offering. We must not mix it up with the thought of anything wrought in us ; it is the wondrous work of Christ alone ; " and the Holy Spirit also bears us witness of it." The Holy Spirit witnesses of what has been effected by the Sin-offering. As to conscience we are purged and perfected ; we can approach God on the ground and in the value of the Sin-offering.

On this ground we have " boldness for entering into the holy of holies by the blood of Jesus." Have we weighed what this means ? It does not say that all

believers go in, but it tells us our privilege, and says,
" Let us approach with a true heart, in full assurance
of faith." A true heart is a heart responsive to God,
knowing His love. In Hebrews 8 : 10 God puts the
mind before the heart, because it is a question there
of knowing God—of intelligence as to what God is as
made known by the Mediator. That is the side of
God's approach to us ; we must be enlightened before
we can love. But in chapter 10 the subject before
the mind of the Spirit is our approach to God, so in
verse 16 He puts the heart first. God secures the
affections of His people so that they may love Him,
and love the great Priest, and desire to approach
because they love. Then understanding follows, and
the more understanding they get the more free they
are to approach.

We approach as having " a great priest over the
house of God." It is the attraction of the Priest, and
the consciousness of having His support, that draws
us in in the power of affection. The One who has
sympathised with me and succoured me in His tender
love and grace in the pathway here, the One I have
" long proved in secret help," attracts me to the
place where He is with God " within the veil." How
" great " is that heavenly Priest ! Great in the glory
of His Person ; great in His love ! What attraction
there is to approach ! We have a Priest who has
gone within the veil, and we approach by Him to God.
If we approach by Him His nearness is the measure
of ours. A better hope has been introduced by which
we draw nigh to God. It is this which gives Christian
approach such a peculiar character ; we approach in the
blessedness of what is within the veil, the present light
and gain of an unseen and heavenly order of things.

The blessing of the heavenly company *within* transcends the blessing of Israel. The Bullock for the priestly house is greater than the Goat for Israel. I believe the Spirit magnifies Christ in Hebrews 1, 2, to give us an apprehension of Him in that greatness that is typified in the bullock. It was without any design or desire on our part that we are in the time of the heavenly ; we have had no choice in the matter. In the sovereign disposition of God He has brought us into being, and into blessing, in the time of the heavenly. What infinite favour ! We can draw nigh now in the light, and consciousness by the Spirit, of all that will be made good actually when we are translated in the condition of purpose.

> " O love supreme and bright !
>   Good to the feeblest heart,
> That gives us now as heavenly light,
>   What soon shall be our part."

The true Aaron has gone in in the power of the blood of the Sin-offering.

> " He's gone within the veil,
>   For us that place has won ;
> In Him we stand, a heavenly band,
>   Where He Himself is gone."

We can draw near, we can take our place with Him and with the blessed God according to what Christ is as having " by his own blood . . . entered in once for all into the holy of holies, having found an eternal redemption," Heb. 9 : 12. The priestly house is privileged to draw near, and to joy in God in the blessedness of all that subsists " within the veil."

Our calling is to those things which are " within " —a spiritual and heavenly order of privilege and blessing. Indeed to get the full character of Christian privilege and blessing we have to bring in the truth of other epistles as well as that to the Hebrews. The types give us a " shadow " but not " the image itself " of the good things that have come in Christianity. 2 Corinthians 5 clearly refers to the sin-offering and its results. " Him who knew not sin he has made sin for us, that we might become God's righteousness in him." It is on the ground of the sin-offering that the saints are " in Christ," and " there is a new creation ; the old things have passed away ; behold, all things have become new : and all things are of the God who has reconciled us to himself by Jesus Christ." This is something altogether outside and apart from what we are according to flesh. The Christ in whom we are is a risen and glorified Man. We are introduced to an entirely new order of things in which all is complacent to God. If we look round in the old creation we see sin and death's stamp everywhere. But in Christ risen and glorified in heaven there is what God can indeed pronounce " Very good." " New creation " is outside the reach of sin and death ; it is the whole order of things which centres in a risen and glorified Man in heaven. Such is the wondrous result of the Sin-offering—the saints become God's rightousness in Him. It has been remarked that this involves the glorified state.

If we turn to Colossians we learn the pleasure of the Fulness of the Godhead " by him to reconcile all things to itself, having made peace by the blood of his cross—by him, whether the things on the earth or the things in the heavens. And you, who once were alienated and enemies in mind by wicked works, yet now has it reconciled in the body of his flesh through death ; to present you holy and unblamable and irreproachable before it," Col. 1 : 19–22. This, again, gives us the Sin-offering and its results.

Then in the epistle to the Ephesians we have the full light of the heavenly. We read there that "Now in Christ Jesus ye who once were afar off are become nigh by the blood of the Christ. . . . For through him we have both (Jew and Gentile) access by one Spirit to the Father," Ephes. 2 : 13, 18. "The blood of the Christ" is the blood of the sin-offering which has been put on the mercy-seat and the golden altar so that we might be made nigh "in Christ Jesus." This gives us an entirely new state and place with God outside everything that was connected with us as living in the world. That we should be before God in Christ Jesus, holy and blameless, and "sons with Him who is above," is marvellous grace indeed. On the ground of the sin-offering God has given to those who believe a heavenly place and relationship according to His eternal purpose in Christ Jesus. Yea, we are "taken into favour in the Beloved," Ephes. 1 : 6. That is in the glorified Man, the Object of the Father's love in heaven, the One who said, "I go to prepare a place for you," John 14 : 2. Have we really taken this in ? That His going to the Father has made that heavenly place ours ? He is coming to receive us actually into the place where He is, but it is *our place now* as much as it will be when we are actually in it.

In Ephesians 2 the saints are viewed as " quickened with the Christ (ye are saved by grace), and has raised us up together, and has made us sit down together in the heavenlies in Christ Jesus, that he might display in the coming ages the surpassing riches of his grace in kindness towards us in Christ Jesus. For ye are saved by grace, through faith ; and this not of yourselves ; it is God's gift : not on the principle

of works, that no one might boast," Ephes. 2 : 5–9.
Have we considered what it means to be " saved by
grace " according to Ephesians 2 ? It means that
we have an entirely new place with God, and that the
place of Christ as a glorified Man in heaven. How
many of us understand that heaven is our present
place ? Not merely that we shall be there when we
die, or when the Lord comes. But that God's salvation by grace has made it our place now, has secured
for us at this present time the place of the risen and
glorified Man—the anointed Head. Is not that
infinitely better and greater than the best place—the
best religious place even—that we could have on earth ?

God would have us to know the character of
approach to Himself which is secured by the Bullock
of the Sin-offering. It is a larger apprehension of
Christ than the Scape-goat, or the Goat for Jehovah.
These will be known by Israel, but the Bullock is for
the assembly. We ought to covet to have the largest
possible thought of Christ, and of what He has secured
for us. Every one who has the forgiveness of sins
and the gift of the Spirit is of the assembly, and God
would encourage each one to say in his heart, I belong
to the heavenly company. There is sometimes a
feeling with believers that it would be presumption to
take such high ground. But has the great love of
God given us that place ? If so, His pleasure must be
that we should know and enjoy it. It has nothing to
do with any worthiness or merit of ours. It is a question of the love of God, the value of the Sin-offering,
and the preciousness of Christ to God. One might
add, also, the riches of His mercy to us.

The blessing of Israel—the earthly company—is on
the ground of Christ as typified by the two goats for a

sin-offering, and the ram for a burnt-offering.   One
goat is for Jehovah, to glorify Him in the highest, for
its blood is carried in and sprinkled upon and before
the mercy-seat.   The other bears away "to a land
apart from men " the iniquities, transgressions and
sins of the people.   In the one we have what meets
the glory of God and makes propitiation ;   in the
other we see substitution—the actual bearing of sins.
The sins are taken clean away, never to return.   " I
will pardon their iniquity, and their sin will I remember
no more," Jer. 31 : 34.

We have to go through the exercises of the day of
atonement, and to learn its lessons, and Israel will
have to take up those exercises in a coming day.   It
is not only that they have broken the law, and turned
to idolatry, but they have persecuted and slain the
prophets, and have become the deliverers up and
murderers of their promised Messiah.   Blood-guiltiness
attaches to them in the most awful way.   Zechariah
describes what they will go through when they realise
this.   " They shall look on me whom they pierced,
and they shall mourn for him, as one mourneth for an
only son, and shall be in bitterness for him, as one
that is in bitterness for his firstborn.   In that day
shall there be a great mourning in Jerusalem . . .
and the land shall mourn, every family apart : the
family of the house of David apart, and their wives
apart ;   the family of the house of Nathan apart, and
their wives apart ;   the family of the house of Levi
apart, and their wives apart ;   the family of Shimei
apart, and their wives apart ;   all the families that
remain, every family apart, and their wives apart,"
Zech. 12 : 10–14.

What a day will that be for them when they look at

their whole history in the light of the fact that they have slain their Messiah ! Whatever glory has been found amongst them in the ways of God—kingly, prophetic, priestly or levitical—has to come down into the dust of self-abasement and mourning. " Ye shall afflict your souls : it is an everlasting statute," Lev. 16 : 31. There is no exemption from the obligation of this, but, thank God ! " a sabbath of rest shall it be unto you." They will learn then to confess their iniquities " and all their transgressions in all their sins." over the head of the Blessed One whom they refused and killed, but who became in grace their Sin-offering.

> " Dark deed ! it was thine to afflict Him,
>   Yet longs His soul for the day
> When thou in the blood of thy Victim
>   Shalt wash thy deep stains away ! "

They will learn that all their guilt has been borne by Him. They will exclaim with wonder, in words which have been prepared for them beforehand by the prophetic Spirit, " Surely *he* hath borne our griefs and carried our sorrows ; and we, we did regard him stricken, smitten of God, and afflicted. But he was wounded for our transgressions, he was bruised for our iniquities ; the chastisement of our peace was upon him, and with his stripes we are healed. All we like sheep have gone astray, we have turned every one to his own way ; and Jehovah hath laid upon him the iniquity of us all. . . . For the transgression of my people was he stricken . . . he had done no violence, neither was there guile in his mouth. Yet it pleased Jehovah to bruise him ; he hath subjected him to suffering. When thou shalt make his soul an offering for sin, he shall see a seed, he shall prolong his days, and the pleasure of Jehovah shall prosper in his hand. . . . *He* shall bear their iniquities . . . He hath poured out his soul unto death, and was reckoned with the transgressors ; and he bore the sin of many, and made intercessions for the transgressors," Isaiah 53. All this expresses most touchingly what was true of Christ as typified on the day of atonement by the goat that was sent away. And as the people enter into it, and rest in the value of Christ as the sin-offering they will find " a sabbath of rest." And this is all true to-day for any guilt-oppressed soul that believes in Jesus.

Then in Leviticus 16 : 24 Aaron, having put off the linen garments and resumed the normal priestly garments, goes back to the brazen altar and offers his burnt-offering, and the burnt-offering of the people. The burnt offering would seem, from its use in Scripture generally, to have in view an acceptance and divine favour in which God's people stand as having a place before Him on earth. The first burnt-offering was Noah's (Gen. 8 : 20) ; it secured God's favour for the earth. The second was Isaac (Gen. 22), and on the ground of it Abraham would be richly blessed, and his seed multiplied. He would have seed for heavenly blessing as well as earthly ; " the stars of heaven " setting forth the former, and " the sand that is on the seashore " the latter. And in his Seed should " all the nations of the earth bless themselves." Then in Exodus 18 " Jethro, Moses' father-in-law, took a burnt-offering and sacrifices for God." This was typically the Gentile taking his place with God in the sweet savour of the burnt-offering—apprehending Christ in his personal and sacrificial acceptability to God as the ground of blessing.

God has had a Man—His own beloved Son—on
earth to do His will, and to be perfect in devotedness
to Him under every conceivable test, even as bearing
sin. The sweet odour of that has gone up from the
earth, and is a ground of acceptance for men viewed
as on earth. We come into it as persons justified by
faith, who now have access through Christ into God's
favour in which we stand (Rom. 5 : 2). Believers
to-day stand in divine favour according to the accept-
ableness of Christ. We are the children of God down
here, the subjects of His Fatherly care and love, His
household ; and we are sons in freedom in the very
place where we were once slaves in bondage. See
Gal. 4 : 6, 7 ; Rom. 8 : 15. Hence we are to be
" imitators of God, as beloved children, and walk in
love, even as the Christ loved us, and delivered himself
up for us, an offering and sacrifice to God for a sweet-
smelling savour," Ephes. 5 : 1, 2. This is not what
we are " inside the veil," but what we are as occupying,
for the time, a place on earth as in divine favour. We
are provisionally in the place where Israel was, and
will be, but we are there in divine favour, and as
knowing the love of God and of Christ. We do not
learn that favour by circumstances or providences,
but by knowing that we are with God on the footing
of Christ, and His death in burnt-offering character.
We perceive love that way, and as we know it we
" walk in love."

Millennial Israel will be on earth in the favour of
God on the ground of the Burnt-offering. Their
circumstances will be happy, for there will be " neither
adversary nor evil event " ; they will have " rest on
every side " ; but even then they will measure the
favour of God, not by the happy surroundings, but by

Christ. They will say when they come to Zion, "Behold, O God, our shield, and look upon the face of thine anointed," Psa. 84 : 9. "Men shall bless themselves in him ; all nations shall call him blessed," Psa. 72 : 17. We, to-day, have not millennial circumstances. Sin and sorrow are all around us. Sufferings mark "this present time." But we stand in favour on account of Christ, and because of the sweet odour of the Burnt-offering.

The bullock of the sin-offering and the goat of the sin-offering were to be burned with fire outside the camp (Lev. 16 : 27). This is what is referred to in Hebrews 13 : 11, 12. "Of those beasts whose blood is carried as sacrifices for sin into the holy of holies by the high priest, of these the bodies are burned outside the camp. Wherefore also Jesus, that he might sanctify the people by his own blood, suffered without the gate." The burning of the bodies of those beasts speaks of the all-consuming judgment with which sin has been visited. The One who knew no sin has been made sin for us, and He has borne the judgment that was due to sin. God would teach us by this holy type that there was something more involved in atonement than suffering at the hands of men—something additional even to the penalty of death. There is the action of the fire. All that God is as against sin, expressed in a holy judgment that would utterly consume it when presented before Him sacrificially, is seen in this solemn type. Christ as the sin-offering has endured it fully. The judgment of God—so far as believers are concerned—has been entirely and eternally exhausted.

Romans 8 : 3 is peculiarly touching. "God having sent *his own Son*, in likeness of flesh of sin, and for sin, has condemned sin in the flesh." It was "*His own Son*" who was sent into the place of sin's condemnation. The utter destruction of the world and all its inhabitants would not have been such a solemn and impressive testimony as that. For it was the righteous and holy One who was forsaken, and who bore the judgment. God has condemned sin in the flesh in the most solemn and public way. Now the order of man which dishonoured Him—the man characterised by sin—is no longer before Him. Another Man is before God, who has glorified Him in bearing sin's condemnation, and every creature under heaven can be blessed through that Man.

But the writer of the epistle to the Hebrews connects momentous present consequences with the blood being carried within the holiest and the bodies burned outside the camp. He introduces the subject by saying, "We have an altar of which they have no right to eat who serve the tabernacle." It seems to me that what is in the mind of the Spirit here is the whole system of heavenly grace which is our part on the ground of the Sin-offering. He would have our hearts confirmed with it. I have connected it in my mind with the "altar of wood" in Ezekiel 41 : 22, which is said to be "the table which is before Jehovah." The fact that it is of wood precludes the idea of it being a fire-altar, either for sacrifice or for incense. It is a food-altar— a table to feed from. It is the only thing mentioned which seems to be within the house, and there is no intimation of any service being rendered at that altar, or of the priests eating from it. They "minister in the gates of the inner court, and *towards* the house," but it is not said that they enter. It is true that there are doors with turning leaves, which suggest abundant entrance, but there is nothing to show that Israel, or the earthly priesthood—" the sons of Zadok "—will enter therein. The fact that " the glory of Jehovah filled the house " would rather preclude the thought of this. The doors with turning leaves, and the " altar of wood " within, might be a witness to Israel that there was another family with the privilege of abundant entrance to a nearer place than theirs, and that that family would have a food-altar connected with what was *within*.

But whether this is so or not, we have clearly a food-altar in Heb. 13 : 10 of which it is said, " they have no right to eat who serve the tabernacle." It is a source of food supply for the hearts of God's people which is connected with the blood of the sin-offering being carried into the holy of holies, and the bodies being burned outside the camp. God would have our hearts nourished upon what stands connected with that. And that for us brings in the confirming power of all that is now to be known through Christ having been the sin-offering, and having now passed through the heavens and entered within the veil as Forerunner for us. The truth of the heavenly calling, and all that is bound up with it, would be the food of that altar.

There are no sins where Jesus is " within the veil " ; He has " made by himself the purification of sins." Man in the flesh is not there ; he has been sacrificially ended in the death of Christ.

> " Glory supreme is there,
>   Glory that shines through all."

But there is a company sanctified by the blood of the Sin-offering, and having the witness of the Spirit to the value of that offering, for whom there is abundant entrance through infinite grace.

" 'Tis Jesus fills that holy place
  Where glory dwells, and Thy deep love
In its own fulness (known through grace)
  Rests where He lives, in heaven above."

The altar of which we have a right to eat is the
Christian altar, as contrasted with what is earthly and
Jewish. It is an altar which stands in relation to
" the better and more perfect tabernacle not made
with hand (that is, not of this creation)." It is connected with " the heavenly things themselves." It is
" the table which is before Jehovah " ; or rather, as we
must say now in the light of full revelation, which is
before the God and Father of our Lord Jesus Christ.
The epistle to the Hebrews does not develop all that
goes to make up the system of " heavenly things,"
but it would prepare those who read it for the epistle
to the Ephesians which gives the full light and blessedness of the heavenly.

We have a Food-altar : are we eating of it ? Are
we being nourished on the grace which has given us a
place and portion within the veil with a heavenly
Christ ? Our approach to God will be practically
according to the measure in which our hearts are
confirmed with that grace. We should consider
much what is before the God and Father of our Lord
Jesus Christ. Is it not that He " has blessed us with
every spiritual blessing in the heavenlies in Christ ;
according as he has chosen us in him before the world's
foundation, that we should be holy and blameless
before him in love ; having marked us out beforehand for sonship through Jesus Christ to himself,
according to the good pleasure of his will, to the praise
of the glory of his grace, wherein he has taken us into
favour in the Beloved : in whom we have redemption
through his blood, the forgiveness of offences, according

to the riches of his grace " ? All the grace of that is ministered to us for the confirmation of our hearts. We have access to the Father in the light and strength of it.

Now can you find anything to correspond with that in the organised systems of christendom which give man in the flesh a place ? Can you, in the light of your place *within*, remain in " the camp " ? If the blood of the Sin-offering has gone within it has secured for those whom it has sanctified a place and privilege that are wholly apart from the man after the flesh, and from everything that could have a religious place on earth—even Judaism, so long divinely sanctioned. Is it that Judaism was not of God ? By no means. *But the man who had religious privileges on earth in Judaism was under death.* Ah ! the " Place of a skull " tells its own solemn tale ! What of a city, be it ever so holy as a divinely-appointed religious centre on earth, if all in it are under death ? What of ordinances, services, ceremonies, sacraments, if the " Place of a skull " is man's place, and the end of his religion as well as of his sins ? If Jesus has suffered without the gate of the holy city, where does it put His " companions " as to everything that has religious status in connection with man after the flesh ?

God acted with patience and forbearance. He gave space for repentance to the house of Israel in the early chapters of the Acts, and there was a transitional period which continued some years. But when the epistle to the Hebrews was written there was a definite call to " go forth to him without the camp, bearing his reproach." Judaism, and all that was connected with it, was to be left, for Jesus was outside it. He had suffered without the gate, and His blood had gone within the veil. The system of things which recognised man in the flesh was no longer to hold the people of God, for Jesus had died and borne the judgment of that man in order to remove him sacrificially, and to set up everything for the pleasure of God in Himself as risen and in heaven, and to set apart a people to be in the light and blessing of it ; but, as a necessary consequence, to be " without the camp, bearing his reproach."

We can see the application of this to " the camp " of Judaism, but it is impossible to forget that the religious world to-day largely takes character from Judaism. It recognises the man after the flesh ; it has set up and maintains an order of things in which he can participate. It will not own in any practical sense that all that is due to that man is the " Place of a skull " and the consuming judgment of God. So that those who do own this in their souls, and who recognise that they have a place within in association with a heavenly Christ, must needs be found in a path of separation. We cannot go outside the Christian profession, as the believing Jew was called to leave Judaism altogether, so that the analogy between their circumstances and ours is not complete. But the path to which they were divinely called affords instruction as to the separation in which God would have His people to walk in the midst of the corruption and departure of christendom. We are to " withdraw from iniquity," to purify ourselves from vessels to dishonour in separating from them, and we are to " pursue righteousness, faith, love, peace, with those that call upon the Lord out of a pure heart," 2 Tim. 2 : 19–22. We are called to a separate path *within* the Christian profession, as those who have the light of the heavenly calling, and who see that the man after the flesh has no place with God. Such a path involves bearing the reproach of Christ.

CHAPTER 17

THE first part of this chapter relates to the fellowship of God's people. In considering chapter 16 we have seen the blessed character of *our approach to God* according to the value of the Sin-offering of the **day** of atonement, and according to Christ as the **One** who has gone within the veil. But peace-offerings relate to the fellowship in which we walk with others in the place where Christ died. And the truth of fellowship involves the whole question of what our enjoyment consist in, and where we find them. God loves His people too well to bear that they should have enjoyments apart from Him.

The elder brother in Luke 15 did not care for the merriment and rejoicing which were going on in the father's house; he had no communion with his father's delights; he had a fellowship of his own. " To me hast thou never given a kid that I might make merry *with my friends*." It was " I " and " my friends " without his father; he " would not go in " to take part in the communion of infinite grace. His fellowship was really an idolatrous one, for it was as much apart from his father as were the self-gratifications of the younger son in the far country.

It is against such selfish and idolatrous enjoyments that this chapter warns us. Every ox, or sheep, or goat slaughtered was to be brought to Jehovah, to the entrance of the tent of meeting, and sacrificed as a

peace-offering to Jehovah. " And they shall no more
sacrifice their sacrifices unto demons, after whom
they go a whoring." Any enjoyments that cannot
be taken up with God, and shared with His people
as in relation to Him at the altar, may be suspected
as likely to open the door to what is idolatrous.

" Neither be ye idolaters, as some of them ; as it is
written, The people sat down to eat and to drink, and
rose up to play," 1 Cor. 10 : 7. They gratified themselves in the absence of Moses, and without God. To
do so is to forget that Christ has died here, and that He
is absent as rejected by the world. In introducing
the subject of fellowship the apostle says, " Wherefore, my beloved, flee from idolatry. I speak as to
intelligent persons : do ye judge what I say. The cup
of blessing which we bless, is it not the communion of
the blood of the Christ ? The bread which we break,
is it not the communion of the body of the Christ ? "
And in contrast with this he says " that what the
nations sacrifice they sacrifice to demons, and not to
God. Now I do not wish you to be in communion
with demons. Ye cannot drink the Lord's cup, and
the cup of demons : ye cannot partake of the Lord's
table, and of the table of demons," 1 Cor. 10 : 14–22.

In a professedly Christian country we have not
idols of wood or stone, but there are a thousand things
which practically rob God of His place in the hearts
of His people. Things which have no connection with
His altar, and no place in the spiritual fellowship to
which He has called His people. All worldly amuse-
ments have this character, and much that is connected
with worldly religion is really idolatrous, because it
tends to please and satisfy men at a distance from
God.

For a man to kill his ox, sheep, or goat without bringing it to the tent of meeting simply meant that he was going to have a feast in which God had no part. " That man shall be cut off from among his people." He had morally cut himself off by making provision to enjoy himself without God. There was no sacrificial character about an animal slaughtered apart from the altar : it did not speak of Christ at all ; it only represented a using of what God had given providentially for self-gratification. This is exactly what the world does, and it is in principle idolatrous. God loves His people, and would have all their happiness connected with Himself. He would have each one of His people to say truthfully, " My God, the spring of all my joys."

Peace-offerings connected with the altar and the tent of meeting can be participated in by all the people of God that are " clean." Everything that truly belongs to the fellowship—all that is of Christ, and hat comes to us through His death; and the holy love of God revealed to us through death—can be shared by all who love God. If I have a source of gratification which is not the common portion of all saints I might well ask, What is its character ? What we can enjoy in common lies entirely outside the world ; it is the fellowship of the body and blood of Christ ; and this puts our enjoyments really on the resurrection side of death. We may enjoy together feeding upon Christ, with the happy consciousness that what we enjoy is the common portion of all who love God, and that we enjoy it as near to God, and in communion with His altar.

" The tent of meeting " was the rallying point for the whole congregation. It would remind us of our relations with all the brethren. We stand committed to a holy partnership, and we have all to be true to it. Should I like to know that all saints were doing what I am doing ? If not, can it be right for me to do it ? If I do what is not according to the truth of Christian fellowship, I misrepresent all the brethren, as well as failing to maintain what is due to the Lord. Each partner is to be a true representative of all the others. Everything that we do either ministers to the support of the fellowship or weakens it. A young believer just starting on a two-years' cruise in a large vessel, lay in his hammock the first night out from Portsmouth, praying about the two years during which he might perhaps hardly have any Christian fellowship, and the thought came to him, Here you are with all these men, and you do not know that there is one believer amongst them to report what you say or do, and yet the way you conduct yourself during these two years will affect for strengthening or weakening the whole company of saints on earth ! It is good to remember that each partner in the fellowship represents all the partners. Sometimes a believer may think he is of no account, and it does not matter what he does, or where he goes, or how he spends his time ! But each believer is one of the partners in the fellowship, and what he does is either true to the fellowship or is a misrepresentation of it. I heard the other day of a brother being seen at a football match ! What kind of witness was that ?

In the wilderness position it is important to maintain what is due to the Lord, and what is consistent with the fellowship to which we are called. So that it is a continual exercise not to take up anything for enjoyment that we do not hold in communion with God, and with those who love Him. But " in the land," as

Deuteronomy 12 tells us, " according to all the desire of thy soul thou mayest slay and eat flesh in all thy gates, according to the blessing of Jehovah thy God which he hath given thee " (verse 15.) Your " gates " are on divine territory now, and your border has been enlarged there (verse 20), and every trace of idolatry extirpated (verses 2, 3). You are in " the rest " and " the inheritance " (verse 9), you love all saints, and you have " gates " in which you can enjoy what your soul desires. The burnt-offerings and the hallowed things are all still connected with the place where Jehovah sets His Name, but what the soul desires can be enjoyed in " all thy gates." This is not " in the camp " or " out of the camp," but souls established, in type, on divine territory. They are wonderful " gates " when you consider what is cherished and nourished there—the Levite, the stranger, the father-less, the widow. See Deut. 14 : 29. When you have " gates " like that you can be trusted. They are the " gates " of a people who are in the affections of sons, and who enjoy a God-given inheritance in a spirit of grace towards those who are dependent. They have " bowels of compassions "—the first feature of the elect of God in Colossians 3. " The desire of thy soul " in Deuteronomy 12 is typically the desire of the new man, and the " gates " are only open to receive the blessing of Jehovah (verse 15), and to administer that blessing in a spirit of grace to others. To enjoy such a portion all the year round is a wonderful preparation for going up to " the place which Jehovah your God will choose . . . to set his name there."

The difference between Leviticus 17 and Deuteronomy 12 brings out the difference between saints viewed as being true to the fellowship in the wilderness, and viewed

as enjoying the inheritance in the land. In one position
constant watchfulness against the intrusion of what
is idolatrous is called for. In the other what is
typified is the enjoyment in rest and liberty of divine
favour and goodness on divine territory where all is
received from God and used for God. What was
killed in those " gates " was not for self-gratification,
but in the enjoyment of what was God-given, and to
minister to others in the spirit of grace. It was there
the enjoyment of the inheritance.

Leviticus 17 : 10–14 renews the commandment against
eating blood, which had been first given to Noah
(Gen. 9 : 4), and repeated in Lev. 3 : 17 ; chap. 7 : 26,
but now the reason is given. " I have given it to you
upon the altar to make atonement for your souls, for
it is the blood that maketh atonement for the soul.
Therefore have I said unto the children of Israel, No
soul of you shall eat blood." The lessons of the blood
were so distinctive, and so vital to all their relations
with God, that He would not allow any use of blood
which might enfeeble them. Blood was always to be
connected in their thoughts with atonement.

It has pleased God that man should be in a condition on earth in which " the soul (or life) of the flesh
is in the blood." If man's blood is shed his life is taken.
In the wisdom of God this is also true of the animals,
that they might be suitable to represent man sacrificially, though they have no spirit that stands morally
in relation to God as man has. Man as in flesh,
having his life in the blood, has fallen, and come under
the penalty of death. If man is to have righteousness
with God, or life, or blessing, it must be on the ground
of the death of Another. The " coats of skin "
(Gen. 3 : 21) were the first lesson as to this, disclosing

the wondrous thought of God that man, the fallen and naked sinner, might be clothed with a divine righteousness through death. Every animal that is killed for man's benefit speaks of Christ, for it is given by God (Gen. 9 : 3) to suggest to man that he may benefit through death.

Then every life that was taken sacrificially emphasised the lesson. The blood was given upon the altar to make atonement. Every animal that is killed for food speaks of man as being sustained through the death of Another. Every animal killed in sacrifice spoke of man being in relation with God through the death of Another. Both remind man that his own life in flesh is forfeited, and that he may enjoy good through a life being taken over which he had not the slightest claim. God originated that life, and alone had rights in regard to it, and if in goodness and mercy He permits the creature whose life in flesh is forfeited to benefit by another creature life being taken, His rights must be owned. He reserves the blood. It is as obligatory upon Christians to abstain from eating blood as it was upon the children of Israel. See Acts 15 : 29. It is a question of the permanent rights of God over His creatures on earth.

But this statement that " the life of the flesh is in the blood " can hardly be considered without our hearts being reminded of the wondrous fact that there has been One in that condition whose life was *not* forfeited. The blessed Son of God took part in blood and flesh. See Hebrews 2 : 14 and the note in the New Translation. He came into that condition absolutely without taint of sin ; He " knew no sin " ; He was the Holy One of God. But He took part in that condition of flesh and blood in which man had

been created and had fallen and become sinful and
subject to death. In that condition of flesh and
blood sin attached *to us* ; our lives were forfeited ;
we were under the penalty of death. In that
condition of flesh and blood sin did not attach to
Him, and therefore *His* life was not forfeited ;
death had no claim on Him whatever. But He
came into that condition where " the life of the
flesh is in the blood " in view of the accomplishment
of atonement. He took part in blood and flesh that
His blood might be poured out, and the life ended
sacrificially that was forfeited by the just judgment
of God upon sin. His blood was given upon the altar
to make atonement. The very condition to which,
in us, sin attached was brought to an end in the
vicarious death of that sinless One. He never resumed
the life in blood and flesh. He was raised having
" flesh and bones " (Luke 24 : 39) but having poured
out His blood for atonement. He has laid down the
life which was in the blood, and He lives eternally
now in resurrection life and a spiritual and glorified
body. The same Blessed Man, unchanged in all that
He was morally, but in a new and eternal condition to
which sin can never attach, and in which He dies no
more.

" It is the blood that maketh atonement for the
soul." We know how the adversaries of our faith
deride the thought of this. They regard it as offensive,
and only suited to an unenlightened age. But man is
a sinner, and under death. No doubt the thought of
this is offensive also. If we set aside the thought of
atoning blood we have not got rid of all that is
offensive ! But, thank God ! the precious fact remains
that the blood speaks of what meets in divine grace

the actual and undeniable facts of the situation. It goes to the very root of the tremendous questions which all men have to face. Men may be, as Peter says, " willingly " ignorant. They may resolutely shut their eyes to the fact that man is fallen and under death. They may dream out schemes of morality and philosophy, indifferent to the fact that they are useless as a remedy for man's condition. They may even profess to accept the moral teachings of the Bible while refusing its doctrine of atonement. But the fact remains that man is sinful ; his life is forfeited ; he cannot put himself right. It is the voice of a Saviour God that says, " The life of the flesh is in the blood ; and I have given it to you upon the altar to make atonement for your souls, for it is the blood that maketh atonement for the soul." Man's life in flesh is forfeited ; he is under the penalty of death. Whatever his views he cannot get away from this, offensive as the thought may be. But if infinite love has considered the situation, and a Sinless One—a divine Person—has come into flesh and blood that an unforfeited life of infinite value might be given in the way of atonement, what a revelation it is of what God is !

Man's life in flesh is in the blood ; if you shed his blood his life is gone. But man in that life is fallen ; he is a sinner under death. Is man content to leave it at that ? If so, he must be prepared to abide the consequences. But if man is content to leave it so, God is not. He has sent His blessed Son in holy Manhood to take part in blood and flesh that His blood might be given for atonement. It is in this way that we know the love and righteousness of a Saviour God.

Blood speaks of life poured out. Man is ever to respect that; it is never to be a common thing to him, or a thing he can use as he likes. Every life taken for man's benefit speaks of Christ and of atonement. The principle of vegetarianism is contrary to Scripture; the real root of it is the enemy's hatred of the idea that man is to benefit through death. But it is only death that can make atonement or secure blessing for sinful men.

———

CHAPTERS 18–20

THESE chapters correspond with what is spoken of in the New Testament as the putting off the old man with his deeds, and putting on the new man. A former order of things is contemplated. "After the doings of the land of Egypt, wherein ye dwelt, shall ye not do; and after the doings of the land of Canaan, whither I bring you, shall ye not do; neither shall ye walk in their customs." "All these abominations have the men of the land done, who were before you, and the land hath been made unclean" (chapters 18 : 3, 27 ; 20 : 23). All connected with that former order is to be absolutely refused. It is positively evil and abominable, and divine authority is brought to bear upon it. Moses is the speaker; Aaron does not appear.

All the features of the old man appear in these chapters—corruption in the gratification of lust, cruelty in giving their seed unto Molech, and falsehood. The old man is morally after the devil. It "corrupts itself according to the deceitful lusts," Ephes. 4 : 22. We must distinguish between the old man and the natural man. There are things in the natural man which are of God—natural affection, kindness, and often a great measure of truth and uprightness in dealing with his fellows. These things serve to show that in natural—that is, unconverted— men and women there are features which are of God. Paul speaks of some who " practise by nature the things of the law," Rom. 2 : 14. The rich young man who came to the Lord was a natural man, but there were features in him which the Lord could value, and which drew out the Lord's love. It is right to recognise even in unconverted people what is good and of God. It is to be respected, for it is a trace left of God's handiwork. Just as in a ruined building you may see bits that show the handiwork of the builder.

But the old man is marked by corruption, cruelty, and falsehood. It sets forth what man is as corrupted by Satan, and corrupting himself ; there is not a single feature in the old man that is of God. The heart of man as fallen is the source of every corrupt and cruel thing (Mark 7 : 21). There may be a certain veneer on the outside, particularly where Christian light is, but within is " all uncleanness," Matt. 23 : 27. The old man is not an individual any more than the new man is. These terms " the old man " and " the new man " are used to designate two totally different orders of moral being. The whole mass of fallen humanity carries the features of " the old man," though those features come out more distinctly in some than others. The saints—" the holy and faithful brethren in Christ "—have " put off the old man with his deeds," and have put on the new. The new man " according to God is created in truthful

righteousness and holiness " (Ephes. 4 : 24), and is
" renewed into full knowledge according to the image
of him that has created him," Col. 3 : 10. That
image is seen in Christ. So that the new man is
according to God as set forth in Christ. " I am
Jehovah your God " necessitates moral correspondence between God and His people. And it is striking
that believers are not told to put off the old man and
to put on the new. It is supposed that every one who
has learned the Christ has done it.

The new man is a divine creation. What the old
man is can be seen on all sides. It is written large on
the history of the world, and in the pages of every
newspaper ! But, thank God ! there is a new man—
a divine creation more wonderful than the material
universe—a man created " in truthful righteousness
and holiness," and according to God as imaged in
Christ. A man who is not only " created " but
" renewed," so that his moral features are preserved
in distinctiveness and freshness. The features of the
new man do not deteriorate or decay. They are not
one hair's-breadth nearer to the features of the old
man than they were at the outset of Christianity.

The new man does not go on with " the doings of
the land of Egypt " or " the doings of the land of
Canaan." It seems to me that the Egyptian element
is prominent in Colossians—" philosophy and vain
deceit, according to the teaching of men, according to
the elements of the world, and not according to
Christ," Col. 2 : 8. But I think the Canaanitish
element would appear in Ephesians. " This I say
therefore, and testify in the Lord, that ye should no
longer walk as the rest of the nations walk in the
vanity of their mind, being darkened in understanding,

estranged from the life of God by reason of the ignorance which is in them, by reason of the hardness of their hearts, who having cast off all feeling, have given themselves up to lasciviousness, to work all uncleanness with greedy unsatisfied lust," Ephes. 4 : 17–19.

It may be added that the new man comes into evidence on earth. " The new man " could have no meaning in heaven, for there has never been an " old man " there. In the place where diabolical corruption appears in the old man the new man comes out as a divine creation. And indeed many of the features of the new man will not be called for in heaven. For example, bowels of compassion, long-suffering, forbearing one another, and forgiving one another ! These are for earth, not heaven.

It is through the affections that God brings us to put off the old man and to put on the new. He brings Christ into the view of our souls as the Anointed Man of His pleasure. Colossians speaks of receiving the Christ ; Ephesians speaks of learning the Christ. The brethren in Christ " have heard him and been instructed in him according as the truth is in Jesus," Ephes. 4 : 21. This shows that believers come under the direct and personal influence of Christ ; and all who have really experienced this have put off the old man and have put on the new.

Chapter 19 stands by itself as the only chapter in this book whose contents are addressed to " all the assembly of the children of Israel." It is the people looked at as forming a moral whole—one might say, in figure, " one new man "—observing in unity all God's statutes and ordinances. God has His new man down here where the Jew and Gentile were. He has wrought in creative power to bring that new man into being, and it takes " all the assembly " to give expression to him. This chapter is a comprehensive summary of what is to mark those who reverence God's sanctuary. There is something more in it than individual obedience, for each one is to be concerned that his neighbour also is kept right. One is to be as anxious for one's neighbour to be free from any evil as one is about oneself (verses 17, 18). We belong to a holy assembly, for it is God's assembly and He is holy, and each one is responsible to maintain the holy character of His assembly.

Much that is written here is almost transcribed into Colossians and Ephesians. " Ye shall reverence every man his mother, and his father." " Ye shall not steal." " Ye shall not lie one to another." " Thou shalt not avenge thyself, nor bear any grudge against the children of thy people." Compare Ephes. 6 : 2 ; chap. 4 : 28, 25, 31, 32.

If " all the assembly " is to be holy because God is holy, every mother and father in that assembly would be marked by holiness, and the influence which they brought to bear in their households would be a divine and godly influence. The children not provoked to anger, but brought up in the discipline and admonition of the Lord. It is very suitable that we should " reverence " those who have cared for us in childhood and youth, and preserved us from the corrupting influences of the 'world, and who have sought our good in relation to God. The older we get the more we " reverence " those who in the place of parents have protected us, and brought divine influences and control to bear upon us. Indeed it is to be noted that it is " every man "—not every child—who is to reverence his mother and father. As long as the parents live they are to be reverenced. Many a wayward boy and girl has longed to be free from parental care and control, but the grace of God would bring salvation to such, and teach them to value the immense privilege of a Christian household. On the other hand it is an abiding exercise for believing parents to maintain that, before their children, which is truly deserving of reverence.

I have no doubt there is a parental influence in the assembly which God would have us to reverence. There is maternal cherishing and fatherly admonition (1 Thess. 2 : 7, 11).

" My sabbaths shall ye keep," refers to the other positive injunction of the law. God's people are to own *His* sabbaths. Jehovah rested on the seventh day, and blessed and hallowed it. He said, as it were, I have hallowed My sabbaths, now you are to hallow them. It tested the people's state of heart as to whether they valued communion with their God. Do you love to think of how perfectly God has secured rest for Himself in Christ ?

The " sacrifice of peace-offering " refers to the fellowship of saints being such as can be accepted. It must not be eaten beyond the second day. Spiritual joys have to be sustained by renewed direct communion with God. We have spoken of the principle of renewing in connection with the new man, and the necessity for renewing is emphasised in the peace-offering. It is not sufficient to be conscious that one has not done anything wrong. There must be a *renewal* with God and with His people of that which is the source and spring of spiritual joy. Many live on the remembrance of joys they have had, but that is not an acceptable ground of communion in the present. We often, perhaps, speak together of things when the heart has no longer a present and deep sense of what they mean as in nearness to God about them. At such a time renewing is needed. We should be exercised that the character of our communion is such that God can be complacent in it at the moment. Every saint who has the Spirit has known spiritual joy in Christ. Many know it was real, and live on the memory of it. People who tell us that things were better, and in more power, years ago are confessing that what they cherish as a remembrance is greater to them than what they are in the enjoyment of now! It is time they brought another peace-offering, and got all renewed with God and with the brethren! One feels the need for renewing very much. It is easy to sing beautiful hymns, and to utter beautiful words, without the affections moving vitally with what we sing or say. We need renewal of spiritual joy and energy. We may know a thing to be true without having the present joy of it with God or with our brethren. How thankful we ought to be that there is such a thing as renewing!

Then in the harvest and the vintage, when the rich fruits of divine goodness are being gathered, " the poor and the stranger " are to be thought of (verses 9, 10). God would never have us to forget that there are " poor " amongst His people—those who are not in possession of fields or vineyards. If we have spiritual substance let us consider them, and try to make some of it available for them. There are tens of thousands of God's Israel who are " poor." We cannot make them come and glean, but we ought to think of them, and have them in our hearts. We can see, at any rate, that gleanings are there for them if they have any desire. Such consideration is " after God " ; if He sees it in our hearts He sees the features of the new man.

Then the " stranger "—one entirely outside God's people—is to be thought of also. Boaz carried this out to the stranger Ruth. How thankful should we be to see more Ruths in the fields of Boaz ! There are rich gleanings there, and the gleaners can have not only the gleanings, but Boaz Himself—the mighty Man in whom all divine wealth is found ! The " poor " would thus become rich indeed !

The following statutes (verse 11–18) bring out in various ways the character that God would impress upon His people by bringing Himself before them as known in grace. Then mixtures are to be avoided (verse 19). Satan often works on this line—putting together two things which should be kept apart, and really spoiling both. We are warned not to be carried away by " various and strange doctrines." I think all such are marked by mixture—part law, part grace, part human philosophy ! How often there are two sorts of seeds in what professes to be gospel preaching ! And in result people appear in garments " woven of two materials " ! A bit of Christ and a good deal of self !

Ten times in these three chapters God says, " I am Jehovah your God." Twelve times He says, " I am Jehovah." He would impress upon His people that their conduct and spirit is to take character from Him. The new man is " according to God . . . created in truthful righteousness and holiness." He says, " Ye shall be holy unto me ; for I Jehovah am holy, and have separated you from the peoples to be mine " (chapter 20 : 26). God would have His people to be entirely diverse from all other peoples. Moses prayed to Jehovah to go with His people, " so shall we be distinguished, I and thy people, from every people that is on the face of the earth," Exod. 33 : 16. If God goes with His people it must be to discipline them, and bring them into accord with Himself, so that they may be for His pleasure.

Chapter 21

THIS chapter brings before us the holiness proper to " the priests, the sons of Aaron." The nearer one comes to God, the more essential it is to maintain holiness. A degree of separation that might suffice for the congregation would not be suitable for the priests. There has to be greater care as to natural influences, though they are not wholly excluded save in the case of " the priest who is greater than his brethren." He is not to uncover his head, nor rend his garments, nor make himself unclean even for his father or mother. But the priest in general might " make himself unclean " for " his immediate relation, who is near unto him."

This suggests that in priests natural feelings are to be under restraint, and there must be exercise as to how far they allow themselves to be affected thereby. There is that which is legitimate, but the priest has to consider how far what is natural has a claim according to God. " They shall be holy unto their God . . . for they present Jehovah's offerings by fire, the bread of their God ; therefore shall they be holy " (verse 6).

The fat of the peace-offering is called " the bread of
the offering by fire to Jehovah," Lev. 3 : 11, 16. The
priest is one who ministers to the satisfaction of God
in bringing Christ before Him, and therefore it is not
fitting that he should be affected by natural feelings
without exercise as to what is comely. He must ever
remember that he is a priest, and that he is called to
minister to God that which God can feed upon, and
his natural feelings have to be controlled in view of
that. When it is was a question of the service of God
the Lord said to His mother, " What have I to do with
thee, woman ? mine hour has not yet come," John
2 : 4. He did not own the natural in His service. His
mother and His brethren were those who did the will
of God.

Then the priest was to keep his affections from
going out to that which had a moral stain upon it—
that which was marked by unfaithfulness or impurity
(verse 7). There are many things in the Christian
profession which bear the mark of unfaithfulness. We
must recognise that it is unsuitable for priests to
come into association with them. It is a question
here of the moral dignity of those who minister to
God. It would be well if God's called ones looked at
themselves more in the light of verse 8. All saints
have the privilege of taking up priesthood, but how
far we have taken it up spiritually is another matter.
God would encourage us to do so.

There is a further thought in verses 10–15. We
come here to " the priest who is greater than his
brethren." This is a type of Christ—the anointed
and consecrated One—who never leaves the sanctuary ; who is apart from all natural influences ; but
who gets a companion of virgin character in the

faithful remnant of His people, or—at the present
time—in the assembly.

But whether we think of " the anointing oil " poured
on His head, or " the garments " of His consecration,
how blessedly are His saints identified with Him !
If He is " the priest who is greater than his brethren,"
that very designation shows that He has brethren.
And His brethren share in the anointing ; they have
a memorial in the breast-plate, the shoulder-pieces,
and the hem of the cloak. It is impossible to detach
the saints from Christ in heaven, or He from them.
The Sanctifier and the sanctified are " all of one."
Our earthly links are broken by the death of Christ
here, and heavenly ones are formed by the anointing
that links us with Him where He is.

Now we have to see that we are identified with the
" virgin " character—not with that which speaks of
unfaithfulness, or of affections that have had another
object. No other but Christ was ever entitled to the
assembly. The Spirit's work is to produce holy
affections in the assembly—affections that never had,
and never could have, any other object but Christ.
We have to see to it that such affections are maintained in freshness and fervour. The serpent would
do his utmost to beguile us by his craft, so that our
" thoughts should be corrupted from simplicity as to
the Christ," 2 Cor. 11 : 3. We are to be presented
" a chaste virgin to Christ."

People talk of " revivals " here and there, but in
truth we are in the time of the greatest revival there
ever was. The Spirit of God is reviving virgin character and bridal affections in the assembly under the
eye, and for the heart, of the One who values that
character and those affections. Does not the thought

of it move us to desire and pray that we may be in the gain of what the Spirit is saying to the assemblies to-day ? The " virgin " character is in contrast to Thyatira, which develops into Babylon, the great harlot, who corrupts herself with all that is great and grand in the world. And bridal affection would come in as a bright and blessed contrast to the indifference of Laodicea. All saints are called to have " chaste virgin " character. Every corrupting influence is exposed in Scripture, and particularly in the epistles to the seven assemblies, that we may turn from those influences with aversion, and allow our hearts to unfold " as the rose to the golden sun " to the One who is coming.

Then none of Aaron's seed with a " defect " was to " approach to present the bread of his God " (verse 17). Note that it is Aaron's " seed " here, not his " sons." This is only found in this section of the book. The " seed " seems to suggest those born again —of new generation morally—but not necessarily " perfect in Christ." Aaron's " sons " would speak of their dignity as consecrated. To use the language of the New Testament the " sons " have received the ministry of reconciliation, but the " seed " may not have. There are many of divine " seed " in the world who do not stand consciously in the good of the gospel ; they are not yet in the freedom and spiritual dignity of " sons." They cannot approach to offer as priests either unto the veil or the altar.

Now for such it is important to know that God is announcing in this world a Person in whom there never was, nor could be, any " defect." Speaking of Christ, Paul says, " Whom we announce." Christ is announced that He may be received, and that souls

may know that they can be with God entirely on the
ground of Another Man in whom there never was any
defect. So Paul announced Christ, and laboured that
he might " present every man perfect in Christ,"
Col. 1 : 28. " The reconciliation " is something to be
received, for it is written, " Our Lord Jesus Christ,
through whom now we have received the reconciliation," Rom. 5 : 11. Through the death of His Son we
can be with God on the footing of One in whom there
was never any blemish.

A " defect " is not necessarily a man's own fault ;
it might be the result of bad teaching, which left one
unconfirmed with grace. A " defect " does not necessarily render one unclean, for " the bread of his God,
of the most holy and of the holy, shall he eat,"
and he could not do this if unclean. See chapter
22 : 4–6. It is blessed grace that permits the one of
Aaron's seed with a " defect " to eat, but such a one
must keep a good conscience, and not touch any
unclean thing. " The bread of his God " is not with-
held from any upright or exercised soul. The holy
things speak of Christ as the Object of complacency
and delight to God. As souls feed on that they are
inwardly formed in the appreciation of the Man who
is entirely for God's delight. In a sense every one
born again can appreciate Christ. The man in
Romans 7 says, " I delight in the law of God
according to the inward man." If Christ were
presented to such a one he would delight in Christ.
Indeed that is how the divine " seed " comes to light.
Christ is presented in the glad tidings, and certain
persons are attracted ; they appreciate Christ as
presented to them. But then He is presented that
souls may know that they can be with God on the

footing of that Man. A divinely exercised soul may feed upon what Christ was as obedient unto death, and upon what He was as having gone into death so that God and His people might have a common joy. That is the oblation and the peace-offering—all that Christ was as here in flesh for God's pleasure, and what He was as going into death to be the Substance of our communion and joy. Indeed the antitype surpasses the type, for I think we may say that eating the bread of God spiritually would remove defects. J. B. S. used to say that *our* High Priest can remove all the defects in the members of His family !

Sometimes a " defect " is the result of one's own lack of spiritual diligence. Peter speaks of some being " blind, shortsighted," and he accounts for it by their lack of diligence to make their calling and election sure. Hebrews 12 : 13 speaks of some as being " lame," but suggests that they may be " healed." Probably the " lame " one might be a Jewish believer of feeble faith, with whom there was danger that he might be stumbled and go back if he did not find grace to help him amongst the Christian company, and particularly if they did not " make straight paths " for their feet.

In Christianity no " defect " need be permanent ; the normal working of grace would be in the direction of removing every defect. There is no necessity now for saints to be permanently incapacitated for holy service. There are many " dwarfs " to-day, but they might grow up to full stature if their desire and purpose was to do so !

CHAPTER 22

No one of Aaron's seed is to approach the holy things or eat of them with uncleanness upon him. If there has been contact with anything unclean, the sun of that day must go down, and the flesh must be bathed with water, before the holy things may be eaten. The whole day is affected by what has taken place, and the soul has to learn by its sorrowful deprivation of "the holy things" how serious it is to contract uncleanness.

Then the seed of Aaron were forbidden to eat of "a dead carcase and what is torn" (verse 8.) It was not forbidden to the ordinary Israelite, but even for him it rendered unclean until even, and necessitated washing (Lev. 17 : 15). "A dead carcase" would signify a source of food which had no sacrificial character ; it would suggest that in which God has no pleasure. And "what is torn" would imply that such food had become available through violence. There is much which sometimes tempts the people of God, of which they would have to admit that there was nothing for God in it, and some of which is the fruit of violence being done to what is due to Him. Such food renders an Israelite unclean, but it is absolutely prohibited to one of the priestly seed.

In verses 10–16 the holy things are restricted to the priestly household. The priestly household has its own privileges. All of that household can eat—the slave, those born in the house, the daughter at home—but no stranger. Neither stranger, sojourner, nor hired servant may eat. It is only those who are of the household by purchase or by birth who can partake. of the priestly food. It is one thing to sojourn with the priest, another to be part of his household. The sojourner and the hired servant represent those who are providentially near to the priest, but do not belong to him. It is a great thing to be conscious that one belongs by purchase to a priestly household ! Such are not casual visitors or strangers. It supposes some who are not up to priesthood themselves, but who can hold themselves as purchased. The feeblest believer can do that ; he can say, I am bought with a price.

Then " he that is born in his house . . . may eat of his food." It supposes that there will be children born there. Where priestly conditions are maintained one would look for children to be born ! And even young converts are entitled to the " holy things." What an unfolding of grace there is in this ! The one with a defect, the purchased one, the child born, all entitled to eat of the " holy things " if clean !

" No stranger shall eat the holy thing." The " stranger " here is one " not of the seed of Aaron," Num. 16 : 40. He is not at home in the priestly household ; he does not belong to it. There are many scriptures which show what grace there is in the heart of God for the " stranger." He need not remain a " stranger " ; he may become " a soul of purchase." " Ye are no longer strangers and foreigners, but ye are fellow-citizens of the saints, and of the household of God," Ephes. 2 : 19. But no stranger *as such* can eat the holy thing.

" A priest's daughter who is married to a stranger may not eat of the heave-offering of the holy things." She is one who has been in the priestly household, and known what it was to enjoy priestly food, but she has entered into an association outside the priestly ·family.

She loses her right to the holy things. This would be a serious consideration for any true-hearted daughter of the priestly house. The principle of this would apply to-day. Any kind of association—marriage or otherwise—that links us intimately with those who have no priestly character or exercises is sure to deprive us practically of our share in priestly food. If we have known what it is to feed on Christ, and delight in Him, let us beware of forming links of friendship or companionship with those who are " strangers " to the priestly family !

But there is an intimation here of restoration. Verse 13 speaks of her becoming a widow, or being divorced, and returning to her father's house, as in her youth ! How many have got away through associations which they have formed, only to find that they lose all that they went after ! Through the sorrow of widowhood they come back to what they need never have left. They may even be " divorced " —disowned and cast off by the very persons who drew them away ! What precious grace to think that such can go back to " her father's house, as in her youth," and " she may eat of her father's food."

The " stranger " here is not exactly an unbeliever ; he is an Israelite, but not of the seed of Aaron. We have to beware that even converted people do not draw us away from priestly privileges and food. We have to be careful what kind of links we form even with believers. As we were seeing in the types of the tabernacle, they must be loops of blue, clasps of gold, clasps of copper, rods of silver ! These things indicate the kind of links that are safe. Heavenly, divine spiritual links will never lead us away from spiritual privilege and food. We can *serve* all believers as we have opportunity, but we have to guard our associations if we wish to retain the privileges that belong to the priestly household.

Barnabas lost much by allowing his natural partiality for his nephew to be greater in his estimation than his link of partnership with Paul. It is sad to think of one who had been a pattern of good works, and a comfort to the apostles—for they surnamed him " Son of consolation "—one who had a large and true appreciation of Paul, allowing his attachment to his nephew to deprive him of so much that might have been his priestly privilege ! It was not that either the uncle or the nephew ceased to be believers, or to be servants of the Lord, but they both lost a priceless privilege. To be associates of Paul was the highest privilege of the moment, and they lost it, at any rate for the time. This shows the dangers of unspiritual links with even true believers.

The closing section of this chapter is the last word in the book about the offerings, and it insists that there shall be no blemish or defect therein whether offered for a burnt-offering or a peace-offering to accomplish a vow. " As a voluntary offering " a bullock or a sheep might be offered " that hath a member too long or too short." This would represent typically a lack of proportion in the apprehension of Christ. One feature of Christ made so much of that it is out of proportion to the rest in our apprehension, or another feature to which due place is not given. But the offerer in this case has no thought of blemish or defect in Christ. He simply has not things in intelligent and divinely adjusted proportion. One can be deeply thankful that such a voluntary offering is accepted, for with how many of us is there a lack of proportion in our apprehension of Christ! God accepts it, for it is *Christ* who is apprehended and offered, but He intimates to us at the same time that such an offering does not come up to what He looks for in a truly spiritual person. "As a vow it shall not be accepted." Where there is that devotedness and spiritual energy of which a "vow" would be the expression there would be much exercise to have the perfections of Christ in their due proportion before the soul, so that we might be able to present them to God with intelligent apprehension, and in such a way as to be accepted, and to give pleasure to God.

<hr/>

Chapter 23

"The set feasts of Jehovah . . . my set feasts" are God's appointed seasons; they make known what is in His mind. They are not voluntary (see verse 38), or obligatory because of sins like sin- or trespass-offerings. They are things which the people of God have to take up *together* for His pleasure. This gives them a very precious character. They were to be proclaimed as "holy convocations"; they refer to what has to be taken up collectively as God's appointed seasons. It is not the thought of what springs out of our exercises or desires, but of what God appoints for His own pleasure.

Each of these feasts would bring all the people together, and if we think of what they typify we must see that they speak of things which would have the effect of bringing all the people of God together morally. No one can say, Mine is a different Passover from yours, or a different Wave-sheaf, or a different

Oblation. They are fixed rallying points for God's people in relation to Himself, that they may be brought together morally. To be brought together merely in an outward way would not be a " holy convocation." It might be possible to get all the believers in a town together in one place, but if they all had different thoughts and views they would not be together morally.

What I understand by a " holy convocation " is that God's people are called together in a real and spiritual sense. They are united in the same mind, and in the same opinion (1 Cor. 1 : 10). All were together outwardly at Corinth, but they were not together morally. Theirs was not a " holy convocation," but the Apostle laboured that it might become one. We are all here in this room, but how far are we really united in the same mind and in the same opinion ? God provides in His set feasts all that is essential to *unify* His people. If we go through these feasts, and keep them with God, we shall not have a divergent thought about anything. A company of persons together without a divergent thought, and every thought in harmony with God, is a " holy convocation." Divergent thoughts are the result of entertaining things which lie outside what is appointed of God.

There can be no doubt that there will be a " holy convocation " at the rapture. If the Lord's assembling shout rang out at this moment the whole assembly would be caught up without one divergent thought in all the myriads that compose it. The work of God goes on now to bring that about morally before it comes about by divine power at the rapture. He would have all His people to know what it is to have part in a " holy convocation " now.

It is instructive to see that " the sabbath of rest " comes first. It is not exactly one of the set feasts (see verse 38), but it comes in as preparatory to them all. It speaks of that restful spirit which God would have in the dwellings of His people. The sabbath was " an everlasting covenant. It shall be a sign between me and the children of Israel for ever," Exod. 31 : 16, 17. The thought of *rest* is essential to the covenant ; it is very sweet that it should be so.

" The sabbath to Jehovah " is a complete cessation from our own activities, that we may contemplate in rest what God has done, and the character of His rest, and how He would have His people to share it. The " sabbath *of* Jehovah " is that God gives and appoints it ; the " sabbath *to* Jehovah " is that His people regard Him in it. The words " to Jehovah " occur often in this chapter, and this shows how His pleasure in the feasts is a paramount thought. Elements of unrest brought in amongst the people of God break the sabbath of rest. We have to see to it that nothing takes us away from a restful attitude of soul Godward ; and this not merely in the meetings, but " in all your dwellings." Persons in a perturbed state of mind could never be a " holy convocation." If you are labouring and burdened—and I say this to my own heart—come to the Son of the Father, and He will give you rest. The sabbath is God calling men into communion with His own rest. But it is irksome to man, because the natural man does not care for communion with God ; he prefers his own works to God's rest in Christ. Our " dwellings " are where we live in a spiritual sense ; there must be sabbath conditions there—restful conditions.

The thought of " the assembly of Israel " was first

introduced in connection with the passover (Exod. 12 : 3). " The assembly " is " the congregation looked at as a moral whole, a corporate person before God." (Note to Exod. 12 : 3 in the New Translation.) And if we consider the passover we shall see that it involves very real and practical oneness. One spotless Lamb has borne the judgment due to the sinful man, and His love in doing it is now the food of the sheltered. All that I was as a fallen natural man was under judgment, but Christ has borne the judgment in love, and I feed on Him now so as to live by Him. I have no longer before me the man after the order of Adam —the man in the flesh. I recognise that man as under judgment, but Christ has borne the judgment that I might live by Him. Is not this true for every believer on the face of the earth ? Have we not all —in the light of Christ being sacrificed, and bearing the judgment due to us—the same divine estimate of ourselves, and the same precious thoughts of the worth of Christ, and of His sacrifice ? As to our-selves we can only say that we deserved death and the judgment of God. As to Christ, we know that He has been sacrificed, and has borne the judgment due to us, that we might live by Him. Is there not perfect and universal accord throughout the whole assembly of God as to these divine realities ? I am not—for the moment—speaking of the shelter and safety which the Passover secures (for that is not the thought in Lev. 23), but of the unity which it estab-lishes throughout the Israel of God.

Then " the feast of unleavened bread to Jehovah " follows immediately upon the passover. Indeed in the New Testament the two feasts are identified— " the feast of unleavened bread, which is called the

passover," Luke 22 : 1. They go together morally,
and are therefore put in the same section of this
chapter. If all that I was as a man in the flesh came
under judgment in the sacrifice of Christ, how can I
tolerate the leaven of self-importance, or any of
those features which God has judged in the death of
Christ ? The one who has truly fed on the Lamb
roast with fire has something inwardly in his moral
constitution which gives ability to estimate things
according to God ; he discerns that what is of the
flesh is " leaven " ; it has a corrupting and inflating
character.

"Seven days shall ye eat unleavened bread." The
unleavened bread is Christ. We see in Him a kind
of humanity which had no corrupting or inflating
elements in it. The temptation proved that He was
unleavened. Adam had taken himself out of God's
hands in distrust and disobedience ; he had coveted
to possess what God had not given him ; he had been
allured by the prospect of being as God ; he had
dared to risk the pronounced penalty on disobedience.
But Christ trusted in God ; He would not act for
Himself, or receive from the prince of this world ;
He would not leave for a moment the place of obedience and dependence ; He would not tempt God by
putting His word to the test. There was no corrupting
or corruptible element there. Nor was there any
inflation or puffing up, or anything in the slightest
degree unreal. His prayer was " not out of feigned
lips " ; His thought went not beyond His word
(Ps. 17 : 1, 3). When they said, " Who art thou ? "
He answered, " Altogether that which I also say to
you," John 8 : 25. He could speak of Himself as
" a man who has spoken the truth to you," John

8 : 40. We may study every act of His, and every word, and we find nothing but " sincerity and truth." That is " unleavened bread " ; and it is to be eaten " seven days "—a perfect period, covering typically the whole of our life here.

One might say, I can never be like that ! But can you eat it ? Have you a taste for that kind of bread ? If you eat it you will become unleavened. The " old leaven " is to be purged out that the assembly of God " may be a new lump, according as ye are unleavened," 1 Cor. 5 : 7. " Old leaven " would be something brought over from the old lump of dough, which corresponds with " our old man." All that is corrupting, and tends to puffing up, and it has to be purged out. The " new lump." corresponds with " the new man, which according to God is created in truthful righteousness and holiness."

In one sense the saints " *are* unleavened," for they are in Christ Jesus by the work of God, and Christ Jesus is made to them " wisdom from God, and righteousness, and holiness, and redemption," 1 Cor. 1 : 30. God cannot own for His pleasure any life in believers but the life of Christ. Then how can we be in fellowship with God if we practically own the life of " our old man " ? Indeed, the very term " our old man " implies that we are not going on with that man now. As saints in Christ we have put him off, and have put on the new man. And now we have to keep the feast of unleavened bread during the whole period of our life here. This is not done by looking to see how imperfectly others are doing it, but by each one in uprightness of heart, and with a good conscience before God, seeking to maintain an unleavened character himself. As we feed on Christ we are nourished and strengthened, and He becomes our life practically, so that we can refuse the old leaven, and the leaven of malice and wickedness, and have with us " the unleavened bread of sincerity and truth."

The whole Israel of God is to move on that line, and that is how assembly conditions and assembly unity are brought about. It is by each one refusing what is of the flesh, and giving place to that which is of Christ. This would bring us all together morally, would it not ? Every day that we " celebrate the feast " of unleavened bread there is " an offering by fire." We know from Numbers 28 that it con- sisted of " two young bullocks, and one ram, and seven yearling lambs " for a burnt-offering, and other offerings. But here it is not specified in detail ; it is simply that there is what goes up as sweet odour. As the people of God refuse the flesh, and give place to what is of Christ, they acquire ability to minister to the delight of God.

A new section of the chapter begins at verse 9 and goes down to verse 22. It will be noticed that this is " When ye come into the land that I give unto you, and ye reap the harvest thereof, then ye shall bring a sheaf of the first-fruits of your harvest unto the priest. And he shall wave the sheaf before Jehovah to be accepted for you ; on the next day after the sabbath the priest shall wave it." Christ risen is set forth in this deeply interesting type as the First-fruits of the land of divine promise and purpose. God's thoughts as to the conditions and blessedness in which He would have His people before Him have reached fruition in One who rose on " the next day after the sabbath." This speaks of a new beginning, but one which stands in relation to what preceded it.

There were promises made to the fathers, and ways of God with Israel which had in view the fulfilment of those promises, but every day of Israel's history only made more manifest that none of those promises or those ways could come to fruition in connection with what they were as in the flesh. That history culminated in their rejection of the Promised One— the One in whom was embodied all " the truth of God " Rom. 15 : 8. They had proved utterly unfaithful— breaking the law, disregarding the covenant, despising the promises, killing the prophets, and last, most terrible of all, betraying and murdering the Just One— so that on what was truly the greatest and most momentous sabbath in their history He was lying in Joseph's tomb. The fact that the wave-sheaf would be a sheaf of barley, for barley harvest came before wheat harvest, might have some reference to the state of Israel as unfaithful, for barley only appears in the offerings in the jealousy offering of Numbers 5. It would suggest that Christ came in to take up the question of the unfaithfulness of those who have had a place as in relation with God. The exercise of having utterly failed as the people of God is a deeper exercise than the conviction of a man who has never professed to know God. Israel will have this exercise, and many of us have known the bitterness of it. But grace entitles us to know that Christ has borne the judgment due to our unfaithfulness. Israel will yet be brought to own that her unfaithfulness has been fully exposed, but that her suffering Messiah has taken it up, and borne the judgment due to it, and that as the Risen One He has become her accept- ance. She will then enjoy without a disturbing element the land which Jehovah has given her, and eat its bread. Israel will start afresh with God on the ground of a risen Christ, and they will get " the sure mercies of David."

But the Sheaf of the First-fruits is for us as well as for Israel. Christ has taken up everything that attached to us as a righteous liability, whether as ungodly sinners or as professing Christians, and He has met every divine claim, and has come forth in resurrection to be accepted for us. There is no question of any title that we might have in ourselves or of anything in which one might differ from another. God's thought of acceptance for the whole of His Israel—for every believer on the face of the earth— is set forth in a risen Man. What a unifying power there is in the apprehension of this ! There is one acceptance for us all, and it is that glorious Person, alive from the dead, in spotless and eternal suitability to the resurrection world which He has entered. In this world there may be a thousand differences between us, but with God we have a risen Christ—Christ only and wholly—for acceptance.

But then, this is not simply that Christ is our righteousness so that we have peace with God. It is an acceptance which sets us at liberty to eat the bread of the land which God has given us. He has prepared wonderful things for them that love Him, but they are not things which eye can see, or ear can hear, or which naturally come into man's heart. They are spiritual things, the fruit of " that hidden wisdom which God had predetermined before the ages for our glory." God has given us a wonderful land, the blessedness of which lies outside all natural ken, but is revealed by His Spirit, and entered into by spiritual persons. The " Sheaf of first-fruits " is

Christ in relation to that land, and as accepted for us
in view of our enjoying the " bread " of that land.
With what supreme liberty of heart, then, can the
people of God, as having kept this feast, enjoy their
unseen and eternal portion in Christ ! A risen Man
is the First-fruits. This shows us plainly that all the
after-fruits—if we may use the term—are after that
order ; they belong to a spiritual region which lies
beyond death ; they are " food which abides unto
life eternal," John 6 : 27.

" Ye shall bring a sheaf of the first-fruits of your
harvest unto the priest. And he shall wave the sheaf
before Jehovah, to be accepted for you." God would
have the whole of His Israel to recognise a risen Christ
as the First-fruits of what is in His heart for them.
He would have them in spiritual intelligence to wave
that blessed One before Him, as knowing that He is
accepted for them so that in liberty of heart they
may enjoy the bread of

> " Life's eternal home,
> Where sin, nor want, nor woe, nor death can come."

This begins a new period with God ; it is " on the
next day after the sabbath." It stands in relation to
a period that has closed ; substantiating all the
promises, securing all that the former ways of God
had in view, but putting all now on the footing of
resurrection. So that all the promises of God are Yea
and Amen in Christ the risen One, and as substantiated
in Him they are known as present realities. It is a
new period marked by the enjoyment of spiritual
realities of which the risen Christ is the First-fruits.

Then on the same day a he-lamb is offered as a
burnt-offering, with its oblation and drink-offering.

I

Along with the blessed apprehension of Christ as the
First-fruits in resurrection these various offerings have
their place. Their import has come before us in
considering the early chapters of this book, save that
of the drink-offering, which is here mentioned for the
first time in Leviticus. It is striking that what speaks
of joy—for the drink-offering is of wine—should be
introduced in this connection. And we may remember that the wine in the drink-offering is the same
measure as the oil in the oblation. It speaks of " joy
in the Holy Spirit," Rom. 14 : 17. God has great
delight in the joy of His people in Christ ; the drink-
offering was to be poured out " in the sanctuary."

The next feast is of peculiar interest, for it brings
before us what pertains to the present period—the
" new oblation " of Pentecost. This clearly sets
forth the assembly as " first-fruits " to God. This
has a definite connection with the preceding feast, for
the day of bringing and waving the sheaf of first-
fruits is the starting point from which the " seven
weeks " or " fifty days " are counted to the day of
presenting the " new oblation." The resurrection of
Christ is the starting point of a course of divine exercise
and education which results in the " two wave-loaves "
being brought out of the " dwellings " of God's people.
I understand this to convey that what is in God's
mind to effect gets such a place with His people that
they can bring it out of their dwellings in a definite
shape for His pleasure. But this is the result of a
" fifty days' " exercise following upon the apprehension of Christ risen as " First-fruits." We know what
filled those " fifty days " historically. The risen One
was seen " during forty days " by those " to whom
also he presented himself living, after he had suffered,

with many proofs." He spoke to them " of the things
which concern the kingdom of God." He " assembled
with them," and " by the Holy Spirit charged " them ;
educating them by His own action to think of assemb-
bling, and of acting by the Holy Spirit. He led them
to think of the Holy Spirit as the power which would
come upon them to constitute them His witnesses to
the end of the earth. Then He was taken up, and
was beheld by them going into heaven, and they were
told that He should " thus come in the manner in
which ye have beheld him going into heaven." Then
there were another ten days during which they knew
Him as having gone into heaven, and were characterised by going " up to the upper chamber," which was
an indication that they knew their relation to Him as
in heaven. The eleven were there, the women, Mary
the mother of Jesus, and His brethren. The true
" Israel of God " was there ; and it was not simply that
they *met* there ; they *stayed* there ; it corresponded
with the " dwellings " of Lev. 23 : 17. " Continual
prayer " marked that dwelling, an enlightened subjection to the Holy Scriptures, and a zealous care for
the witness and service which had been committed to
them. " And when the day of Pentecost was now
accomplishing, they were all together in one place.
And there came suddenly a sound out of heaven as of
a violent impetuous blowing, and filled all the house
where they were sitting. And there appeared to
them parted tongues, as of fire, and it sat upon each
one of them. And they were all filled with the Holy
Spirit, and began to speak with other tongues as the
Spirit gave to them to speak forth," Acts 2 : 1–4. It
was out of that dwelling that the " two wave-loaves "
were brought.

We have not in this type the truth of the assembly
as one body ; that, as we know, is symbolised by the
" one loaf," 1 Cor. 10 : 17. The " two wave-loaves "
would set forth rather the saints in their witness here
to Jesus as made Lord and Christ in heaven. They
are presented for God's pleasure as " a new oblation."
They take the place of Jesus here under the eye of
God, for He was the Oblation in all His perfection in
the power of the Spirit. But now there is " a new
oblation," not unleavened as He was, but " baken with
leaven " to intimate that it is composed of those in
whom there has been a former working of sin, but in
whom that working has ceased through the action of
fire—self-judgment in the power of the Spirit. Jesus
is no longer here personally, but He is maintained
here in witness in the " new oblation " for the pleasure
of God. The *two* loaves might have reference to the
mutuality and sympathy which marked the relations
of the saints one toward another, of which Acts 2 : 42–
44, 45 ; chap. 4 : 32 bear such blessed witness.

The " two wave-loaves " are " first-fruits to
Jehovah." This helps to define the aspect of the
assembly which is set before us in this type. It is
not the assembly in those heavenly relationships and
privileges which are peculiar to it, but the assembly
viewed as taking the place of Israel on earth, and
maintaining in testimony here what will be brought
forth for God in the great ingathering of the world to
come. On the day of Pentecost the kingdom of God
was here in the power of the Spirit, and there was
adequate witness to the One who is made Lord and
Christ in heaven. A witness not only in word, but in
the manner of life and mutual relations of a company
of men and women in this world. The substance of

that witness was " fine flour "—the life of Christ in His saints, taking form through self-judgment, and through the spiritual influences and education of those wonderful " fifty days," culminating in all being filled with the Holy Spirit. Such a result can only be brought out of " dwellings " that have the character seen in Acts 1 and 2. The " two wave-loaves " are the product of saints dwelling in the blessed conditions which are seen there. We have to know the power of those conditions in order to be true to the character of the assembly as set forth in the wave-loaves. Then the saints will be " first-fruits " ; they will express the features of Christ in the interval between His being " taken up " and His coming again.

God would have His people to come unitedly to the apprehension of what the day of Pentecost means, and what is involved in the bringing forth of the " new oblation." It raises the question of where we dwell, and what we can bring forth as " first-fruits." God would have us to think much of the assembly as filling up in witness this present interval during the absence of Christ in heaven, and before He resumes His ways with Israel on earth. If we do not cherish it in our " dwellings " we shall not be able to bring it forth as having taken form. Those who are known as " high church " people train their disciples to think much of " the church." But their " church " is the mustard tree or the leavened meal rather than the " treasure " or the " one pearl of great value," Matt. 13. It is the public professing body, in which people are supposed to be born again because they have been baptised, and to maintain a vital link with Christ by sacraments. In that system all depends on the validity of so-called " orders," so that it exalts a

human priesthood to a place of supreme importance.
And it makes all uncertain, for there is not a " priest "
on earth who can prove the validity of his " orders."
The Anglican claims to have such ; the Pope will not
acknowledge that he has ; and with the highest
authorities in the " church " disputing about it, who
can be sure ? In contrast with all this, let us think
much of the assembly as composed of all those who
believe on the Lord Jesus Christ, and love Him, and
as indwelt by the Spirit are in His life, and are really
" first-fruits " to God. Let us be more and more
exercised that this should be brought forth in testimony here ! We shall then be true churchmen ! The
tendency amongst some Protestants has been so to
recoil from the pretensions of a corrupt church that
they make individual blessing the great thing, and do
not think enough of what is collective and corporate.
Let us be good churchmen in a true and spiritual
sense ! God would bring His people into unity in
regard to the assembly. Every true believer cherishes
the thought of Christ ; then let us cherish the thought
of the assembly, for it is Christ's. Paul says, " I
speak as to Christ, and as to the assembly." The
assembly is of Christ, and for Christ.

Then with the bread are presented " seven he-lambs
without blemish, yearlings, and one young bullock,
and two rams : they shall be a burnt-offering to
Jehovah with their oblation, and their drink-offerings."
The saints as having the Spirit have a remarkable
capacity for the apprehension and appreciation of
Christ. I believe that no company will ever have
such apprehensions of Christ as the assembly. God
delights that we should take up His perfections and
bring them as " sweet odour." There is a sin-offering,

and peace-offerings also. God would bring us into perfect accord in the appreciation of Christ, and give us " to be like-minded one toward another, according to Christ Jesus ; that ye may with one accord, with one mouth, glorify the God and Father of our Lord Jesus Christ," Rom. 15 : 5, 6. The " offering up of the nations " as " acceptable, sanctified by the Holy Spirit " (Rom. 15 : 16) would be much like the wave-loaves.

The peace-offerings introduce the thought of the fellowship. The teaching of the apostles makes everything of Christ, and that forms the fellowship (Acts 2 : 42). The fellowship derives character from the appreciation of Christ, and the refusal of all that is inconsistent with the life of Christ. Then we can get near to one another, and there are all the elements of a " holy convocation " in love and liberty, nothing " servile " about it ; the saints by love serve one another.

This section of the chapter ends with a lovely touch of gracious consideration for " the poor " and " the stranger." It shows the spirit of grace which God would have to mark His people ; it is His own character reproducing itself in them. There will always be those who answer to " the poor " and " the stranger," and they are always to be thought of when God's people are reaping the rich harvest of their blessings in Christ.

Verses 23–25 are another section of the chapter, and this, and what follows, refers to what takes place " in the seventh month." The " seventh month " brings things to spiritual completion ; the set times or appointed seasons end in that month. Indeed it is definitely spoken of in Exodus 23 : 16 as " the end

of the year." So that there is a very marked difference between the feasts we have been considering and
those which now come before us. The passover, the
feast of unleavened bread, the wave-sheaf, and the two
wave-loaves presented fifty days later at Pentecost,
are all in relation to the *beginning* of the year. But
the seventh month has the *end* of the year in view.
The one set of types has to do with the *beginning* of
God's ways, the other set with the *end* of those ways.
To see this clearly is essential to the spiritual understanding of what is here set before us. All has a
primary reference to Israel, but it is not confined to
Israel, for the passover, the feast of unleavened bread,
Christ risen as the wave-sheaf of first-fruits, are all
seen in the New Testament to stand connected with
the assembly. And the " new oblation " of Pentecost is
clearly so also, though it does not regard the assembly
in its own peculiar privileges, but as " first-fruits " of
the great harvest which God is going to reap from the
earth.

The " seventh month " brings us to contemplate
the *end* of God's year—the end of His ways with His
people. His ways must reach the " expected end,"
for His thoughts toward His people are " thoughts of
peace, and not of evil, to give you in your latter end a
hope," Jer. 29 : 11. As regards Israel God has not
forgotten His ancient promises, and His gifts and
calling are not subject to repentance. Israel is in the
darkness of unbelief to-day. They broke the law,
despised the promises, persecuted and killed the
prophets, betrayed and murdered their Messiah, and
refused the Spirit's testimony to Him as risen and
glorified. But the promises must be fulfilled ; God's
end must be reached ; and the time is drawing near

when Israel will enter upon her " seventh month " and come on the first day of that month as the new moon into the shining of Christ. What " a memorial of blowing of trumpets " will there be on that day! " Blow the trumpet at the new moon, at the set time, on our feast day " (Ps. 81 : 3), will then be fulfilled. The Spirit of God will cause to sound afresh in Israel's ears all that is connected with the promises and covenant of God, and all that depends on her long-rejected Messiah for its realisation. What an awakening for Israel then, and for myriads of Gentiles, as the trumpets sound forth that Christ is in heaven, but that He is about to come back, and that the kingdom is almost immediately to be established!

Peter told them on the day of Pentecost that what they then witnessed was the very thing which the prophet Joel had said should be in the last days. The light of a risen and heavenly Christ was shining for Israel then, and the remnant came into it by God's electing grace, and there was a wonderful " blowing of trumpets." And wherever the apostles went " to the Jew first " they blew the trumpets, but the " joyful sound " fell on heedless ears save as there was " a remnant according to election of grace."

But " in the seventh month, on the first of the month," after the translation of the assembly, God will cause the light of a risen and heavenly Christ to shine again on a remnant in Israel, and the trumpets will sound to awaken Israel to the One who is coming in kingly glory to His city and His land. God will have the *end* of His ways in view, and He will work effectively to bring that end to pass.

Now while the primary application of this is to Israel, we can see that there has been something analogous in the ways of God with the assembly. A long period elapsed from Pentecost during which things went from good to bad, and from bad to worse. There was a long course of declension and departure. But God never lost sight of the assembly's heavenly portion and destiny, and I think we may say reverently that it was morally impossible for God to leave things in the state to which man's unfaithfulness had brought them. He had His own *end* in view—the return of the Bridegroom, and the translation of the raised and changed saints. It was morally impossible—that is, it was unsuitable to God—that Christ should come without a people being prepared for the rapture. The " blowing of trumpets " will awaken the remnant of Israel to their coming Messiah-King. In principle the midnight cry of Matthew 25 : 6 was a " blowing of trumpets " for the assembly.

If the assembly was no longer practically in the light of her glorious Head, nor answering to that light by an ungrieved indwelling Spirit, she must have what answers to the " seventh month " of revival, and of restored heavenly light and testimony. I have no doubt that " seventh month " in this sense began in those spiritual movements which preceded what men call the Reformation, and the light of Christ and the sound of the trumpets has been increasing ever since. And particularly during the last hundred years God has given a wonderful ministry of revival—a more glorious presentation of a risen and heavenly and coming Christ than has been known since the days of the apostles. How wonderful that God should have come in to give the assembly, as it were, a new start, in view of the end before Him ! So that the saints might take up afresh the character which pertained to the beginning—" unleavened bread " and the " new oblation." And that we might be prepared for the moment when " the Spirit and the bride say, Come ! "

Then the next section of the chapter (verses 26–32) gives us " the day of the atonement." This is " the tenth of this seventh month." We might have thought that the month should begin with this, but that is not the divine order. It is an awakened and revived people who keep the holy convocation of the day of atonement, and afflict their souls. I have no doubt that it will be in the light of Christ in heaven, and in the grace of the Spirit as poured out on them, that the remnant of Israel will learn the marvellous reality and import of the death of their Messiah.

The day of atonement, as we have seen in considering chapter 16, gives a unique presentation of the death of Christ. It comes in as meeting the glory of God after the complete failure of that which had stood in relation to Him. It supposes the breakdown of everything according to the flesh in a people who had a place in relation to God. It meets the exercise awakened by a history of departure and corruption, and the ruin of the outward order as set up by God. We have to take things up now in the light of the departure and complete failure of the people of God and the priesthood. Such will be the exercise of an awakened and enlightened Israel, and such is ours to-day. Each one must " afflict " his soul, for each one has been involved in the common sin of a ruined profession. Not one of us can say that we are not involved in the sin of christendom's departure from God. Most earnest Christians will admit there has been, and is, great failure, but the remedy which is generally proposed is increased activity. It is thought that if Christians were more earnest and energetic, things would be put right. But the case is too serious to be met that way. "Ye shall do no manner of work on that same day; for it is a day of atonement, to make atonement for you before Jehovah your God." It has to be met by the solemn recognition that all on our side has failed and come to ruin. This is a humbling exercise, but it leads to a great appreciation of the death of Christ and of the Mercy-seat. Everything that is for God is the fruit of mercy, and stands in the value of the death of Christ. The remnant includes all that is for God, and such have to learn that all blessing is the fruit of God acting from Himself when every title to blessing has been forfeited by man. It was so at the beginning; God brought in blessing not because there was anything in man to deserve it, but because of what He was, and because of the delight He had in Christ, and because of the value of the death of Christ. Now at the end of His ways He brings in recovery on the same principle.

One cannot but be impressed by the fact that the Spirit of God has greatly magnified the death of Christ in the spiritual apprehensions of saints in these last days. The true import of that death could only be apprehended in the light of Christ glorified, and by giving place to the Spirit. One of the greatest spiritual gains of recent times is the enlarged and deepened understanding of that precious death in its varied aspects, in its wondrous results for God and man, in its blessed import as bringing to an end the history of the man after the flesh, and giving full expression to the holy love of God, and also disclosing all the perfections of Christ in the fullest way, and revealing

His love for the saints individually and for the assembly. The way the Lord's Supper has been restored, and the revived affections of the saints in relation to it, is a very striking feature of the present ways of God, and it has greatly served to magnify the death of the Lord before the hearts of His own.

The closing section of the chapter brings before us " the feast of booths," which commenced on " the fifteenth day of this seventh month," and lasted seven days. It is referred to in Exodus as " the feast of ingathering," and here it is said, " when ye have gathered in the produce of the land." It thus looks on to the time when all the promises will be fulfilled, and Israel will be in the enjoyment of their full fruition. The moon would be full on the fifteenth day of the month, which suggests Israel having come into full-orbed splendour in the light of the Sun of righteousness. They will then be settled in the land, but their generations are to know that Jehovah causes the children of Israel to dwell in booths when He brought them out of the land of Egypt. They have reached the consummation of the ways of God, but they are not to forget the former history of those ways. Jehovah will then have praise from Israel, not only for the millennial blessedness which they enjoy, but for all those wilderness ways of grace by which He led them, and in which He cared for them in the past. In the actual presence of those ways they were murmurers and rebels, but they will eventually give Jehovah the praise that is due to Him for His ways, and for the end to which they have led. The " beautiful trees, palm branches and the boughs of leafy trees, and willows of the brook " speak of the luxuriance of the land, and its restful shade, while reminding them of a care that was equally wonderful in wilderness conditions. This is pre-eminently the feast of joy. " Ye shall rejoice before Jehovah your God seven days."

If the " feast of booths " brings us, in type, to the *end* of God's ways with Israel it remains for us to ask if there is anything that corresponds with it as the end of His ways with the assembly ? I have no doubt there is. The assembly has her own relation to the time which is prefigured by " the feast of booths." She has had made known to her " the mystery of his will, according to his good pleasure which he purposed in himself for the administration of the fulness of times ; to head up all things in the Christ, the things in the heavens and the things upon the earth ; in him, in whom we have also obtained an inheritance, being marked out beforehand according to the purpose of him who works all things according to the counsel of his own will, that we should be to the praise of his glory who have pre-trusted in the Christ." Then addressing Gentiles he adds, " In whom ye also have trusted, having heard the word of the truth, the glad tidings of your salvation ; in whom also, having believed, ye have been sealed with the Holy Spirit of promise, who is the earnest of our inheritance to the redemption of the acquired possession to the praise of his glory," Ephes. 1 : 9–14.

" The feast of booths " is typically that side of " the fulness of times " which relates to " the things upon the earth." To get the side which relates to " the things in the heavens " we must read the epistle to the Ephesians. We see there the assembly's part in Christ, and the inheritance which the saints of the present period have in Him. And the Holy Spirit of promise is the earnest of our inheritance. As sealed

with the Holy Spirit we have the enjoyment now of
the inheritance, for He is the " earnest " of it. He
gives us some of the value and blessedness of it beforehand ; we have some of the *substance* of it, so that it
is even now an " acquired possession," though we still
await the actuality.

In God's " great love wherewith he loved us (we
too being dead in offences)," He " has quickened us
with the Christ . . . and has raised us up together, and
has made us sit down together in the heavenlies in
Christ Jesus." The rapture is thus anticipated in
spirit ; the saints, quickened, elevated, and seated,
have reached in spirit the *end* which divine love has
purposed. And this in order that God " might display
in the coming ages the surpassing riches of his grace
in kindness towards us in Christ Jesus." We sit down
under all the beauty of a heavenly Christ in what may
be spoken of as " the eternal tabernacles." This is
the *end* of God's ways and working with His saints,
to which He would bring us in spirit even now. As
the saints reach this by the work of God they are
ready for the rapture, for they are already in spirit
where the rapture will put them actually. They have
reached God's *end* spiritually ; the rapture will bring
them to it in actuality. They are fully ready, in
concert with the Spirit, to say, Come !

Then there is a beautiful hint in the chapter before
us of something even beyond the " feast of booths."
That feast lasts seven days, but at the end of it there
is an " eighth day." I believe the joy of the millen-
nium will lead the saints on earth to desire and look
for what is eternal, and I have no doubt they will
reach " the eighth day " in the new earth, when the
tabernacle of God will be with men, and God will be

all in all. Indeed, as we know from Numbers 29, there will be a measure of decline through the seven days of the " feast of booths." No actual departure, but a measure of decline, so that there will not be the same wealth in the affections Godward at the end as at the beginning. The full moon of the fifteenth day —how true a figure of Israel !—will soon begin to wane. The flesh and blood condition was not God's eternal thought for man, and I think He will manifest this to faith by allowing it to appear that man in that condition even in millennial circumstances is not able to maintain full or perfect response to God. This will make the " eighth day " necessary for faith, as it surely is for God. Its being " the eighth day " shows that it has a connection with what has gone before, but adds a perfection that could never be found while men continued in the flesh and blood condition. They will look for the new earth with its eternal conditions, and its abiding rest. There will be no decline there, for God will be all in all. Every vessel will be filled with God—God known in His eternal rest.

We, too, through infinite grace, know something greater than " the fulness of times." Even the blessedness of the world to come must give place to God's eternal day. And our characteristic day is " the first day of the week." That is the beginning of what is wholly new, spiritual, and eternal. " In the last, the great day of the feast, Jesus stood and cried, saying, If any one thirst, let him come to me and drink. He that believes on me, as the scripture has said, out of his belly shall flow rivers of living water. But this he said concerning the Spirit, which they that believed on him were about to receive ; for the Spirit was not yet, because Jesus had not yet been glorified,"

John 7 : 37–39. The Lord thus connected the " eighth day " with the gift of the Spirit, and with Himself glorified. This introduces what is eternal. " The great day of the feast " is typical of God's eternal day.

It is by these wondrous things, which cover all the ways of God founded on redemption right on to His eternal rest, that God would bring His people together in unity. And this, as we have seen, not only in relation to His original thoughts, but—and this especially in our days—in relation to His blessed movements of recovery when all that He set up originally had been departed from. The " seventh month " speaks of recovery brought about by the renewed shining of Christ upon His people, by the sounding out of a special testimony, and by the exercises of the day of atonement, leading to the possession of that which God has given to His saints as their inheritance, and the ingathering of its fruits.

The unity of the people of God is brought about in a special manner in a day of departure. It is not only that God would have His people to be in unity as to the original basis of fellowship, but they are to be in unity as to the peculiar conditions of a day of revival and recovery. From Joshua's day to Nehemiah there was no celebration of the " feast of booths." In a day of recovery it was taken up by the returned remnant. We know how this history repeated itself in the assembly. The true *end* of God's ways was kept before the saints in those victorious days of spiritual conflict when the apostles were led in triumph in the Christ. That answered to Joshua's day. But for many centuries the " end " of God's year was little thought of. But now that that end has drawn nigh

He is bringing His people back from Babylonish
captivity to build the house and the wall, and to keep
the feast of booths. What a voice this has for those
who have " ears to hear " !

CHAPTER 24

THE teaching of this chapter has reference to a time
of general darkness, for it is " from evening to morning " that Aaron is to dress the lamp ; and in the
reviler we see a figure of apostasy. The whole chapter
is one section, for, as we have remarked before, each
section of this book is introduced by the words,
" Jehovah spoke to Moses." In the presence of surrounding darkness spiritual light is to be maintained,
and in presence of conditions which will culminate
in open apostasy the reality of how God would
retain His people before Him for His pleasure is
to be maintained in faith and love. These are
exercises which are peculiarly appropriate at the
present time. For it is still the night of Christ's
rejection, and apostasy is imminent in the Christian
profession.

It is the exercise of all saints to bring " pure beaten
olive oil " for the light, to light the lamp continually.
The shining of the light depends on each one ; every
one of us is either contributing to the light, or more or
less hindering and obscuring it. Not even an apostle
could bring a spiritual ministry among a carnal people.
Paul told the Corinthians plainly that he could not
speak to them " as to spiritual, but as to fleshly ; as to
babes in Christ. I have given you milk to drink, not
meat, for ye have not yet been able, nor indeed are

ye yet able ; for ye are yet carnal," 1 Cor. 3 : 1–3. Amongst a carnal people the ministry even of the greatest gift is restrained and limited, and unless there is extraordinary spiritual power in the vessels of ministry what is ministered soon drops to the level of the people.

The ministry of Christ is still here in the power of the Spirit, but it is maintained in human vessels, and through the spiritual exercises of the saints generally. We are all responsible to bring oil for the light. This supposes that we have bought oil for ourselves (Matt. 25 : 9), and have it in our vessels—that we have a supply of the Spirit, and are able to pray in the Holy Spirit. The saints, as possessed of the Spirit, are furnished with that which alone will maintain the light. The fact that we have the Spirit should beget peculiar and intense exercise ; this is suggested in " beaten " oil. It is as we give place to the Spirit ourselves that we can bring oil for the light. We are to be interested in the testimony, and prayerfully concerned about the servants and the ministry, not supposing that it rests with the gifts to supply the oil. The three thousand converted on the day of Pentecost " persevered in the teaching and fellowship of the apostles, in breaking of bread and *prayers*." No doubt their prayers would be largely of the same character as the prayer in Acts 4 : 29, which had its answer in verse 31. When Paul asks for the prayers of the Ephesian saints " in order that utterance may be given to me in the opening of my mouth to make known with boldness the mystery of the glad tidings . . . that I may be bold in it as I ought to speak," he is calling upon them to contribute to the maintenance of the light !

All through the night of Christ's rejection and absence He is to be maintained as light amongst the saints in a ministry which is wholly in the power of the Spirit. We have all to be concerned that the purity and brilliance of the light should not wane. It is striking how purity is emphasised in these verses— " pure beaten olive oil for the light," " the pure candlestick," " the pure table," " pure frankincense." There needs to be holy jealousy in a time of darkness and departure merging into apostasy that all connected with the light and the table should be maintained in purity, uncontaminated by human admixtures. This is " outside the veil."

Bringing beaten oil for the light suggests a spiritual exercise to be taken up by all saints, but it is instructive to see that *Aaron* was to dress the lamp continually from evening to morning. The priestly service of Christ in connection with the maintenance of the light is indispensable. Each vessel of ministry must prove that His grace alone suffices, and that His power is perfected in weakness, and that it is only as His power tabernacles over one that there can be a shedding forth of " pure " and spiritual light (2 Cor. 12 : 9). " The Lord stood with me, and gave me power, that through me the proclamation might be fully made, and all those of the nations should hear," 2 Tim. 4 : 17. It is sweet to know that the priestly dressing of the lamps, and their arrangement before God, will be carried on by the skilful hand of Christ until the " morning." Indeed all is of Himself, and by the grace of God. If spiritual conditions are brought about in the saints which enable them to contribute " oil for the light " it is the fruit of divine grace ; and then the living activities of Christ secure the continual shining of that precious ministry which is the light of the holy place.

We learn from Exodus 30 : 7 that whenever Aaron dressed the lamps he burned " fragrant incense " on the golden altar—" a continual incense before Jehovah throughout your generations." The maintenance of the light is associated with that which speaks of the intercession of Christ—an intercession in which the " holy priesthood " can have part with Him. Spiritual light cannot be maintained without prayer.

In the early days of the assembly the light was undimmed. There were spiritual and prayerful conditions amongst the saints, and the apostles and other gifts ministered Christ in purity, and in the power of the Holy Spirit. And I believe God is working now to bring about faithful and devoted affections in His people, so that spiritual conditions may contribute to a full shining of the light. He would have the light undimmed at the end even as it was at the beginning. The words " before Jehovah " occur four times in verses 1–8. It is a question of what is preserved in spiritual reality and power as before God for His pleasure. Is it not a great delight to God that there should be the shining forth in spiritual light of the preciousness and beauty and glory of Christ amongst His saints in the holy place while all around is darkness ? And while the very air of christendom is filled with the spirit of the coming apostasy ? If things are secured first before God for His pleasure there can be no doubt they will be effective as witness here.

Then the " twelve cakes " of " fine wheaten flour " speak of the saints as having Christ as their life. We cannot be too simple in recognising that God has brought in everything for His own pleasure in Christ,

and that nothing else can come under His eye with
complacency. It was once all here in " one loaf," but
now it is in " twelve." God is going to make what
was in Christ appear in the whole company of His
people. It would be well for every young convert to
get the idea at the very beginning, ' God has taken me
up that Christ might be my life, and that He might
make me like Christ.' Such a thought would have a
profound effect on his whole subsequent course.

" Christ . . . who is our life," is a wonderful statement. I understand it to mean that what the world
is to the unconverted, Christ has become to the
Christian company. He has become our life. An old
man was asked, " If I could prove that there was no
such person as the Lord Jesus Christ, what effect would
it have upon you ? " His answer was, " I should fall
to pieces " ! Every true lover of Christ would say,
" If you take away Christ you have taken all that is life
to me." The pleasure of God at the present moment
is found in those to whom Christ has become life.
Christ is cherished in their hearts as the Man of God's
pleasure, and therefore they cannot go on now with
what is not after Christ. It is their continual exercise
to give place to Christ, and to refuse what is not Christ.
In that way the " fine wheaten flour " comes into
evidence. It is remarkable that the twelve cakes
should be spoken of as " an offering by fire to Jehovah "
(verses 7, 9), for they were not burned as a sweet
odour, but eaten by the priests. As baked they had
been subject to the action of fire, and perhaps this
indicates that there are testings which result in what
is of Christ taking a definite shape in the saints for
the pleasure of God. They come before Him as the
fruit of exercises which they have passed through,

involving severe testing, but resulting in their having
value as an offering.

The " two wave-loaves " of Pentecost typify the
saints as found here in testimony—the " first-fruits "
to God of that great harvest which He will gather
from the earth. But the " twelve cakes " of shewbread give the thought of what is before God as " a
bread of remembrance." They bring before God the
remembrance of what Christ was under His eye for
His delight, and they indicate that God has it before
Him in view of public administration. That character
of things is soon to be in universal ascendency, and
the world to come will be under its administration.
" When the Christ is manifested who is our life, then
shall ye also be manifested with him in glory," Col.
3 : 4. Think of being in the secret of this while all
is darkness around, and the elements of apostasy
present !

The " two tenths " in each cake would suggest
uniformity. We do not see here a figure of the saints
as differing in divine sovereignty, having " distinctions
of gifts," as in 1 Cor. 12 or Rom. 12, but, as being
all alike morally because Christ is the life of all. What
we get in Colossians down to chapter 3 : 17 are things
in which the saints are characterised by uniformity.
It is the grace of Christ in features which are alike in
all. We can all be alike in " bowels of compassion,
kindness, lowliness, meekness, longsuffering," and in
" love which is the bond of perfectness." All that is
" fine wheaten flour." The saints are thus seen in
spiritual uniformity, as taking constitution and
character from Christ. What a delight for the heart
of God !

The " two rows, six in a row " suggest to my mind

the thought of mutuality. In Colossians the words " one another " recur again and again. " Do not lie to one another " ; " forbearing one another, and forgiving one another " ; " in all wisdom teaching and admonishing one another." This is not *fellowship*, which is our common bond in a hostile scene, but *mutuality*—the way we act towards one another in the Christian circle.

" Pure frankincense upon each row " would refer, I think, to the Spirit of Christ coming out in the way we pray for one another, and for all saints. Paul had deep exercise for the Colossians, and those in Laodicea, and for as many as had not seen his face in flesh (Col. 2 : 1). And he looked for the saints to " persevere in prayer, watching in it with thanksgiving ; praying at the same time for us also." He reminds them, too, the Epaphras was " always combating earnestly for you in prayers, to the end that ye may stand perfect and complete in all the will of God," chap. 4 : 2, 12. The saints are thus before God in the fragrance of a spirit of dependence and confidence in which everything is sought from God that will be for His pleasure. It suggests that the saints cannot be upon the pure table as a bread of remembrance apart from the fragrance of a spirit of intercession that confides in God, and draws all from God. I do not believe that a single grace of Christ appears in the saints under the eye of God, or is maintained, apart from prayer.*

The one who " blasphemed the Name " (verses 10– 23) represents that amongst the people of God which is really apostasy. It is the product of a mixture of what is of God with what is of the world ; for he was

---

* For other remarks on the candlestick and the shewbread, the reader is referred to " An Outline of Exodus," chapter 25.

" the son of an Israelitish woman, but withal the son of an Egyptian." Where such a mixture is found it leads to strife, and ultimately to blasphemy. When that point is publicly reached in what has been the Christian profession it will come under the unsparing judgment of God.

CHAPTER 25

CHAPTERS 25 and 26 bring out the conditions on which " the land that I will give you " could be held and enjoyed. God would have His people ever to remember that the land was *His*. They were not to be independent proprietors of the freehold. They were to hold it as the gift of sovereign love, and to hold it in relation to the Giver ; it was His inheritance (Exod. 15 : 17), and they were " to him a people of inheritance," Deut. 4 : 20. Their title was one of absolute grace, but the rights in grace of the Giver were always reserved. This brought out the state of their hearts. Apart from a right attitude of heart towards the One who had conferred the inheritance there could be neither true appreciation of the inheritance, nor any right possession of it. They might be actually in Canaan through God's providential ordering and His forbearance, but if the land were not held in relation to the Giver it morally ceased to be the inheritance.

On Jehovah's part all that He claimed were rights of grace. The Pentateuch does not contain a more touching expression of God's rights in grace than is set forth in this chapter. The sabbatical year, and the year of jubilee with its provisions of liberty and

complete restoration show the character of the Giver
of the land, and the spirit with which He would have
all His heirs imbued. And they bring out, typically,
the ultimate issue of His ways with His people. The
" sabbath of rest " speaks of what remains to be
entered into, and the " year of jubilee " of that
complete restoration in grace under new covenant
conditions by which Israel will return to all that they
have forfeited by their sin and unbelief ; and, indeed,
by which they will for the first time truly enter into
God's rest. For, as we know, Joshua did not really
bring them into the rest of the inheritance (Heb. 4 : 8),
though they came in an outward way into the land
of Canaan. The true fulfilment of God's promises
and purposes as to Israel's inheritance and entering
into His rest awaits a yet future day.

In the meantime the love of God has given to the
partakers of the heavenly calling a wondrous inheritance in Christ. But it can only be enjoyed with Him
as we hold it in a sense of the love that has given it,
and with reference to His will in the use we make of
it. We are tested as to how we take up the spiritual
blessings which God has given us, and whether we
really hold them in relation to Him, and to all that
is before Him for His pleasure. What God has given
us in Christ is the expression and witness of His love,
and as we thus hold it we wish to take up the great
gain of it in relation to His pleasure. Otherwise the
abundance of the blessing may turn to self-consideration, and the joy of it with God be lost. We may
be occupied with what " the land " is to us, and not
hold it in relation to the love and pleasure of God.
There is a warning as to this in the fact that the
sabbatical year probably ceased to be observed about

Solomon's time, as we gather by reckoning back 490 years from 2 Chronicles 36 : 21.

The " sabbath of rest " in the seventh year was a wonderful testimony to what was in the heart of God. *Love* gave the land, and love would have it to be held in relation to what was before God. His thought was to bring in rest. God was the great Worker in Genesis 1, but He worked in view of rest on the seventh day, and when that day came He blessed and hallowed it " because that on it he rested from all his work which God had created in making it," Gen. 2 : 3. God ever has in view His own rest, and His pleasure that His people should share in it. Sin has made Him a Worker for well-nigh six thousand years, but He cherishes the thought of rest for Himself and His people. God would bring us under the influence of His love into sympathy with what He delights in.

I have no doubt that God uses the toil and burden of things here, and even labour and travail in the Lord's interests and service, to develop desires that are in harmony with His own. The young are energetic and think of work, but the older we get the more we cherish the thought of rest. Read J.N.D.'s hymns, and see how often the thought of *rest* comes in ! His desires were formed in harmony with God's.

The weekly sabbath was continually saying to the people that God delighted in rest, and in having His people in rest before Him. And the sabbatical year said the same thing in a larger and more impressive way. " A sabbath of rest for the land, a sabbath to Jehovah . . . a year of rest shall it be for the land." We may be sure that God would not reiterate the sabbath thought so frequently if it had not a great place in His own mind. He has cherished all through the thought of that blessed time when He " will rest in his love," Zeph. 3 : 17. He was ever saying, as it were, ' My great thought is that you should share My rest, and enjoy My love in that rest.' A toil-less year of rest would yield abundant food (verses 6, 7) ; instead of losing by keeping the sabbatical year, they would only the more prove the wealth of the land. It was a whole year undisturbed by toil—no sowing the field, no pruning the vineyard, no reaping even what sprang up from scattered seed, no gathering of grapes even from undressed vines ! Nothing to do but to enjoy in restful obedience that which love had freely given !

The great pleasure of God is that we should be restful, and enjoy what He has given us in His great love. He would have us near to Him to know what He values, and to be in the light and gain of His rest in Christ. The people went into captivity for seventy years because the land had not " enjoyed its sabbaths " (2 Chron. 36 : 21) ; and if we do not keep our sabbaths we shall, sooner or later, fall under the power of what is of man. To enter into God's rest is a greater pleasure to God than any labours of ours could be ; it is presented in Scripture as complete blessedness. It will be entered into by Israel in millennial conditions ; it is anticipated in spirit by those who believe (Heb. 4 : 3), who enter into that which will characterise the world to come, when the rest of God will be publicly introduced. The sabbatical year is a typical fore-shadowing of that period.

I suppose that the sabbatical year and the " year of release," in Deuteronomy 15 were probably con-current. In the year of release every creditor remitted his claim. A people whose many transgressions have been forgiven, and their sins blotted out and remembered no more, should not find it difficult to " make a release " even of what might be a just claim. We are to be " compassionate, forgiving one another, so as God also in Christ has forgiven you," Ephes. 4 : 32. People say sometimes, " But I want righteousness ! " Well, righteousness at the present time is to act toward others on the ·same principle as God has acted toward us. We see this in Matthew 18 : 21–35. As to what may be personally due to us let us not hold anything in our hearts against one another. Let us " make a release," let us " relax " our hand. " He shall not demand it of his neighbour, or of his brother ; for a release to Jehovah hath been proclaimed," Deut. 15 : 2. It is a " release to Jehovah " ! It is a little opportunity to show to the blessed God that we appreciate His wondrous forgiving grace, and that we are in the spirit of it towards our neighbour and brother.

Then after " seven sabbaths of years, seven times seven years . . . shalt thou cause the loud sound of the trumpet to go forth in the seventh month, on the tenth of the month ; on the day of atonement shall ye cause the trumpet to go forth throughout your land " (verses 8, 9). The " year of jubilee " speaks of liberty, and the restoration in pure grace and sovereign mercy—based on atonement—of all that has been forfeited by Israel. It looks on to that day of restoration when " the great trumpet shall be blown ; and they shall come that were perishing in the land of Assyria, and the outcasts in the land of Egypt, and they shall worship Jehovah in the holy mountain at Jerusalem," Isa. 27 : 13.

" And ye shall return every man unto his possession,

and ye shall return every man unto his family " (verse 10). This supposes that the pessession has been forfeited, that the people on their side have lost their inheritance. But God says, so to speak, " I will have the last word ; I will not give up the thoughts of my love ; every man shall return to his possession." What a comfort to know that God will have the last word in relation to Israel ! After all their unbelief, unfaithfulness, and rebellion He will in sovereign mercy cause the trumpet of jubilee to sound, and they will return to their possession. They will come into their inheritance on the footing of atonement and of Christ. I do not suppose that any of them will be able to prove their genealogical title. They will have to get their title from Christ, who as the heavenly Priest has the Urim and Thummim (Nehem. 7 : 64, 65). Israel's title and genealogy are preserved in the breast-plate of that glorious Priest who has never forgotten them, though they have at present no thought of Him.

And if God will have the last word in relation to Israel, we may be sure He will have the last word in relation to saints of the assembly, and to every other family of the redeemed. How much was given to the assembly ! It was set up in all the blessedness of the love of God, known by the Holy Spirit. It was enriched with the unsearchable riches of the Christ—the glorious Head in heaven. It was blessed with every spiritual blessing in the heavenlies in Christ.

A long history of failure has come in, but it has not changed God's thoughts, or the purposes of His love, and He will eventually bring His saints into all that He has purposed for them in Christ. At the rapture He will place them all in the everlasting possession and enjoyment of what His love has given to them in Christ. A trumpet is very soon to sound which will " in an instant, in the twinkling of an eye," introduce the saints into " the glory of the children of God." The dead raised incorruptible, the living changed, and both caught up together in spiritual and glorified bodies to meet the Lord in the air, and to be ever with Him. 1 Cor. 15 : 51, 52 ; 1 Thess. 4 : 15–18. It is delightful to think of the saints being actually introduced by divine power in an incorruptible condition into all that divine love has purposed for them. The full possession and enjoyment of their incorruptible and undefiled and unfading heavenly inheritance will then be theirs, never to be alienated.

" The anxious looking out of the creature expects the revelation of the sons of God . . . the creature itself also shall be set free from the bondage of corruption into the liberty of the glory of the children of God," Rom. 8 : 19–21. The sons of God will be revealed in company with the Firstborn, and the creature will be freed from bondage, and brought into the liberty of the glory of the children of God. What a jubilee will that be ! What a triumphant last word on God's part after all the unfaithfulness of men ! The assembly glorified in its heavenly portion, Israel reinstated on earth in the land of her possession, and the whole creation liberated from thraldom, and set in the value of reconciliation ! And all this brought about purely by divine mercy and grace on the basis of atonement, and by a power that gives effect to all the purposes of God.

No question is raised at the jubilee as to how a man came into bondage and lost his possession. The past, with all its sorrowful history of failure, is blotted out ; the day of atonement meets it all ; and the exercises of the people on that day justify God, and prepare them for blessing which is wholly of God. It will be so with Israel : it will be so with saints of the present period. *They* lost the land of their possession by unfaithfulness. And how many saints of the assembly are practically not in possession and enjoyment of their blessings in the heavenlies ! Indeed it may be said that the church, as a whole, has sold its heavenly possession for earthly things. But the assembling shout of the descending Lord, with archangel's voice and trump of God, will place the heavenly saints in complete and everlasting possession of their inheritance ; while shortly afterwards the trumpet of jubilee will sound for the reinstatement of Israel. But this chapter suggests to us the possibility also of returning to our possession even before the jubilee, as we shall see presently.

A section comes in here which has a very practical bearing. Buying and selling were to be according to the nearness or remoteness of the jubilee (verses 14–16). Our estimation of the value of things will show pretty accurately whether we regard the jubilee as near or distant. There are " sufferings of this present time," but they " are not worthy to be compared with the coming glory to be revealed to us," Rom. 8 : 18. The jubilee was not distant to Paul's heart when he spoke of his affliction as " momentary and light " ; the " eternal weight of glory " was near —the things not seen (2 Cor. 4 : 17, 18). He took a light estimate of the affliction because the glory was near ! And as to earthly advantages—the acquisition of wealth, position, name—what would they all be to us if we were momentarily expecting to hear the assembling shout of our Lord ? Alas ! I am afraid we often say in our hearts, if not with our lips, " My Lord delayeth His coming." The Lord said, " I come *quickly.*" Did He not know that nearly two thousand years would elapse ? Yes, He did, but He said, " quickly " because it was going to be near *His* heart all the time, and He wanted it to be near ours.

During a great part of the last century there was much ministry about the coming of the Lord ; it occupied the attention of saints very largely ; and the novelty of the teaching awakened a more or less deep interest in thousands. Now the freshness attaching to a newly recovered truth has passed ; we no longer need pamphlets or addresses to enlighten us as to the truth of the Lord's coming ; it is an accepted teaching with us. But there is now the danger of accepting and holding the truth without being much practically affected by it. How does it affect our practical outlook ? Are we estimating the value of things here in relation to the jubilee ? Whether it be sufferings or advantages, are we soberly taking account of them in view of the nearness of the rapture, and of " the times of the restoring of all things, of which God has spoken by the mouth of his holy prophets since time began " ? (Acts 3 : 21).

It has often been pointed out that there is an analogy between the seven weeks ending in Pentecost (Lev. 23 : 15) and the seven times seven years followed by the year of Jubilee. Pentecost brought to light that which is " first-fruits," in the power of the Holy Spirit sent down from heaven, of the great result for God in the world to come. But the year of Jubilee is typical of the complete restoration of Israel

J

—" liberty in the land unto all the inhabitants thereof "
—when their fulness will be the world's wealth in a
way far surpassing what their fall and loss have been
(Rom. 11 : 12–15). Pentecost was the fiftieth day, and
it was " the morning after the seventh sabbath." It
was the beginning of a new period, when all the
promises of God were known as substantiated in a
risen and glorified Christ, and the Holy Spirit was
here to be the power of witness to Him. The jubilee
is the fiftieth year, and it will bring in the fulfilment
of all the promises by the " times of refreshing "
coming from the presence of the Lord. It answers
to " the fulness of times " in Ephes. 1 : 10. " The
acceptable year of the Lord " was preached by the
Son of God (Luke 4 : 19), and it was made known
here spiritually in the testimony of the Holy Spirit
who came down at Pentecost, but it will be introduced
actually when the Lord comes again.

I think the fiftieth day in each case indicates that
a new element is brought in as connected with the
ways of God on the earth, but not exactly forming
part of those ways. The presence of a glorified Christ
in heaven was plainly spoken of in the Old Testament
(Ps. 68 : 18 ; 110 : 1), and such a wondrous fact
brought in a new character of blessing and testimony.
The Holy Spirit came down to make good in men the
influence of what was established in a glorified Man in
heaven, and thus the Pentecostal " first-fruits " were
brought forth. The Messiah glorified in heaven was
a new starting point for all blessing. All the promises
were confirmed and established, not by being fulfilled
in the ways of God on earth, but by being substantiated
in the Person of Christ as a risen and glorified Man in
heaven.

And the jubilee is " the fiftieth year." I think it
indicates that the consummation of the divine ways
on earth will come about as a result of divine actings
which are additional to those ways. The sons of God
—the joint-heirs with Christ—have been called during
this wondrous interval between the descent of the
Spirit at Pentecost and the calling up of the heavenly
saints at the rapture. A company has been called
and secured for a place in heaven according to eternal
counsels of love—a company of many brethren pre-
destinated to be conformed to the image of God's
glorified Son, that He may be the Firstborn among
them. This is outside the weeks of earth ; it is
above and beyond the sabbath periods, which always
refer, I believe, to God's works and ways on earth,
and their consummation in the introduction of His
rest in millennial blessedness. But that consummation will be connected with the shining forth of the
glory of a heavenly Christ, and with the revelation of
the sons of God who have been called to have a place
in heaven with Him. This will give a peculiar
character to the liberty into which " the creature "
—that is, everything connected with this creation
which now groans under the bondage of corruption—
will be brought. It is " the liberty of the glory of the
children of God." So that there is not only the
intensified perfection of the " seven sabbaths of years,
seven times seven years ; so that the days of the
seven sabbaths of years shall be unto thee forty-nine
years." That would suggest the winding up in
perfect rest of the ways of God with man on the earth.
But there is a " fiftieth year," which suggests that the
earth will also partake in the wondrous gain which
will come to creation through the shining forth of that

company of sons who are the fruit of the eternal purpose of God's love, and who have their place in heavenly glory outside God's ways with the earth. So that the liberated creation will not only have the fulfilment of all the Old Testament promises, which bring in sabbath conditions where the vanity, bondage, and groaning and travailing in pain have been. But they will enjoy those conditions in the light of " the revelation of the sons of God." The shining forth of the heavenly families will give an additional glory to the scene, and will give character to the liberty which pervades it. I think this is suggested by the fact that the jubilee is " the fiftieth year."

The Old Testament contains hints of the blessed fact that God intended to bring the earth under the influence of what He established in heaven. Daniel 7 : 22 speaks of the Ancient of days coming, and judgment being given " to the saints of the most high places "—clearly the heavenly saints. And the New Testament tells us that " the righteous shall shine forth as the sun in the kingdom of their Father," Matt. 13 : 43. And that " at the revelation of the Lord Jesus from heaven . . . he shall have come to be glorified in his saints, and wondered at in all that have believed," 2 Thess. 1 : 10. The place which the heavenly saints have in the kingdom is thus a most important feature of it. Their calling and heavenly place are something additional to God's ways with the earth, but not unconnected with those ways, as it is the revelation of the heavenly sons which will give character to the restoration and liberty of earth's jubilee. My impression is that this is intimated in " the fiftieth year." It will secure not only Israel's blessing, but the emancipation of the whole creation.

It will mean the undoing of all that has come in by sin and Satan's power.

Jehovah says, " And the land shall not be sold for ever ; for the land is mine." It is *His* land. The people may refuse " the waters of Shiloah which flow softly " (Shiloah means " sending forth " ; it probably refers to the prophetic word of promise in regard to Christ) ; and they may rejoice in " Rezin and in the son of Remaliah "—kings of Syria and Israel—and in divine judgment the Assyrian may come and over-flow the land, but it is still " thy land, O Immanuel," Isa. 8 : 5–8. The Turks have had it for centuries, the British have it now, but it is still Immanuel's land. He will not enjoy His land until His people enjoy it. I think this must be the force of " ye are strangers and sojourners with me," Lev. 25 : 23. When Immanuel came in He had no possession in the land that was His ; He was the true Stranger and Sojourner ; He had not where to lay His head. He came in to be with a disinherited remnant, and to have them with Him. He was Immanuel—God with us. He was with repentant ones, with those who were poor in spirit, mourners, meek, hungering and thirsting after righteousness, merciful, pure in heart, peace-makers, those persecuted on account of righteousness. In view of the redemption of the purchased possession it is important to see the kind of heirs that can take it up. It is a people of this kind who are the children God has given Him. " Immanuel " speaks of the grace in which He was *with them*, but " *with me* " speaks of their great and peculiar privilege—though having lost possession of the land—of being *with Him*, and sharing His Stranger-ship.

Does it not touch our hearts to think that the One who is entitled to everything here—the One who can say, " The land is mine," and who is claiming that land claims the right to dispose of the earth as He will—is a Stranger and Sojourner ? He is not in possession of His rights here, so the place of the joint-heirs is to be " strangers and sojourners " with Him. Peter addresses the people of God in this character (1 Peter 1 : 1; chap. 2 : 11). It has ever been faith's place here, and ever will be until Immanuel takes up His rights in the true year of jubilee. We " have been sealed with the Holy Spirit of promise, who is the earnest of our inheritance "—and that a heavenly one—but as to our place on earth we are " strangers and sojourners."

Verse 25 shows that if one who has sold his possession has a wealthy kinsman he may have it redeemed, and may return to it before the jubilee. This is very interesting, for it sets forth what is available at the present time. Israel grew poor and sold his possession. A blessed Kinsman came in with the right of redemption ; but Israel—save a small remnant—spurned the Kinsman-redeemer, and lost his golden opportunity. He will have to wait now until the jubilee to return to his possession. But in the meantime the remnant who received the Messiah got a better inheritance—a heavenly one—in association with Him. And a day is coming when the remnant, as having forfeited all right to the promises, and therefore typified by Ruth the Moabitess, will cast herself upon the grace of Christ as the true Boaz —the " mighty man of wealth "—and will learn what a Redeemer He is.

Many a Christian to-day has practically sold his

possession. He has become spiritually impoverished, and got his mind on " the things that are on the earth." He has sold his possession at a very low price, for he has given up the spiritual and the heavenly for a bit of the world or the earth. It may be that " there was a famine in the land " ! For some reason in the government of God there was a shortage of spiritual food, and the believer went to sojourn " in the fields of Moab," only to be disciplined there, and to find that all turns to bitterness. But then there comes a gracious report " how that Jehovah had visited his people to give them bread," and a desire is awakened to return. Is there any means of being restored to his possession now, or must he wait for that assembling shout which will be, in a certain way, our jubilee ? Thank God ! there is still a Boaz for every returning Naomi and Ruth—a Kinsman who can redeem what has been forfeited or sold ! Our Kinsman loves us, and it lies in His ability to secure for us now a return to the full possession and enjoyment of our spiritual and God-given possession. He is the " mighty man of wealth " in Bethlehem (the house of bread) before He is King in Zion. " In him is strength " to reinstate an impoverished one in possession of an inheritance which has been sold. This speaks not of the original gift of divine love, but of the peculiar strength of that love in granting recovery and restoration when that gift has been departed from. If there is a desire to return on the part of one who is conscious of having got away, grace would encourage that one to come back and lay down at the feet of the true Boaz. Put yourself absolutely in His hands. He will spread His wing over you, and secure all for you, though you may be conscious that you have no title to anything. The only claim you have is that which *grace* gives. The grace of the jubilee can be known beforehand in the Kinsman-Redeemer. We are " not left . . . this day without one that has the right of redemption." He can reinstate even one who has sold his possession ! What precious grace ! The Book of Ruth brings Christ before us in this blessed character.

The whole character of the Lord's ways with saints of the assembly at the present moment is one of recovery, and restoration of lost privilege. The saints are soon going to be translated, but in the meantime a great spiritual revival is going on. The presence of the Holy Spirit—so long practically ignored—is being recognised by many. The affections of the saints are being stirred up to hold the Head, and to love one another, and to reach after the possession and enjoyment of what is spiritual and heavenly. In this way they are returning to their possession in anticipation of that moment when they will be actually with Christ in the heavenlies.

If one sold a " dwelling house in a walled city " there was a limited period during which the seller had the right of redemption ; if he did not exercise that right he lost it for ever. It was a warning to the Jew that there was something which he might lose for ever—which not even the jubilee would restore to him. " The fields of the country " would speak, I think, of earthly blessing ; but the " walled city " speaks of what is enclosed. It speaks of a community with its own exclusive privileges. A " walled city " has a distinctive character and collective life of its own, with a definite separation from all that surrounds it. It typifies the place which the assembly has here. God gave the Jew an opportunity to have a house in that " walled city," but he sold his dwelling, and he did not redeem it within the " full year." The book of the Acts shows us, I think, the " full year " during which the dwelling might have been redeemed, and then it passed into the hand of the Gentile.

Have we " bought " a dwelling in that " walled city " ? It costs something to have a dwelling in that city, but it is worth more than all it costs. We are tested as to whether we prefer earthly things—" the fields of the country "—or a dwelling in the " walled city." In the assembly viewed as the " walled city " everything is made of Christ ; nothing else has any importance or standing ; its walls exclude all that is of man after the flesh. His wisdom, his righteousness, his religion, every part of his glory are outside its walls. That city stands in holy separation from the world, and from all that is earthly in a religious way.

It is good to see that " the Levites shall have a perpetual right of redemption " (verse 32). The Levites had cities, but they had no inheritance among the children of Israel (Num. 18 : 23) ; they typify " the assembly of the firstborn ones who are enregistered in heaven," Heb. 12 : 23. The portion of a heavenly people can never be alienated ; it is " a perpetual possession." " The field of the suburbs of their cities shall not be sold." God will secure to us as much of earthly mercy as we need so long as we are here, but the place we hold here is that of a people whose inheritance is a heavenly one.

Then we have the thought of a brother grown poor, and " fallen into decay " (verse 35), or even " sold unto thee " (verse 39), or sold unto a wealthy stranger (verse 47). The whole chapter contemplates in different forms a reduced and impoverished state—a state in which the original wealth of the inheritance has been forfeited. But it is full of the spirit of grace. The poor brother is to be cared for, the one sold is not to be treated as a bondservant, and if sold to a wealthy stranger there is still to be " right of redemption for him," and full liberty in the year of jubilee. Jehovah says, " They are my bondmen." It is as much as to say, You must be considerate for them because they are Mine. How touching the grace of it ! Does it not teach us tender and gracious consideration for those who belong to God, however impoverished and decayed they may be ? There is perhaps with us a tendency not to care enough for those who do not get on spiritually. We feel it is their own fault that they have " fallen into decay," and this may be true ; but do they belong to God ? If so, they are to be cared for. It is due to God that they should be the subjects of considerate and kindly interest.

This chapter magnifies the grace that deals wondrously with those who have, on their side, lost their possessions. The whole chapter is coloured by the grace of the jubilee. God will have the last word. Whatever happens on our side, His unfailing grace will assert itself, and every one will return to his possession. When the trumpet of jubilee sounds the power of sovereign divine love will place the heirs in possession and enjoyment of the inheritance. It will be known then that " of him, and through him, and for him are all things : to him be glory for ever. Amen."

CHAPTER 26

CHAPTER 25 is a wonderful unfolding of *grace* which
restores to the people of God's election all that has
been forfeited or unworthily surrendered. God had
the first word with them, and He will have the last.
But chapter 26 comes in also, and it sets before us
God's ways in *government*. It is a continual exercise
to hold these two great principles of the divine ways
in their full weight and power without allowing the
one to enfeeble the other. We shall see that both
combine to reach the same end. For God's governmental ways issue in His people accepting the punishment of their iniquity, and confessing their unfaithfulness. Then He remembers His covenant and His
land (verses 40–45). Both His grace and His government will result in His people enjoying all that His
heart delighted to give them, and being suitable to
enjoy it.

It is a great thing to be brought consciously to God
as revealed in grace in His beloved Son. God began
with us in grace, and grace begun will end in glory.
But He would have us to be kept in sobriety and godly
fear as knowing also that we are the subjects of His
government. God would have this ever to be a happy
thought to us, because if we keep His commandments
His government ensures that we shall be recompensed
in the fullest way. See verses 3–13. It pays well, if
we may be allowed to use such an expression, to walk
in obedience and faithfulness. God has set " glory
and honour and incorruptibility " before us in our
Lord Jesus Christ, a living Man out of death ; and if,
" in patient continuance of good works," we seek for
those things He will render to us life eternal. There

is " glory and honour and peace to every one that works good," Rom. 2 : 6–11. " If, by the Spirit, ye put to death the deeds of the body, ye shall live," Rom. 8 : 13. " Whatever a man shall sow, that also shall he reap . . . he that sows to the Spirit, from the Spirit shall reap eternal life," Gal. 6 : 7, 8. This is the good news of the government of God. We are apt to think of the government of God as always operating against what is wrong, and not to think sufficiently of how it operates to bring in spiritual gain when we move according to the Spirit. It is our privilege to reach God's end in a happy way, and to have continual prosperity because our course is such that God's government is always in our favour. Part of the blessedness that we have come to is " God the judge of all." He is taking account of every bit of response to His love, of desire to follow Christ, of purpose to walk in the Spirit, every manifestation of love to His people, every wish to contribute to their edification. He will in His government seal to us the fruit of every spiritual movement of this kind.

God is concerned most about the state of our hearts with reference to Him. Hebrews 12 tells us that He is " the Father of spirits " ; He is concerned about our spirits. What He looked for in Israel was that they should have no idols, and that they should observe His sabbaths, and reverence His sanctuary (verses 1, 2). These things tested the people as to the place Jehovah had in their hearts, and they still test us individually and collectively. Is God the supreme Object to us, as revealed in Christ, or have we other objects which practically control us and displace Him ? I would not like to impoverish my soul by falling under the power of an idol. Do we love to answer to the thoughts of God's heart, and value the opportunity of being restful with Him ? And do we reverence His sanctuary ? God would have the whole divine system which was set forth in the tabernacle reverenced in our affections. If people go into a religious building they take off their hats·; they reverence the material structure. But God would have us to reverence His sanctuary in a spiritual sense. The sanctuary is the whole order of things which takes character from the holiest, and from God dwelling there ; it is " the abode of his holiness."

There are infinitely great blessings which come in according to this chapter, on the line of God's govern-ment. " Rain in the season thereof, and the land shall yield its produce, and the trees of the field shall yield their fruit, etc." There is peace, victory, God's face is towards His people, He sets His habitation among them. " I will walk among you, and will be your God, and ye shall be to me a people." This scripture is quoted in 2 Corinthians 6 : 16 to induce the Corinthians to come out and be separate from the idolatrous and unbelieving. God loves to set His tabernacle among His people, and to dwell there restfully, but this demands holy and spiritual con-ditions. Then " I will walk among you," indicates that divine movements are found among the people of God. The assembly is " the assembly of the living God " ; it is the place where His movements and activities are known. He overrules and controls the affairs of nations in the world, but what we see there are the movements of men. It is only amongst His separate and obedient people that the movements of God are known ; it is there He walks.

But if His people do not hearken to Him, or do His commandments, His government becomes adverse to them. See verses 14–39. There is a solemn contrast between the sabbatic sevens in chapter 25 and the four-times-repeated " sevenfold " in chapter 26. Yet even in this we see the patience and persistence of God. He moves deliberately from one stage of corrective discipline to another until He reaches His end. There are five distinct stages of correction in these verses. He will have the last word in His government as well as in His grace, and a refusal to hearken on the part of His people only prolongs and intensifies His correction. All that He so faithfully forewarned Israel of in this chapter has come to pass. They have now perished among the nations, and the land of their enemies has eaten them up (verse 38). But He will yet reach the end of His ways in government with them. They will yet confess their iniquity, and their uncircumcised heart will be humbled, and Jehovah will remember His covenant with Jacob (verses 40–42). Jacob is put first here because in Jacob we see God's disciplinary ways and their result. The book of Job is typical of how God will reach His end with His people Israel through prolonged and painful discipline. They will be brought in the end to abhor themselves, and to glory in the fact that they know God, and that His covenant is the security of all blessing for them.

If we " walk contrary " to God we shall find that His government is contrary to us, and the longer we persist in self-will the more severe will the operation of that government become. But we may be sure that God will overcome in a conflict between our wills and His ; He will reach His end, though it may be through much suffering to us which might have been avoided. The sooner we submit, and humble our uncircumcised hearts, the better it will be for us. Confession, the acceptance of God's ways in righteous government, and turning to Him, lead to recovery. God remembers the covenant, and can righteously bestow on a repentant and humbled people its wealth of blessing.

The spiritual famine in a great part of the Christian profession to-day, the way the world has dominion, the superstition and infidelity which threaten to sweep away the last remnants of faith, so that christendom is wellnigh ready to open its doors to the strong delusion and to utterly apostatise, are solemn evidences of how men have walked contrary to God in the Christian dispensation, even as Israel did in hers, and of how they suffer now under His government. That government is going on, as yet, in view of repentance and recovery. Whenever and wherever an uncircumcised heart is humbled, and confession is made, there is nothing on God's part to hinder a return to the original ground of all blessing. *Christ* is the Covenant, and He is the God-given Title to blessing. God never forgets Christ, and where there is self-judgment, and turning to Him, He delights to bless according to all that Christ is. He is available for every one in the Christian profession to-day, even as He will be for Israel in the day when they will be brought under God's government, and by His gracious working in them, to say, " Blessed is he that comes in the name of Jehovah " !

CHAPTER 27

THIS chapter deals with what is devoted or hallowed to Jehovah by His people. It concerns the spontaneous fruit of divine grace, maturing in a willing-hearted people. It is an attractive subject to those who love God.

Hannah's prayer (1 Sam. 1 : 11) was the prayer of a devoted heart. Such prayers do not fail of an answer. She prayed for " a man child," not to have the gain of him for herself, but that she might " give him to Jehovah all the days of his life." She devoted him by a vow in a day when the priesthood was feeble and undiscerning in Eli, and corrupt in his sons, and the kingdom was shortly to be introduced. I think that we may say that Jehovah, and Israel too, got the value of that vow. The prophetic word came in by Samuel, and the way for the setting up of the kingdom was prepared. There is much in common between Hannah's day and our own.

We are called upon to yield ourselves " to God as alive from among the dead, and your members instruments of righteousness to God," Rom. 6 : 13. We are privileged to present our " bodies a living sacrifice, holy, acceptable to God, which is your intelligent service," Rom. 12 : 1. If we have not yielded ourselves to God we are not yet in normal Christian relations with Him. Paul says of the assemblies of Macedonia that " they gave themselves first to the Lord, and to us by God's will," 2 Cor. 8 : 5. That is the starting point of what is for God—a self-dedication which has definite spiritual value.

But this chapter teaches us that there is a graduated scale of spiritual value even in what is devoted. All devotedness is not alike. It may be feeble and immature, as seen " from a month old even unto five years old " ; it may be growing up in increasing strength, as typified " from five years old even unto twenty years old " ; it may be in the maturity of full growth " from twenty years old even unto sixty " ; it may be of " male " or " female " character—a greater or less measure of active energy ; or it may, alas ! be weakening or decrepit, as " from sixty years old and above."

There is such a thing as spiritual growth, and no doubt John's three grades of babes, young men, and fathers would correspond with the three different ages here with their increasing " valuation." " From sixty years old and above " is a sorrowful picture of decline. It is very sad when a man's spiritual value drops, but it is by no means an uncommon case. Look at Ephesus ! There was, perhaps, the highest possible spiritual value there at one time, but Revelation 2 shows how terribly it dropped. It should be a constant exercise with us to be on the line of increase rather than diminution. There is no reason on the divine side why we should ever get above " sixty " in a spiritual sense. Decline is not inevitable. Moses' eye was not dim, nor his natural force abated, at one hundred and twenty (Deut. 34 : 7) ; Caleb was as good a warrior at eighty-five as he was at forty (Josh. 14 : 7, 10). Paul, John, and Peter never dropped in the scale of spiritual value ; and some of us have known what it was to be in contact with men and women whose spiritual value did not drop to the very end of their course. What encouragement there is in this !

The valuation of Moses would typify the Lord's

estimate of our true spiritual value ; that is, of what
we really are by divine grace. There is often a great
disparity between our natural age and our spiritual
growth. It does not follow that because I have
been breaking bread forty or fifty years I am full
grown. I may be spiritually under " five " ! But
even in that case I have a definite spiritual value, and
my happiness will very largely depend on my answering to it in true devotedness. The Lord does not
value us by our natural abilities or mental powers or
acquirements ; He values us according to what we
are by the grace of God. Paul could say, " By God's
grace I am what I am " (1 Cor. 15 : 10), and every
truly converted person can say that. What we are
by God's grace is the measure of our spiritual value,
and the Lord takes account of it ; He makes no
mistakes in His " valuation."

Many persons may overvalue me, and some may
undervalue me, but my comfort is that the Lord does
neither. He knows exactly my true age spiritually,
and values me accordingly. Now I want to answer
to that so that God may get the full value of it from
me. If people overvalue me they only put me in a
false position, for I cannot yield fifty shekels if I am
only worth twenty ! If they undervalue me they rob
themselves of some of the gain which they might
derive from me through grace. It is safer *for me* to
be undervalued, but if my brethren were to undervalue me—which they do not—*they* would be the
losers ! How much the blessed Lord Himself was
undervalued ! They weighed for Him thirty silver
pieces—" a goodly price that I was prized at by
them." Jehovah says, " Cast it unto the potter." He
absolutely repudiates their valuation. " Chosen of

God and precious," " a name, that which is above
every name," " crowned with glory and honour," and
all heaven filled with worshipping myriads, tell God's
valuation of Christ !

Each of us has to be exercised that God
gets the full value of what we are by His grace.
None of us need wish to be somebody else, but we
have to see to it that we come up to the measure
of the grace, or faith, or gift which God has bestowed
upon us. The question is, Are we devoted to God
according to the " valuation " which the Lord has
made of us ?

As to service we find the Lord giving talents " to
each according to his particular ability," Matt. 25 : 15.
He estimated the value of each for service. But
what we have before us in Leviticus 27 lies behind
that ; it is a question of our value in devotedness of
heart. If that is there as a basis God can confer gift.
I am sure if there were more devotedness there would
be more gift ; for gift comes in answer to desire (1 Cor.
12 : 31 ; chap. 14 : 1). It is probable, too, that there
is already much gift, and God-given ability, amongst
Christians which does not come into activity because
devotedness is not sufficiently energetic. I am con-
vinced that God would have us more exercised to
grow in devotedness, so that our spiritual " valuation "
might increase. Romans 16 is a beautiful illustration of spiritual valuation. Paul does not lump
together all those mentioned ; he has something
different to say of almost each one.

Leviticus is a book of wonderful grace ; grace
comes in at unexpected places ; and there is a beautiful
touch of it here in relation to the man who is " poorer
than thy valuation " (verse 8). Every Israelite ought

to have been able to answer to the valuation of Moses. To be poor in Israel would indicate some failure to utilise the wealth of the land. But, notwithstanding this, there is a compassionate consideration of the actual means of one who is poorer than the valuation. He is not deprived of all opportunity to be devoted. " He shall present himself before the priest, and the priest shall value him : according to his means that vowed shall the priest value him." The priest valued a poor man, not according to what he ought to pay, but according to his actual means. His devotedness was accepted, through priestly grace, even though its value was not so great as it might have been, or ought to have been. I have no doubt there are many who, from different causes, are actually " poorer " than they ought to be. But if this is owned compassionate priestly grace is available, and a measure of devotedness may be accepted as being what is within the " means " of the poor person. These things are very touching ; they magnify the grace of our God, and give us to know Him better.

If you are conscious that you are poorer than the " valuation," go to the Priest. You will find priestly grace that estimates the devotedness of which you are capable, and it is permitted to you to be as devoted as you are spiritually able to be. Many a young believer has prayed earnestly that he might be wholly for the Lord. I suppose that we have all done so at some time or other. There was devotedness in that ; but we may not have fully followed it up. Through unwatchfulness and lack of spiritual diligence we may find that practically we have not " means " to carry out what we desired and intended. We have fallen off in earnestness, and divine resources have been

neglected, or but partially utilised. Let us go to the
Priest in true exercise of heart ; He will value us
according to our actual means at the moment, and
there will be something really for God, and accepted
by Him. But then in honouring God according to
our means we shall come in for great spiritual gain
according to Proverbs 3 : 9, 10, and our " means "
will rapidly increase. So that one who really judged
his past slackness and want of purpose, and had to do
with Christ about it, would find his " means " increase,
and if spiritual diligence were maintained he would
come up to his true spiritual valuation. It is a
comfort to know that the Lord makes the best of what
is there. We see that in the epistles to the seven
assemblies ; He puts the full value on what is there,
though He calls attention to the deficiency. But then
when there is true exercise He makes divine resources
available in Himself and in the Spirit, and the
deficiency is made up.

The Lord as Man here was fully devoted to God ;
the vows of God were upon Him. But He was
absolutely cast upon God for those resources of divine
strength by which alone devotedness could be preserved and carried through. He set Jehovah always
before Him, and was never diverted a hair's-breadth.
He was always in the spirit of " Preserve me, O God :
for I trust in thee," Ps. 16 : 1. We can only be
devoted as we follow Him in that path of prayerful
dependence, divinely strengthened and maintained.
There are wonderful " means " available for us—Christ
and the Spirit and all divine resources. We may
have neglected to draw upon our resources, and
therefore our " means " in a practical sense may be
reduced, but the deficiency can be supplied. Let us

not forget the Priest in all His compassion and consideration. I have often been touched by the grace
which He has shown to me, when I have had to own
that I was poorer than the " valuation." And I have
seen His grace to others who have felt in the later
years of their lives ashamed that they had not been
more devoted. The enemy might use the consciousness of this to cast us down. But the grace of Christ
is wonderful, and where there is an upright acknowledgment, and a true turning to Him, He can secure
to the heart what it desires in the way of devotedness.

" And if it be a beast whereof men bring an offering
unto Jehovah, all that they give of such unto Jehovah
shall be holy " (verse 9). This would, I think, typify
an apprehension of Christ as held by the heart of the
believer in true devotedness to God. There is no
" valuation " here, for it is the preciousness of Christ
Himself that is set forth in such a beast. It is not to
be altered or changed. The purpose of heart which
devoted what it apprehended of Christ to the pleasure
of God is to stand. Even another, and perhaps a
better, apprehension of Christ cannot be substituted
for it, though it may be added to it. Each apprehension of Christ that is devoted is " holy," and it is
so pleasurable to God that He will not forego it. This
shows how God values every movement of devotedness in the hearts of His people in relation to their
apprehensions of Christ. What has been devoted to
Him cannot be recalled, but this is because of the
pleasure God has in retaining it for Himself. It is
really a lovely touch of grace. He says, as it were,
You may add a better beast if you can, and if your
heart prompts you to do so, but I value your first

movement of devotion too much to allow anything to be substituted for it.

An " unclean beast, of which they do not bring an offering unto Jehovah " (verse 11), would, I think, apply to anything which had not " holy " character which might be surrendered in devotedness to God. Not something sinful, but something on the line of the natural. This must be valued by the priest because it expresses a heart-movement which yields something definitely for God. That yield may be more or less ; all surrenders have not the same value. The Priest knows exactly how to appraise all such devoted things. Many have made surrenders which all could see—giving up earthly prospects and advantages, and comforts and family ties, to serve the Lord. Others have made surrenders for the Lord's sake only known to themselves and to Him. All such surrenders are appraised by the Priest. There may have been mixed motives in some of them which have diminished their value, but the Priest takes account of their true worth Godward. There are no mistakes in His valuation. " According to the valuation of the priest, so shall it be."

In this case the thought of redeeming the devoted beast is brought in. " And if they will in any wise redeem it, then they shall add a fifth part thereof unto thy valuation " (verse 13). Probably the thought of redemption looks on to the future. The spirit of devotedness in the day when the Messiah is in reproach and rejection leads to surrender, as the Lord so plainly intimated in the Gospels. But in a coming day Israel will take up on redemption ground what the faithful remnant surrendered in their devotedness, and they will so hold these things in relation to Jehovah that He will get His added " fifth."

The hallowing of a " house " would speak of devotedness coming out in relation to the conditions in which God's people dwell together. We have seen " a leprous plague in a house " in chapter 14, but here we have the thought of a hallowed house. I suppose every believer has some idea that there is a " house " character of things ; that is, that Christians have the privilege of being together. Generally speaking they *do* get together in some way, but the question is raised here of the value of the " house." It may be a " good " house or a " bad " one, and its value will be correspondingly high or low as an expression of devotedness. The Priest does not value an unhallowed house. There may be associations in which there is no element of devotedness—of being " holy to Jehovah." This scripture does not concern such associations, and one would trust that no true saint would wish his " house " conditions to have that character. But if there is a true desire that the " house " should be hallowed it becomes a serious exercise to know what value Christ puts upon it. *How much* devotedness does it really express ? *How much* spiritual value is there in it ? The Priest makes no mistake. Let us not be content without getting His valuation of our " house."

The one who hallowed the house could have it for his own by paying the price of redemption. This suggests that to dwell in a hallowed ." house " costs something ! When it came home to the people of God that a great corrupt profession united with the world was no suited " house " for them, and they sought to have a " house " which could be held as truly hallowed, they had to pay the price. Every hallowed " house " costs something if it is to be possessed in a divine way. The greater the spiritual value of the " house "—the more true devotedness it expresses—the more it costs to secure it as our own.

God has given great light in these last days as to the " house " conditions in which He would have His people to dwell. Many have been enlightened as to assembly truth and principles. We cannot plead lack of light as an excuse for the " house " being " bad," for in the grace of the Lord, and by the Holy Spirit, there has been a great opening up from Scripture of the spiritual conditions that make the house " good." We have to see that those conditions get place with us in a practical way, and that they are maintained in a spirit of true devotedness. Our " house " should be a hallowed one, and we should be prepared to pay the price so that we may hold it as having made it our own. I have no doubt there has often been great devotedness with little light ; the Priest knows how to value it aright. It is for us to see that with much light we do not fail in devotedness.

The hallowed " field " (verses 16–21) would refer, I believe, to Israel's portion on earth, which he failed to " redeem," and to which he has lost all title. It has reverted to Jehovah and to the Priest. Israel has no longer any claim or right to the land. They will inherit, but it will be through the blessed Priest whom they have so long despised and rejected, and through Jehovah's sovereign mercy under new covenant conditions. It will be to them Immanuel's land, and as a devoted people they will hold it as hallowed, and all that is due to Jehovah will be rendered.

" The firstling " (verse 26) cannot be hallowed, because " it is Jehovah's." " And as to every tithe . . . it is Jehovah's " (verse 30). There is that which

God claims as His due, and which must be rendered to Him. The voluntary devotion which is set forth in a " vow " is very acceptable to God, but He reminds us in the closing verses of this book that He has definite claims which cannot be righteously ignored. We must all feel how desirable it is that the spirit of devotedness should be increased in our hearts. But while we think of this let us not forget that there is much which is not left to be suggested by voluntary devotedness, but which is a matter of simple obedience, and of rendering to God and to our Lord Jesus Christ what is due. If we are not faithful in such matters we certainly cannot take the ground of being devoted.